Winding Roads

Winding Roads
A Bicyclist's Journey through Life and America

John Frederick

Copyright © 2018 — John Frederick

ALL RIGHTS RESERVED — No part of this book may be reproduced in any form or by any electronic or mechanical means, including information storage and retrieval systems, without permission in writing from the authors, except by a reviewer who may quote brief passages in a review.

Originally published by Deeds Publishing in Athens, GA
www.deedspublishing.com

Printed in The United States of America

Cover design by Mark Babcock

Cover photo by Mark Frederick

ISBN 978-1-947309-17-3

Lyrics from the song "Born to Run" by Bruce Springsteen. Copyright © 1975 Bruce Springsteen, renewed © 2003 Bruce Springsteen (Global Music Rights). Reprinted by permission. International copyright secured. All rights reserved.

Landforms of the United States, Sixth Revised Edition 1957
Copyright © 1957 by Erwin J. Raisz (1893-1968)

The maps are also reprinted and slightly modified by permission.

The amazing maps, drawn by the famous American cartographer long before the days of satellite imagery, are true works of art and are still sold by his family. Visit www.raiszmaps.com to peruse the selections and order maps. Tell them you discovered the maps in Winding Roads.

Books are available in quantity for promotional or premium use. For information, email the author at johnfrederick@atlanticbb.net. Visit www.johnjfrederick.com.

First Edition, 2018
Second Edition, 2023
10 9 8 7 6 5 4 3 2 1

Dedicated to my wife Kathy and my sons Jared and Mark. They patiently listened to the stories, no matter how many times they had heard them before.

Contents

Acknowledgements & Notes	i
Introduction	v
A Lightning Flash Forward	vii
An Unexpected Beginning	**ix**
Staying Upright	1
It's Pirate Baseball Time	5
A Neighborhood as It Should Be	11
An Age of Innocence	16
The Worst of Times	22
The Beat of a Different Drummer	28
Keep It Between the Ditches	35
A First Time for Everything	**39**
On the Road	40
Under the Neon Lights	46
I'm Eighteen	51
Working on the Railroad	54
A Dark and Stormy Night	58
From Journalism to Geography	63
The Man of Steel	67
Headed for the Coast	**73**
A Random Act of Kindness	74
A Blue Eagle	79
A Cyclist's Vision of Heaven and Hell	82
Discovering Unexpected Connections	88
It's Cold Outside	91

Moving on Up	**95**
To the Head of the Class	97
Riding Across Penn's Woods	105
I Don't Eat Animals	113
The Blue Ridge Mountains of Virginia	121
Marathon Rides and Giant Hemlocks	127
Good Times, Bad Times	131
Let It Snow	137
A Time for Firsts	144
New Explorations	**149**
When the Levee Breaks...	151
In the Summer Time	161
Life's Been Good to Me	164
A New Racing Experience	168
A Winter of Discontent	176
Take It to the Limit	180
Growing Your Own	187
A Grand Adventure Begins	**195**
Ramblin' Man	197
Have You Ever Seen the Rain?	207
Hummingbirds and the Old Man	210
The Leader of the Pack	215
The Wind at My Back	222
Take the Long Way	230
A Mysterious Disappearance	238
Next Gas 43 Miles	246
If the Phone Doesn't Ring, It's Me	249
Rocky Mountain Way	259
A Close Encounter	264
Headwinds and Flatlands	**273**
Hells Half Acre	276
The Van Tassell Hassle	281

High Plains Drifter	291
Scenes of Visionary Enchantment	297
The Glory of Suicide Machines	300
Light at the End of the Tunnel	**307**
A Field of Dreams	311
Some Way Out of Here	316
The Good Samaritan	324
All Alone on the Road	328
Epilogue: Another Story	333
Endnotes	337
About the Author	341

Acknowledgements & Notes

PUTTING A BOOK TOGETHER THAT IS PART MEMOIR CAN BE a surprisingly insightful experience in its own right, especially when one is writing about things that happened decades before. That could have been very difficult, yet I managed to find background and details from a broad spectrum of sources.

I gleaned much from my own training logs, trip journals and newspaper clippings. The ride summaries and photographs from my good friend Ken Steel were a treasure trove of information, brought back a flood of memories and filled in many details that had drifted into the deep, dark recesses of my mind. I could not thank Ken's widow, Kathy, enough for allowing me to actually borrow the sacred documents so that I could scan them.

Beyond those journals, the miracle of on-line maps and streetview images from Google and Bing (unheard of when I made my cross-country ride) were invaluable. They allowed me to retrace many miles of several of my longer trips even though the journeys had been enveloped in the fog of time.

While acknowledging the relatively recent development of online maps and photos, I must also recognize a much older source of geographic images. Irwin Raisz may have been the most talented cartographer of the 20th Century, his landform maps showing phenomenal detail long before the days of satellite imagery. Raisz's grandson, Jonathan, and his wife, Mali, graciously permitted me to use the maps to trace the route of the cross-country trek in a way no other maps could.

Perhaps the biggest thanks go to my two sons, Jared and Mark, and wife, Kathy, who ultimately urged me to write of the broader story of a lifetime of adventures (and misadventures). It did not take me long to realize they were right, for there were many people and things that pushed me to do the things I did and see the places I saw. While my cross-country ride might have been the culmination, what led up to it was an important part of the story.

My mother deserves a posthumous thank you for saving all that she had saved from our family's early years. When her health forced her to leave her home of nearly 55 years, my three siblings and I began the arduous task of cleaning out the house. We found an almost incomprehensible accumulation of papers, records, bills, cancelled checks, letters, cards, pictures, books and items from the previous 60 plus years of our lives, some of it predating my own existence by a decade. Though the massive accumulation of stuff (that was strewn from cellar to attic) was overwhelming to clean up, it serendipitously filled in another bundle of voids in the story.

Mom's obsession with saving stuff had provided us with an opportunity to rekindle old memories or gain insights into our family in general, and my own childhood and adolescence in particular. The nuggets left behind by my mother helped clarify the earliest parts of the story. As is so often the case in any life story (or any portion thereof), our parents often play a very notable role, even if they don't save things from a half century before.

Both my parents instilled an interest in traveling in me and my siblings. Though my mother became a homebody as she grew older, both Mom and Dad were adventurous in their younger days. My father's love of travel never faded and he went on a cross-country cycling adventure of his own after he retired. Our family vacations (every single summer) bestowed the love of travel upon us early in my life and reinforced it throughout.

Finally, I must express gratitude to those that took on the sometimes tedious task of looking over the book, especially for lassoing me in when my inevitable digressions went too far afield. Too often I wanted to convey every detail and their help assured that the story did not bog down in minutiae. My sister P.J. (who also caught the grammatical errors in the early editing stages), my friend Bill Moore (who brought a publishers perspective), my sister Bonnie (who let me know when my childhood recollections got too personal) and my wife (who could bluntly tell me that something was superfluous) were especially helpful.

They also reminded me that I might want to "change the names to protect the innocent," as Jack Webb so often said in the old *Dragnet* television shows. I realized, with some amusement, that in a few instances the name changes ended up protecting the guilty.

The folks at Deeds Publishing were so incredibly helpful. Bob Babcock took a chance on an unproven author because he liked the story and the way I told it. Ashley Clarke was a patient editor, who no doubt wore the labels off several keys on her keyboard adding all those missing commas and hyphens from my manuscript. Mark Babcock deserves many thanks for making it *look* like a book you'd want to read.

Even though many others are also mentioned in the book, I must recognize four particular people whose influence and encouragement took my interest in the sport to another level. There wouldn't have been much of a story to tell without them. Roddy Gerraughty, my college cycling class teacher, was the one who first ignited the glowing embers of my cycling interest. The topographic maps on the walls of his office still fresh in my mind, he helped cement the connection between the bike and the geography. My frequent riding partners, Ken Steel, Gary Kephart, and John Bradley, experienced a bundle of cycling adventures that are deeply embedded, not just in my memory, but in my very soul. Ken and Gary both left us much too soon and I miss them both. My only regret connected with the book is that we all won't have the opportunity to get together and laugh as we recall those most amazing tales.

Introduction

THE BICYCLE IS AN AMAZING BIT OF TECHNOLOGY. THERE is no more efficient way to move a human being from one place to another. But beyond efficiency, it is also an amazing way to see the world. A bicycle, some have said, is the just-right, Goldilocks mode of transportation — not too fast, not too slow.

While the speed and efficiency of a bike bring some interesting twists to any cycling story, there is another factor separate from those. The bicycle is the transportation of our younger days, the way we got from one place to another, independent of our parents and on our own in many other ways. Especially in the mid-20th century, it played an important part in many children's play, travel and adventure. As I considered telling the story of my cross-country adventure after college graduation, I realized the story began long before that trip. The journey was one that began during the days when the bicycle was a toy of my youth.

The endeavor to tell the story began more than a decade before the actual publication of the book on the occasion of my birthday. During dinner, the discussion turned toward the subject of a book, as it often did when an impassioned point or amusing recollection tumbled into our conversation. As I ate my birthday dinner at our kitchen table, I recollected two birthday meals from the road that were much different than the one that evening. Though the birthdays had been more than three decades before and very far from home, I still humorously recalled the stories with incredible clarity. My older son, Jared, declared that these stories needed to be written down. I should start writing or shut up.

I began college with the intentions of majoring in Journalism but a fear of a lifetime of writer's block and an interest in the environment prompted a change to Geography. Ironically, four decades after graduation, I found myself blending my two academic interests and writing a book with a distinctly geographic perspective.

Everyone that aspires to write shares the anxiety that they will write something that no one wants to read. But I was convinced this really was a good story, one that might entertain and enlighten the readers. For while there have been many enjoyable travel logs written over the years, the bulk have been written from the perspective of explorers, hitchhikers, walkers, pioneers, or those on horse, in a car or on a train. Relatively few have looked at the world from the sometimes uncomfortable saddle of a bicycle.

This book is not just about a single trip. It's a book about people, geography, the roads we travel on, the mechanism by which we move about, the natural world, the man-made landscape. Such research and writing can prompt one to become particularly introspective. This could be both a blessing and a curse. Many times I laughed, many times I smiled, but many times I cried, too. Many memories were joyful, but even some of those made me melancholy when I realized that a time or a person was gone forever.

Some of those smiles and tears came when my siblings and I were cleaning our mother's house just before and immediately following her passing. Many voids in the chronology of the book were filled in during that time, as we came across pictures, letters, clippings and notebooks which I had forgotten about or that I feared had disappeared. Among the many things I found was my paperback copy of the book, *I See by My Outfit*, the story of two friends who rode their motor scooters from New York to California in the early sixties. It was the first book I had read about what seems to be a uniquely American experience, the Road Trip. As I read it, I never imagined that I would strike off on my own bicycle ride across the country just seven or eight years later. It seemed just as unlikely I'd ultimately have the chance to tell the story of my own *Winding Roads*.

A Lightning Flash Forward

THE DARK, NEARLY BLACK SKY WAS ENVELOPING ME IN A way only Jonah trying to avoid the whale could have fully understood. An ever-shrinking spot of sunny sky faded on the eastern horizon and I could not make my bicycle go fast enough to escape the rapidly closing jaws of the storm. The almost daily thunderstorm had become routine as we rode across the High Plains and this onslaught would be yet another in a long line of meteorological inconveniences we were forced to deal with.

My college classmate and current riding partner was somewhere between Bassett and Newport and I was stranded in the Nebraska countryside to fend for myself. When I saw the historic marker for Spring Valley Park, Nebraska's first roadside rest, along US Route 20, I was relieved to find cover just as the worst of the rain began to fall. Spring Valley Park, a vestige of roadside parks of an earlier day, would not be mistaken for the roadside rest areas typically found along interstate highways today. The small corrugated metal building had a roof but offered little more in the way of protection or amenities. As the rainstorm developed into a full-fledged thunderstorm, I feared the shelter could be more a liability than an asset.

It was July 4, 1978 and Mother Nature was supplying all the fireworks I needed, perhaps more than I wanted. By 10:00 p.m. the thunderstorm seemed capable of spawning a tornado and I recalled a warning from the day before. The fire chief in Wood Lake had invited us to stay in their firehouse because of the threatening weather and warned us to get under the firetruck if we heard a noise that sounded like a locomotive. "The train doesn't pass through Wood Lake anymore, so if you hear one, it's a tornado. Under the fire engine is the safest place if things start to blow around," he calmly conveyed in a manner only a seasoned tornado survivor could.

As I lay wrapped up in my sleeping bag (as if the bag could protect me from the violent and persistent lightning), I prayed I would not hear the sound of a train. I had never been in a storm like this one and it made me think back to the tornado-flattened street I had witnessed in Gordon, Nebraska just a few days before. If a similarly violent tornado touched down here, I'd need much more than a sleeping bag and a picnic shelter built long before I was born.

Usually the eternal optimist at times like this, I wasn't just pessimistic about my plight, I was genuinely terrified. The hail pounded against the metal walls of the shelter, the wind howled through the trees, and branches scattered across the park. I thought of all the ways I could be maimed or die. When I heard the sound of a train coming from the east, my optimism evaporated into the oppressively humid July night. For the first time in my relatively sheltered life, I sensed imminent danger and had no idea how to avoid it. Now more than halfway across the continent on our cross-country bike trip, it had already been a grand adventure. It seemed the wildest ride of my life was on the verge of becoming a bit wilder.

An Unexpected Beginning

Staying Upright

"Life is designed to knock you down. It will knock you down time and time again, but it doesn't matter how many times you fall—it matters how many times you get back up."

—Canadian Comedian Lilly Singh

AMONG THE MANY THINGS STOWED AWAY IN MY MOM'S HOUSE were a bunch of pictures from my early childhood. An old favorite of mine has me astride my first tricycle on Christmas of 1959. My dad had a stereo optic camera so you can even see me in three dimensions. It's a cute picture but shares a conspicuous peculiarity with all those early cycling photos of me: I never seem to be peddling. I don't think this was simply because I was three years old either, because I have another early childhood memory that reinforces the recollection of this youthful handicap.

Santa brought me a pedal-powered blue army jeep a few years later. Despite my future mistrust of the Military-Industrial Complex that President Eisenhower talked about in those days, I loved that army jeep. I rode it up and down the sidewalk in front of our house on Sixteenth Avenue in Altoona, Pennsylvania for long hours. Being the years that seat belts first appeared in full scale cars, Dad honored my request for such a safety feature in my vehicle, took an old leather belt and made a seat belt for the jeep. But I could never seem to master peddling the thing. Instead, I would push it up the sidewalk with my feet, just the way I watched Fred Flintstone do it every week on the cartoon show. I let gravity take the jeep back down the hill on the return trip to the driveway. Despite my peddling ineptitude, I loved the jeep and got teary eyed when my parents sent it to the scrap yard when I outgrew it.

On my sixth birthday, Mom and Dad got me my first two-wheeler, a 24-inch green and white Kent Convertible. They paid $26 for it, including tax, at Dean Phipps Hardware Store. I found out in later years that Kent, an English company, actually made racing bikes but this machine shared none of the features of its more expensive siblings. It was called a convertible because it had a removable top tube. This feature seemed attractive to my parents, especially since most worry their young sons will endanger their procreative capacities if they fall on those important anatomical parts in their early years.

But it really didn't matter if the bike had the top tube or not, for I was destined to fall off it many times before I learned how to ride it. My dad took me up and down the avenue for the next two years in what must have been a terribly aggravating process for him. I can't recall anything of those lessons but falling down. I even fell down when we still had the training wheels on. This became a rather traumatic experience for me, particularly since everyone else in the neighborhood my age had been riding a two-wheeler for more than a year, some of them since before kindergarten.

Despite a deep desire to learn how to balance my bike, I still could not keep it upright the summer before third grade. Someone needed to try something different, and it was my neighbor and classmate, Bob Cassarly, who would figure out what that would be. Our part of town was particularly hilly and this made the bike balancing efforts even more difficult for an uncoordinated klutz. Thinking someplace flat and unpaved would make it easier, he suggested we try the dusty little baseball field three blocks down the avenue from home. Bob had a slightly smaller bike that he allowed me to use, too, and that change of venue and equipment allowed me to finally conquer the seemingly insurmountable undertaking. Bob managed to do in an afternoon what my poor dad had been unable to do for two summers.

Though Bob had performed a great service, he omitted one important lesson and forgot to show me how to use the brakes. When I got on Sixteenth Avenue for the first time I had a hard time stopping. Since there was a modest hill on the avenue, I didn't need the brakes simply to stop; I needed them to keep from careening through a stop sign and down the steep hill to Nineteenth Street. I thought that I could just drag my feet to stop. Though this feet-dragging was surprisingly effective in stopping the bike it was hard on the tips of my shoes. I did not use my actual pedal brakes at all that day and by early evening my wing tips had no tips. When my frugal mother saw the two-inch hole on the toes of my shoes, she nearly passed out. To think that I had ruined a pair of shoes in one afternoon made her sick. I was still guilt ridden about the incident 40 years later.

I can't remember for certain who passed on the secret of reverse pedaling and the braking action that resulted. It might have been my next-door neighbor and very best friend Jerry Hirt. Jerry was not just my best friend but the guy that was always helping me through difficult times. I clearly remember him trying to help me shoot a basketball and properly swing a baseball bat during those same years. No matter how awful I did (and I was a very bad baseball player at the time), I can never remember him getting mad or impatient with me.

Before bicycling and baseball, our lives were uncomplicated and the physical challenges were simple. Our favorite pastime from age four to seven had been playing with Tonka trucks in the piles of topsoil that one of us always seemed to have in our yard. Both our houses were built the years we were born, his in 1955 and mine in 1956. So when we were little tykes, our fathers were still trying to get grass to grow in our miserable clay soil. This guaranteed that we had a new pile of topsoil to play in every year.

The unbridled joy of playing in the dirt piles may have been great fun for a couple of preschoolers but when Jerry started riding his bike, the world became a different place. Jerry had a blue and white 20-inch bike and to me it seemed like he went directly from his stroller to his bike. By age seven, he was riding it more and more and coming to the dirt pile less and less.

I did not sense it at first, but his bike had transported Jerry to a new place in life. After he and Bob Cassarly taught me to stay upright and even stop on my bike, I, too, came to realize there was a whole new world out there. Even though it was only a few blocks at the time, being allowed on the street with our bikes was a freedom of almost incomprehensible magnitude.

But life was not all fun and games. School would rear its ugly head each September and, like it or not, the bicycling, hiking, and baseball would be drastically scaled back once school began. Going to a small Catholic school and being raised by staunch Catholic parents in a very Catholic neighborhood, it is not surprising that much in our lives, somehow or another, had a connection to church. From an early age, this was part of our lives. In early elementary school, we still went to church every single school day. The school day started with a Latin mass at 8:00 a.m., ended with a prayer at dismissal and had a generous sprinkling of other religious indoctrination throughout the day.

Those early years are fragments of many memories — the smell of the new book bag on the first day, the competition to stay near the smart end of the vocabulary bench in the front of the room, the buckles flapping on your boots on the first big snow of the winter, exploding out the front door at the end of the day when spring finally broke.

Those days also brought the first traumatic experiences to our young lives. Even though in just second grade, I, like nearly every American, can clearly remember where they were and what they were doing when they heard that President Kennedy had been shot. I was sitting in Mrs. Mann's second grade classroom when the principal came into the room and passed the news to the teacher. Though only eight years old, there was a comprehension even in our young minds that a terrible thing had happened.

Death came closer to home the next year when one of our school mates was killed by a car in front of his house. Just like the Kennedy news, I can also still remember the distinct spot where I was when I learned that Bobbie Yeager had been hit by a car. Standing on the front steps of the school next to the rectory, I stood in shocked disbelief. The first unexpected death of a contemporary is a surreal experience. It just does not seem possible that a second grader could die and certainly not one that you know personally.

It's Pirate Baseball Time

"It's Pirate baseball time! Hello again everybody. This is Bob Prince along with Jim Woods and Nellie King bringing you tonight's game from Forbes Field."

—Bob Prince
Introduction to the Pittsburgh Pirate radio broadcast
KDKA Radio, Pittsburgh, Circa 1966

WHILE THERE ARE MANY SCENES FROM THE NEWS, BASEBALL memories, and neighborhood happenings that I recall, it is the summer of 1966 that still sticks out in my mind above any other. This was the summer that I became enthralled with two additional pastimes beyond the bike… baseball and rock and roll. The three were mostly unrelated but equally fascinating diversions. Each of them could be all-consuming for a young boy, so to dive into all three in the same eventful summer was especially momentous.

Like so many boys our age, we were baseball fans and that was the thing that occupied much of our summer as we approached our double-digit years. In fact, one of the most traumatic ordeals of those years was a series of baseball events at the end of the 1966 Major League Baseball season. As we entered the last week of the season, the Pirates, Giants, and Dodgers were embroiled in an incredible pennant race for the National League title. Most of us were Pirate followers but Jerry Hirt was a hard-core Giants fan. The worst possible scenario came to pass, as the Dodgers won the title in the last couple days of the season, shutting out the entire neighborhood. Little did I know that pennant race would spark an enthusiasm for baseball that burned brightly in to my young adult years.

Authors Doris Kearns Goodwin and George Will have often noted that baseball was one of those rare threads that could weave generations of Americans together. Such was the case for my maternal grandfather, Pappy Weakland, and me. We were both fans in the seventies, yet he was old enough to remember Pittsburgh Pirates and baseball stories the whole way back to the twenties. He remembered Babe Ruth playing an exhibition game at the old Cricket Field in Altoona and saw Josh Gibson and the Homestead Grays of the old Negro Leagues. To hear those stories was better than reading any book.

Pap listened to every inning of the Pirate games he could and once he reached retirement age, it became his most important daily ritual from April to October. I would ride my bike the three blocks up to Pap's place and sit on the front porch and listen to the games on the radio through many of those summers in the late sixties and early seventies. Taking the cue from long-time Pirate broadcaster Bob Prince, Pap was among the legendary second-guessers and he would criticize Pirate manager Danny Murtaugh whenever the opportunity presented itself. Though his jovial Irish personality made him well liked by his players, Murtaugh seemed to be a strategic buffoon. Pap, having been a student of the game for many decades, would jump on Murtaugh's ineptitude every chance he got with a flurry of curse words and disdainful looks of disgust. We got only one television channel in the early sixties and it did not carry the Pirates. So when it came to baseball, the radio still held the stature that it did when it was the only electronic media available for sports, music, or entertainment. And just like those olden days before television that our parents and grandparents would reminisce about, we would sit in front of the radio imagining the scene even though we couldn't see it.

I can still remember particular radio games for which I sat attentively, visualizing every pitch, anticipating (sometimes praying fervently) the next pitch would bring us closer to a win. Though the Bucs struggled after the near miss of 1966, Pappy Weakland and I continued to religiously listen and watch. Some of the other cousins had been big fans before I caught the bug and all of them were better baseball players than I was, but as the years passed, baseball became a special bond between Pap and me. While many grandchildren are dragged kicking and screaming to visit their grandparents, I looked forward to every evening visit. And it was the old Kent bicycle that took me the three blocks to Granny and Pap's house. When I got the new generator light, it also meant that I could safely make the return trip after dark when the night games were over. The bikes changed over the years but the ritual continued even into my high school years. We would sit on the front porch and listen to the flamboyant Prince night after night through good years and bad.

The summer of 1966 was day after day of baseball, bicycling, adventures in the woods, endless afternoons of playing board games, and listening to music. In one of life's funny ironies, we played the war game, "Hit the Beach" as our infatuation with rock music began. Just a few years later, we would be listening to anti-war songs and watching the protests and riots on television. It really was an age of innocence.

While baseball may have tied us to the past, one of our other diversions would send us the other direction. For it was also 1966 when we awakened to the wonder of rock and roll music. This was the birth of truly modern rock and roll and 1966 still seems to boast the most impressive list of memorable songs by some of the most notable (and a few less notable) rock artists. Anyone with a pulse and between the ages of 10 and 20 in 1966 remembers that year of music.

Despite our infatuation with the national pastime and a newfound passion for rock and roll, the bike remained our other notable diversion and we rode often, even if our range was limited by our protective mothers. My mom was the most worrisome of the lot. Yet despite her overprotective tendencies, she apprehensively allowed me to go further from the roost over the next few years. By the time I was eleven or twelve, I was allowed on both Fifteenth and Sixteenth Avenues and from my grandparents' house at 20th Street to the last street in the city, 26th Street. This was more than a square mile!

Many would laugh that this really was not much freedom, but it opened up a whole new world for me. We could hang our baseball glove on our handlebars and ride to the Cub Scout Field to play baseball. Or we could mess around in the nearby creek (pronounced "crick" in our parts). I could go to Granny and Pappy's house for marshmallow circus peanuts, wintergreen lozenges, or a drink of cold water from the tin cup Pappy made in the metal shop at the Pennsylvania Railroad. This was real adventure to an eleven-year-old from Fifth Ward.

As we got older, we wanted to be more like grownups (which we know now is not always a good thing). That meant that we just didn't want to ride bikes; we wanted to ride motorcycles. Nowadays, parents will run out and buy their eleven year olds some battery driven vehicle or, worse yet, one of those child-sized all-terrain vehicles. But in those simpler times, we had to fend for ourselves if we wanted to be more grown up. So we would buy balloons from Paul's Store or Romerowicz's, blow them up and attach them to the rear fender bracket so they would rub against the spokes. This made a great motorcycle sound that could be heard from all around, at least until the balloon would break. But we didn't do this too often because balloons cost a penny a piece and we would have much rather had a piece of penny candy than a noisy bike.

Besides, a baseball card could be attached to the fender bracket with a clothes pin and get the motorcycle sound for a lot less expense. The trick, of course, was to find a baseball player that wasn't worth anything and you were certain that no sane kid would ever trade for. One such player was Tito Francona. Though Tito had a few impressive years earlier in his career, he had become an obscure platoon player by 1966. Not having heard much of him, I called him "Titto" the first time I saw his card. I was sitting on Jerry Hirt's front porch step when I first came across his card and when I used a short "i" in his first name, Jerry almost wet himself laughing. Jerry always seemed to be better versed on worldly issues and saw my pronunciation as an accidental obscenity. Besides the funny name (that I made funnier), Tito had a funny looking flat-top haircut. So he ended up being one of those cards that you were happy to stick on your bike.

More advanced equipment came our way over the next few years. Our older sisters had lights on their bikes but they were the battery powered variety. The cutting-edge guys wanted a generator driven light that also looked a lot like a motorcycle headlight. When the lever on the generator roller was flipped down, the little drum would snap onto the side of the tire. Every time the tire would move, the generator would power the light and, voila...the light would go on. The nice sets even came with a red tail light that attached to the seat stay. I was overjoyed when Santa delivered one of those deluxe sets for Christmas.

The bike speedometer was the next big thing we got excited about. Like so much of the equipment in those days, these 1965 era contraptions were much different than their modern-day counterparts. The speedometers were big gaudy instruments with a heavy metal cased cable that connected to the hub of the front wheel to register each revolution. Crude or not, those speedometers and odometers gave us something to shoot for, in both speed and distance.

One of the steepest hills we were allowed to ride on was a short but nasty incline at Sixteenth Avenue and 25th Street near the Cub Scout Field. While my older sister P.J. was always enthralled by the daffodils that grew on the field at the top of the hill, we boys were always excited about speeding down the hill as fast as we could. When we all got speedometers, the hill took on a new significance. Since the downhill was at the beginning of the block, this was really the only stretch that we could speed down recklessly without the concern of rushing through a stop sign or unprotected intersection.

It did not take much to hit 30 miles per hour on that hill and we soon endeavored to go even faster. A good head start up near Ray McCall's house enabled us to come close to maxing out the speedometer. This might not have meant much to our older car-driving siblings since "off the dial" on these instruments was only 40 miles per hour. Just the same, we thought this was quite the accomplishment and would boast about it when given the opportunity. Though we would brag to any of our peers that would listen, we would have never told our mothers. We had learned early on that it would be better to beg for forgiveness than ask permission. And if we never crashed, we figured we would never have to beg for forgiveness.

While the speedometers pushed us to go faster, the odometers gave us new motivation to pile on the miles. Not long after we got them, the competiveness crept into how far we were riding, too. Another of those crazy childhood memories that still remains vivid in my mind is the moment I surpassed the two-mile mark in a single day. I remember the exact spot on Sixteenth Avenue, near the street light in front of Gartman's house when the hallowed event came to pass. Two miles in one day! I even told my mom.

A Neighborhood as It Should Be

"Community, as it once existed in the form of places worth caring about, supported by local economies, has been extirpated by an insidious corporate colonialism that doesn't care about the places from which it extracts its profits or the people subject to its operations."

—James Howard Kunstler
Home from Nowhere
Touchstone Books (1996)

KEEP IN MIND THAT THOSE TWO MILES WERE LOGGED ON less than fifteen city blocks and most were done on the same five block stretch of Sixteenth Avenue. One becomes particularly familiar with the territory and the people that live within it when repeating so much of the path time after time. But that did not seem like such a bad thing at the time, and I seldom felt unwelcome on those neighborhood streets. Those were the days when neighborhoods were real neighborhoods in all the positive connotations the term implies.

At the risk of sounding like my parents, I lament the passing of that era. Suburban sprawl would ultimately replace these traditional neighborhoods with suburbs isolated from where we worked, shopped, and went to school. This would undermine the pedestrian and bicycle transportation that had been part of urban America for many decades. (Most of the suburban developments didn't even have sidewalks.) This was an especially noteworthy change for kids. More cars, fewer quiet neighborhoods with lighter traffic, video games, organized sports (all subjects for another book), and suburbs not connected to much of anything at all have conspired to knock kids off their bikes, literally and figuratively. It has made them considerably fatter as well, childhood obesity now the most common childhood health problem in America. What a sad commentary indeed that we found the cure for polio and smallpox, only to be done in by the Big Mac, Game Boy, and suburban sprawl.

But I digress. Despite riding throughout those fifteen city blocks, I did not really know people much beyond the few blocks around my house. But we knew our immediate neighbors very well and many of them were permanent fixtures. The Gartmans, who owned the biggest and best bake shop in Altoona, built a new house soon after I started bicycling around the neighborhood. Not wanting to leave the neighborhood, they built it just 200 feet from their little bungalow across from Hirt's. It was a beautiful brick place, pretty upscale for our middle-class street. Among other things, they had it professionally landscaped, something that made my mom shake her head in disbelief, even decades after it was done. The real shock came, though, when it was discovered that they had installed an intercom at the front door, evidently so Mr. Gartman didn't have to wander too far from his recliner.

Beyond those memories, it would be hard to forget their bake shop. It was on Eleventh Avenue when downtown Altoona was still a hopping place. They seemed to have every baked good known to man and the place always seemed to be crowded with hungry customers. Thank God that I rode my bike and played baseball, for all those baked goods I ate could have made me a fat kid.

The Swovicks lived in the house between the Gartmans' old house and their new one, directly across the street from us. Their younger son Mark was my age and went to Saint Leo's School with me. Beyond being one of the Sixteenth Avenue bikers, he was part of the two-on-two baseball games we played during those summers. Perhaps the thing I remember most about Mark was his incredible artistic talent. We had art exhibits in grade school every spring, and Mark was always the first-place winner. He used to stick his tongue out the side of his mouth when he colored or drew. I figured that was part of a successful art technique and started sticking my tongue out in the hopes of duplicating Mark's work. But I was a lost cause, and my inability to stay in the lines when I colored would develop into truly mediocre drawing abilities in subsequent years. In one of life's great ironies, my two sons became tremendous artists.

Besides the baseball and bicycling, we would spend lots of time in the woods behind my house. The entire half block across the alley from the Hirt's house and ours was vacant, most of it covered with trees. We could have adventures in the wilderness without even having to cross the street. We would hike on the trails, play hide and seek, or climb trees. Of course, I didn't climb very far since my lack of athletic prowess spilled over even to the most basic of boyhood endeavors.

Our hide and seek games could be intense affairs and I recall being pretty adept at finding excellent hiding places in the underbrush so common in such woodlands. I still laugh about the day I was so well hidden that nobody could find me. Before the seeker hollered the final concession, "Ollie, Ollie in free," I realized that I had to pee like a race horse. I shook and hopped up and down in my rather cramped quarters, hoping to postpone the biologically inevitable. But, I came to learn, the will to "hold it" is not strong enough to prevent a full bladder from emptying once it finally reaches its ultimate capacity. I sat there crouched in the brush, unable to hold it any longer and peed myself. But, by God, they never found me. I managed to sneak down to the house undetected. The ultimate embarrassment for an elementary school aged kid was to wet himself and I still consider myself extremely fortunate not to have been found out—until now.

Those woods were great fun until a neighbor on Seventeenth Avenue, Mr. Lynch, told our parents that he had shot or otherwise killed a half dozen snakes in the grass and brush. Mom forbid us from wandering into the woods when she heard that news, certain that we would be bitten by a Pennsylvania Python or strangled by the rare Appalachian Boa Constrictor. It was no matter to her that neither snake existed in reality; she was convinced that the presence of these reptiles in our woods would bring our certain demise.

Though we eventually gained permission to venture back into our chunk of wilderness in the city, my Aunt Sally and Uncle Pete would further undermine our adventurous spirit by building a new house on the grassy field at the west end of the woods. But I was so excited that my cousins were moving in across the alley from me, the loss seemed inconsequential. Four city lots remained wooded and we still had plenty of nature to explore. A peculiar wedge shaped piece of ground at the edge of their property was left wooded, too. This proved to be a great spot for us as well, and my cousin Tom and I constructed a tree house in one of the trees that even I could climb. (Our dads may have actually had a big hand in the project but the details of the actual division of labor are fuzzy after all these years.) The area around the tree was still overgrown and had a few patches of poison ivy. Despite a hardy constitution otherwise, Tom had a horrible reaction to poison ivy if he was even downwind of the stuff. It seemed that he was covered in calamine lotion almost continually throughout several of those summers. I would walk through the same brush as Tom and come out unscathed while he would be covered in a rash the next day.

Poison ivy aside, we loved that tree house. Technically it was more of a tree platform than a true tree house. It really did not have much of a roof and the sides were like railings rather than walls. We had great fun and many adventures during those summer days.

It was about this time that Helen Hamburg, our next-door neighbor opposite the Hirt's, decided to move away. She was a single woman and kept to herself. So it was a particular shock when the Constantine family and their bratty son Paul moved into the house. I played with him often in the handful of summers that they lived there, but I do not recall fighting with any kid as much as I battled with him.

To make matters worse, he had a bully of a cousin that would visit occasionally. Though his name escapes me 50 years later, I can still remember his scowl. It was the scowl of a true hoodlum, as my mom and dad would call them at that time. He was the prototypical bully: bigger, meaner, and a good bit dumber than most of his peers. It did not matter, though, that he was dumber because the meaner and bigger part more than made up for his mental deficiencies.

One dreaded day that he visited the Constantines, Paul gave him orders to wreck the tree house. Paul was sore at us for some thing or another (which was more the rule than the exception) and thought that his cousin should teach us both a lesson. He had broken his left arm, presumably in some sort of a tiff with one of his fellow bully fraternity members. We could not imagine that even he could damage our tree house in his debilitated state. But alas, we had overestimated our construction prowess and stood at a distance in helpless horror as he tore the thing apart, one poorly fastened piece of wood at a time.

Construction of the Colledges' real house was quite an adventure in itself. Still a fairly young family, they embarked upon the project themselves and much of the work was done by family and friends. Though we were quite young, they let us pound a few nails along the way; but, as we later exhibited in the construction of the tree house, we were not up to union standards.

Tom and I were the same age and best friends through much of elementary and early junior high school. A year older than Tom, Jeff and I were close throughout our college years. Some of my first long distance bike adventures were with Jeff and Tom. As younger kids, we rode around the neighborhood a great deal and were always comparing odometer readings. The Colledges' house was up the hill from our house and forced us to start riding up steeper inclines if we wanted to ride from one house to the other. The hill was nearly insurmountable to ten year olds on single speed bikes weighing 40 pounds. But as time passed and we watched the older kids, we figured out that it was possible to zig-zag up the hill, making the climb more gradual. As each of us conquered the climb, we wore the accomplishment as another proud badge of honor.

An Age of Innocence

"Our innocence goes awfully deep, and our discreditable secret is that we don't know anything at all, and our horrid inner secret is that we don't care that we don't."

> —Dylan Thomas (1914-1953), Welsh poet
> Letter, 1936, to Caitlin, later his wife
> *The Collected Letters of Dylan Thomas* (1985)

THE EARLY SIXTIES REALLY WERE AN AGE OF INNOCENCE, not just for the Sixteenth Avenue Boys but for the nation. One might argue that the national innocence was more about being oblivious than innocent, though. There was initially a national denial over the injustices of racism, the fiasco that was unfolding in Vietnam, the environmental struggles and the social decay of the nation's cities.

That state of denial was as evident in Altoona as it was anywhere else. Though the blatant racism that was prevalent in the South was not as bad in Pennsylvania, there was a subtle racism that plagued Altoona. The city always had one of the lowest percentage rates of African Americans of any urbanized area in the state. And it was no coincidence that a very large portion of them lived in one part of town. It so happened that it was my part of town. The other end of Fifth Ward and the adjacent portions of the next ward north of ours contained more than three quarters of all the blacks in Altoona.

Though nobody can prove it now, the story goes that whenever a black family would set off house hunting, the realtors would always take them to the Fifth Ward. The fine realtors of that day would never admit to this sin, but it seems certain that it happened. One only needed to look at the census data from the middle of the century to confirm that subtle racism.

While Altoona never had slums in the most extreme sense of the term, we still had some pretty dumpy neighborhoods. Many of them were white folks but, on a percentage basis, a much greater portion were black. There were no black families on my block, but there were a number fairly close by. My mom's childhood home was three blocks closer to the predominately black part of Fifth Ward and she had grown up with several black families. Dad was in the Navy and came to be acquainted with a pretty diverse group of shipmates as well. Among other black acquaintances, they came to be adult friends with neighbors Jim and Mildred Moore. They eventually left Altoona to pursue better opportunities in Philadelphia. But they visited our home whenever they were in town until our families grew out of touch in the early sixties.

They had two little girls at the time who were very close to the ages of my two sisters. My sisters enjoyed the visits as much as my mom and dad. I have many times heard the story of my sisters discovering that the Moore girls had palms that were as white as their own and my mom laughed about the surprise in P.J. and Bonnie's voices for decades afterward.

While none of us had many black friends, it seemed like all of us simply saw them as everyday people that just happened to be a bit different. I remember Tony Patillo best. A classmate of mine at Keith Junior High, Tony came to play baseball and football with us and came swimming at my house when we got to be teenagers. (The way the pool water would glisten in his frizzy hair made us chuckle and he proudly proclaimed that he was the only one of us that could pull off that trick.) He fit in with the group and would have probably hung around with us even more had he not lived eight blocks from us. It was a long walk and a really difficult bike ride over two hills that most kids had to push the bike up. So we didn't see him as often as we might have had he lived a few blocks closer.

While many of us viewed our black friends and classmates as simply friends and classmates, we certainly heard plenty of mean and hateful references and comments made about blacks in general and the Fifth Ward in particular. Though Rosa Parks had embarked on her acts of civil disobedience a decade earlier, the civil rights movement had begun to be a bigger and bigger part of the headlines by the mid-sixties. Tension between blacks and whites grew across the country. While we did not have race riots in Altoona, they were part of Walter Cronkite's evening news many nights through those years. The summers of 1967 and 1968 were particularly unpleasant ones in many of the nation's largest cities, and some smaller communities found themselves in dire straits as well.

One of the riots that did touch the Fredericks, even if ever so slightly, was the Cambridge Riot of 1967. Cambridge, Maryland was on the way to Ocean City and was just one of the towns on the way to the beach. But in July of 1967, civil rights activist H. Rap Brown and Maryland Governor Spiro Agnew got into a nasty verbal battle that ignited riots in the small Delmarva Peninsula community. The riots were long over by the time we cruised through Cambridge in our 1966 Chrysler Town and Country station wagon, but our parents were still extremely uneasy about having to drive through the town. Despite temperatures well into the nineties and no air conditioning, we were ordered to roll up our windows as Dad sped through the downtown. We had taken the additional precaution of fueling up before we got there to further assure that we would not have to stop. Though there was little to be concerned about by that time, I was still petrified. We lived a sheltered life in Altoona and even the remote possibility that we would find ourselves in the midst of social unrest of that magnitude was scary.

We tried to go on a vacation every summer and those Ocean City trips were among the most memorable. We had gone to Atlantic City, New Jersey when I was younger, but with highway improvements, the Maryland beaches became more popular in the late sixties. Atlantic City had been popular among Pennsylvanians through the fifties because it was easy to take the train there. When the automobile became a more common mode of transportation for longer trips, Atlantic City became a victim of the change. Ocean City, Maryland, and neighboring Rehoboth Beach, Delaware, had fashioned themselves after Atlantic City, building boardwalks and beach-front motels and hotels.

Though my mom was deathly afraid of the ocean, P.J., my dad, and I loved the water. It's a wonder that I did enjoy the waves so much because my first ocean experience was not so positive. It is said that the only experiences that can be recalled from your early childhood are the most joyous and traumatic of events. My baptism to the ocean was one such traumatic memory. On one of those trips to Atlantic City in the late fifties, Dad took my hand and walked me toward the ocean water. I was enthralled by the waves as they lapped onto my feet and ankles, and I recall my joy and laughter at the novelty of them. But waves, behaving as they so often do, can vary greatly in size from one to the next. Adults, being of greater stature than the typical four-year-old, don't often contemplate the magnitude of those differences in wave height. So as Dad waded into knee deep water, I was wandering into the great abyss. As the first big one approached me, I opened my mouth in a gasp of amazement, just in time to get my first mouth full of salt water. Being overcome by the water was bad enough, but ingesting the foul-tasting stuff put me over the edge. Though Dad had me by the hand, I was tossed about and came out of the water crying hysterically. Try as my father might, I would have nothing of the ocean for the rest of that vacation.

All of that changed as I grew older and those Ocean City trips became the highlight of the summer. The trips were met with even greater anticipation once I learned how to ride a bike. The boardwalk was open to bike traffic for several hours in the morning and bikers of all ages would take advantage of the opportunity. This was before the days of bike trails, and having a place to ride without the anxiety of being run over by a motor vehicle was rare. Bike rental places could be found every block or two at the south end of Ocean City and machines of every size and shape could be found.

I had a very ordinary bike back home, so when I got to the bike shop at the beach I wanted to get radical. I would go straight to the Stingrays. My cousin, Ed Heverly, had a hot orange Stingray, but I wasn't allowed such a luxury. So when I had the chance to rent one, I went for the gold, or should I say orange? Stingrays had 20 inch wheels and the back was equipped with a wider slick tire. The seat was a longer "banana" seat that was designed to allow the rider to slip forward and backward so that it was easier to do "wheelies." The handlebars were fashioned after those found on "chopper" motorcycles, curling up much higher to make it easier to pull up the front wheel. This setup also made them the first bikes designed to jump small obstacles.

Cousin Ed became very adept at such cycling acrobatics but those skills were far beyond me. Still, I rented the Stingray and set off for adventure. The first few years, I had to stay close to our motel, much the way I was limited to the few blocks around my house when I was back home. Though never out of the sight of my mother or sisters in those early years, Mom finally allowed me to ride down the boardwalk by myself one summer. I suspect it might have been the year after the Cambridge Riots, when I would have been nearly twelve. This was another one of those landmark events, one which I would especially cherish given my mother's overprotective nature.

I got up particularly early since I decided I would ride the length of the boardwalk, from the northern end (where the hotels and condos ended at that time) to the southern end of the long barrier island upon which Ocean City sat. Mom gave me the money to rent to the bike and off I went. There was a place called Mike's Bikes that was near where we stayed and it was there that my ill-fated adventure would begin.

As I embarked on more outdoor adventures, I would come to realize that bike rides and hikes would periodically end in less than ideal circumstances. Like most of those rides that would bring anguish of one sort or another, this one began pleasantly enough. It was one of those incredibly peaceful mornings at the beach. The sun was shining, the waves were lapping onto the sand, and the crowd was small. I had several hours to complete the trek, about six miles round trip.

After riding the hills of central Pennsylvania, the pancake-flat boardwalk was easy cycling. The miles passed quickly and I had time to stop and take in the sights and enjoy the glorious morning. After getting to the southern end of town, I turned around and started back to Mike's Bikes. I had lots of time left on my rental and thought that I would ride a little longer if I got back to the bike shop a little early.

But a funny thing happened on the way to the forum. Somehow, I had missed Mike's Bikes as I saw the southern end of the boardwalk ahead of me. Being only twelve, I had not paid particular attention to the specific street on which the bike shop was located. When I couldn't find the side street, I was sure that I had ridden into the Twilight Zone. I kept riding back and forth and could not understand how I could have possibly ridden to the end of the boardwalk and missed the bike rental place.

After riding back and forth what then seemed like dozens of times, I finally rode to the apparent end of the boardwalk and came to realize that it wasn't the end after all. A twelve-year-old perceives the boardwalk as a straight line following a perfectly straight beach. But, alas, like most beaches, this one has gentle curves almost imperceptible to casual observers and certainly beyond the understanding of a kid that just recently finished the fifth grade.

What looked like the end of the boardwalk from 50 yards away was simply the curve about half way up the boardwalk. Once I got past the "end" of the boardwalk, I found that I was only a couple of blocks from Mike's. Though greatly relieved that I had solved the mystery, I was still panic stricken because I was 20 minutes past my rental limit. When I embarrassingly explained my stupidity to Mike, he was gracious enough to give me the overtime without charge. I was still horrified because I now had to explain my tardiness to my mother. I just prayed that she had not called the police.

By the time I got into college, I was taking my own bike with me when we went to Ocean City. When most guys were looking for girls at the beach, I was doing a hundred miles before lunch. But we'll get back to that untraditional practice later.

The Worst of Times

"It was the best of times, it was the worst of times, it was the age of wisdom, it was the age of foolishness, it was the epoch of belief, it was the epoch of incredulity, it was the season of light, it was the season of darkness, it was the spring of hope, it was the winter of despair."

—Charles Dickens,
A Tale of Two Cities (1859)

THOUGH I DID NOT CROSSOVER INTO MY TEENAGE YEARS until the last few months of the sixties, memories of the politics, culture, and music of those tumultuous years remained vivid in my mind for many years. The innocence of 1966 evolved into the upheaval of 1967 and 1968. As ten and eleven year olds, we did not realize that 1966 marked the beginning of socially-conscious music that we would listen to in high school and college. We listened to it in 1966 because of how it sounded. As we got older, what it said became important, too.

Some of what we liked in those days was pretty inane, musically and lyrically. We played Hanky Panky (by Tommy James and the Shondells) until it died of exhaustion on the turntable. But such stuff was not particularly good music in the end and would certainly not stand the test of time. Of course others had great messages and lyrics that we didn't fully appreciate until a few years later. Even some of the songs that just sounded great became classics, too, and still find their way onto the oldie stations. Many still end up on movie soundtracks.

I suppose that 1966 was the year of transition, for rock and roll and for a little squirrelly kid. It was 1966 when music became the rock and roll of the Beatles, the Rolling Stones, the Who, Bob Dylan, and

Jimi Hendrix. Though the music of 1966 still included James Brown and some Motown artists, the rock and roll of the Elvis era had faded away by then. The songs of 1966 were all about electric guitars, organs, and drums played by long-haired musicians. For the first time, people were not just singing about love and heartbreak. They sang about death ("Paint it Black"—The Rolling Stones) and war ("Hey Joe"—Jimi Hendrix). The Beatles sang about isolation in "Eleanor Rigby." The Lovin' Spoonful's "Summer in the City" and the Kinks's "Dead End Street" sang about life in the city.

As we listened to rock and roll, played baseball, and rode our bikes around the neighborhood, we were, at first, oblivious to what was going on around us. As the nation fought an unpopular war, battled over civil rights, and became aware of dreadful environmental problems and urban decay, growing social awareness gave rise to even more protest, both on the streets and on the radio. Just as jazz flourished during Prohibition and the Depression, the worst of times, it would seem, could inspire the best of music.

My perspective on these things and the music that came from this unrest would ultimately be shaped by my sister P.J. Had I been the oldest in the family, the music I heard and the issues that would confront me and our family would have been much different. By the late sixties, P.J. had become, not just a rock and roll fan, but a closet hippy as well. Though she was the daughter of two socially conservative Catholic parents (who themselves were the children of very socially conservative parents), P.J. would secretly attend peace marches, wear bell-bottom blue jeans to class, and befriend anti-war activists and classmates who really didn't spend much time in class. That this would happen to college kids in those days should really not be surprising. It was, after all, their friends and classmates that were going to Vietnam. Many did not come back and those that did often came back different people, some physically and others emotionally.

While we were riding around the neighborhood on our bikes and playing "Hit the Beach," Rosebud and Faye Gartman's son Rodney was really hitting the beach in Vietnam. When his tour of duty ended and his dad picked him up from the Pittsburgh airport, Rodney refused to talk about his war experience. In no uncertain terms he told his father that it was not worth talking about, and he had no desire to tell any war stories of any kind.

The war, and all the civil unrest that resulted, made even apparently uncontroversial things controversial. While still somewhat oblivious to the war in 1966, this divisiveness hit me where it hurt—right in my television viewing schedule. Yes, even something as mundane as television became a source of disagreement.

Now to fully appreciate how badly things had degenerated, one must recall what television was like in the mid-sixties. Those were the days of Andy Griffith and the Wonderful World of Disney, hardly the stuff that would arouse controversy. They never even said the word sex (or hinted that anyone on the telly would engage in it). Curse words were taboo and violence was strictly limited. Ironically, the most violent and objectionable thing on the television was news from Vietnam. So aside from the news, it would be difficult to fathom that anything would prompt a parent to forbid a child from watching. But it was not the theme of a show that led to the first television show ban in the Frederick house. It was an actor who spoke out on the Vietnam War and angered my father.

The show was *The Man from U.N.C.L.E.* and the actor was Robert Vaughn. Vaughn, a liberal Democrat, became one of the first of the "Hollywood Elite" to speak out on the war, in January of 1966. My father, though also a Democrat, was a patriotic World War II veteran that still went once a week to his Naval Reserves meetings and training. When he heard Vaughn's comments, he took particular offense to them and said that I would not watch any show on which such an unpatriotic American would be a part.

This was one of those things that seem now to be so trivial, but at the time it was one of those traumatic wedges shoved between a child and parent. I was so upset with my father. I was just a nine-year-old kid that wanted to watch a spy thriller every Friday night. I did not yet understand why this war would be such a source of consternation to so many on both sides of the fence. Alas, Vietnam became a point of divisiveness, not just among politicians but among parents and their "Children of the Sixties," even those not yet ten years old.

This was perhaps one of the first signs that life was becoming much more complicated. As the mid-sixties became the late sixties, the age of innocence really did fade for me *and* the country.

If things had been stewing in America in 1967, they boiled over in 1968. Beyond the war, the riots, the civil rights struggles, and the looming environmental mess, this was also the year that Martin Luther King and Robert Kennedy were assassinated. Kennedy's death shot down the hope for new leadership that would surely get us out of Vietnam. King's death struck a blow to the nonviolent resistance that had made the civil rights movement what it was—a powerful, meaningful and empowering thing in a time that seemed quite the contrary.

Politically, things had been rough even before the assassinations. But things went from bad to worse in a hurry, and the divisiveness could be seen everywhere. One of my most vivid memories was the Democratic National Convention in Chicago that summer. I remember staying up until 3:00 a.m. to see the final coverage. But it was not the proceedings in the convention hall that made the biggest news. Outside, in what was one of the biggest anti-war protests ever, tens of thousands of demonstrators got into a melee with the Chicago Police in front of a national television audience. While still not fully understanding the implications of the war in Southeast Asia, I knew, at the very least, that what was going on in Chicago did not seem quite right. A year or so later, I would be listening to Crosby, Stills, Nash, and Young singing about the week in Chicago as my father cursed the hippies and my sister marched in anti-war protests. Our lives were like an episode of the nineties television show, *The Wonder Years*, that recounted the struggles of the all-too-real Arnold family in the late sixties and early seventies.

Kevin Arnold and I shared many things, including our bikes. Also like Kevin, our struggles went beyond what was in the news.

When it was too cold to bicycle, we looked for other diversions. Though I was not a very good player, I still loved to play basketball and it filled the void left by not being able to ride the bike or play baseball during those especially cold months. Though it had been a tough year on many fronts, our sixth-grade basketball season was one incredible win after another. We easily won our division of the Altoona

Biddy League, going through the regular season undefeated. I was at the bottom of the depth chart but it was still one of the memorable parts of our last year together.

It was around that time we found out Saint Leo's School would be closed the next year and consolidated with two other schools. Parents screamed protests of dissatisfaction over the consolidation plan and many, including my parents, sent their kids to public school in protest. As many lives go, this would not seem to be such a traumatic event, but it turned my life upside down.

I was more upset about being forced to go to Keith Junior High than I had ever been about anything in my life. It was an enormous building and full of more than a thousand kids that I did not know and had no interest in getting to know. The cafeteria was a zoo, the food was awful and they gave us about 20 minutes to eat. To add insult to injury, I was perhaps the worst athlete in my seventh-grade gym class. And the gym classes at the public junior high were jam packed. So being the worst in a class of that size was even more embarrassing. When Mom went to parent-teacher conferences, my Physical Education teacher, Jay Perry, conveyed to her that some boys were just destined to be nonathletic. Mom came home and told me this in an effort to console me and let me know that she didn't love me any less. It was okay just to be a good student.

Much about the first year at Keith Junior High was awful but it was gym class that was the worst part of this living hell. There were upwards of a hundred kids in the class and some of them were not very nice people. What was worse was that some of them did not know the word hygiene even existed, let alone have a concept of what it meant or how one might practice it. The musty smell of sweaty pre-adolescents, gym clothes on their third go-round without being washed, and the filthy locker room turned gym class into an even more unpleasant experience.

The only athletic things I was able to do with any degree of success was ride a bike and swim. As luck would have it, the only sports I showed any degree of competency in were not part of junior high physical education in Altoona. No school district in the county even had a pool at the time. Though I loved basketball, I was even atrocious at that in early junior high school. Among the many embarrassments of those seventh-grade gym classes was the day we shot free throws for a grade. I missed all 25 attempts.

When the wrestling unit began, I was sucked even further into the vortex of athletic failure. For heaven sake, I loved basketball and failed that. What would happen when I tried a sport I hated? I would find solace in any degree of success, no matter how small it might appear. That success came in the form of Fred Dunson, a similarly challenged athlete in my class. So when it came time to have our final wrestling match for a grade, our teacher Mr. Perry, paired Fred and me against each other. If you were pinned, you got an F and if you lost a decision you got a D. The winner got a B. So when I stepped onto the mat, I said a prayer that I would not get pinned. I quickly realized that Fred was better and stronger than I was and found myself prone on the mat in short order. I spent the entire match squirming and contorting my body to keep from getting pinned. My grade was already so terrible, I simply had to get a D in the wrestling match. When the whistle blew, Fred and I actually got applause from our classmates and I was ecstatic with my D.

Yet it got even worse. Just after the start of the second semester, we started a unit on tumbling and gymnastics. I had managed to squeak by with C's the first two marking periods despite my basketball and wrestling struggles. But when I realized that I had to do somersaults, stand on my head, spin on the rings, jump over the pommel horse and climb a rope to the ceiling of the gym, I knew I was in deep trouble.

I did everything I could to get out of gym class. If I had a cough, I asked Mom to write an excuse that I was having trouble breathing. Even a slight pain in my leg justified the "pulled muscle" excuse. I had headaches that were "incapacitating." I became a gym-class-induced hypochondriac. But those gym teachers had a way of catching up with you and if you missed one of the tests, you had only delayed the inevitable. The only two D's in my life came during the third marking period of my seventh and eighth grade years when we had gymnastics. Little could my classmates have imagined that any manner of athletic success would be in my future.

The Beat of a Different Drummer

"If a man does not keep pace with his companions, perhaps it is because he hears the beat of a different drummer."

—Henry David Thoreau
Walden; or, Life in the Woods (1854)

I WAS SO RELIEVED WHEN THE WARMER WEATHER CAME and we ran up to the athletic field for gym class. To get out of that dank and overcrowded gym was reward enough but to actually be able to run around outside was like the pointless playing you did as a small kid. Especially in seventh grade, the half mile run uphill to the Keith Athletic Field was a bit overwhelming for a skinny, nonathletic twit. But even then, I was always able to beat a few kids in the race that inevitably developed on our way up the hill. In eighth and ninth grade I got closer to the front. By the spring of ninth grade, I was finishing in the front group of kids nearly every time.

I thought this a bit odd at the time. How could this kid that was so awful in so many things, the kid that was laughed at, the poor emaciated thing that could not make a foul shot, how could he possibly finish among the fastest long distance runners in a gym class of more than a hundred kids? I was, after all, the same person that Mr. Perry described as being one of those poor unfortunate nonathletic types that would have to be content in just being a fine student and a good boy. I was confused but proud that I finally could do something athletic. I was certainly not the best runner in the class, but by the end of ninth grade I could see the winner when we got to the gate of the field. I had not realized it at the time, but this was the first indication that God had given me an extraordinary heart and set of lungs. It would be a long time until the cycling ability was fully manifested, but that was surely the first sign of things to come.

Despite the traumatic seventh grade year, by the time ninth grade came along other things started to fall into place, too. I would not realize any of them would mean much later in life, but the newfound running ability, eighth and ninth grade science classes, and my favorite extracurricular activity would set the stage for many things that became important parts of my life years later.

Something or someone talked me into joining the Newswriting Club, the initial training ground for the school newspaper staff. The seventh graders, a year away from rigorous newspaper work, were taken through the fundamentals of newswriting. A young English teacher, Mr. Ed Barr, was the moderator and he would walk us through the finer points of gathering and writing. He made the exercise fun, rather than a painful classroom experience. One day he played the role of an old lady that had witnessed a fire. In a caricatured elderly woman's voice, he told us about her dozen cats, her arthritis, her constipation, and a host of other silly things that had nothing to do with the subject of the story.

In his own quirky way, Mr. Barr was teaching us to sort out the silliness from the important facts, the stuff that did not matter from the information that did. Most importantly, he wanted us to get the facts straight and report the important story, not the drivel or how we felt about the issue. (I have often thought it odd that Mr. Barr could instill that principle into a bunch of thirteen-year-old seventh graders, when so many journalists are unable to grasp the concept decades later.)

At the start of seventh grade, I was counting the days until I could get out of what began as a hell on Earth. But as I got to know people, make friends, and experience some successes, my disdain for the place was transformed into an unexpected enthusiasm. Winning a citizenship award and being named as one of the co-editors of the school paper helped change my outlook on school life. Becoming editor of the school newspaper forced me to get beyond the shyness that had plagued me for the first fourteen years of my life. It was also about this time that I started in earnest to play basketball, hike, and ride my bike beyond my backyard. The world became a bigger place in every way.

Who knows how or why it happened, but the foundation had been laid for a rather atypical teenager. In some ways, such a plight would have seemed unlikely, given my early propensity to spend endless hours in front of the television, the lack of athletic ability, and a family that had little interest in outdoor activities. But it's clear that we all find our own way in the world and are driven there by unforeseen forces and others we know beyond our immediate family. I suppose it means there really are no truly independent thinkers, just untraditional thinkers who follow unusual paths. For the overwhelming portion of our ideas come from others. Sometimes they just come from others that do, indeed, follow the beat of a different drummer.

Part of my untraditional path may have been mapped out by my nerdy pre-adolescence and part of that by a coddling mother. Had I been one of the "cool" kids in school, where would I have wandered? Would I have gone a different direction had I been part of the popular clique? What about the place where I grew up? Certainly, my interest in nature would have been less likely had I lived in the middle of the city. Perhaps I would have hardly ever ridden my bike at all had I lived along a busy highway. But two of my cousins contributed to that interest as well. Jeff Colledge's hikes in the woods and Ed Heverly's explorations on our bikes were part of the puzzle, too.

Where would I have gone politically and philosophically had it not been for my socially conscious sister P.J.? What if I had grown up in one of the truly bigoted parts of Blair County instead of on the fringe of the only black neighborhood in a two-county area? Would a less politically knowledgeable and engaged father have pushed me toward political apathy? How would my political perspectives and musical tastes have evolved if I had been the oldest in the family? Would I have read as much if I could not walk or bicycle to the library? Would I have paid attention to my grades if my mother was less engaged in my schoolwork?

Had I not been blessed with unusual endurance, would I have ever been enthralled by the bike? Had I not met people like Roddy Gerraughty or Ken Steel, would I ever have gone to the next level of cycling? There are thousands of factors and hundreds of people that push us to where we end up. Sometimes we forget that we are a product of all of them. It is equally easy to forget the importance of taking the best from each. Those that do take the best usually end up going the right direction and are blessed with a most interesting and rewarding life experience.

The next part of my life's journey literally took me down the wooded path, for walks in the woods near our homes became more common as we moved into the second half of high school. My cousin Jeff, at the prompting of his ninth-grade Biology teacher, had developed an interest in birding. Though I never came to have the expertise and level of enthusiasm he had, I would join him frequently for early morning hikes to look for birds on the ridge west of where we lived. The solitude that one enjoys in that setting, especially early in the day, is extraordinary. Beyond a feeling of isolation from people, the sound of birds just after a summer day's dawn is hardly one of silence. I remember one morning joking that we should have worn ear plugs — the birds were that loud.

We joked around and laughed often on those hikes. We would make bird-like sounds, using the name of the bird whenever we would see one. I'm sure some thought us to be odd and it was unquestionably silly. But it was the sort of goofy thing that can make teenagers laugh. It was another sign of a simpler time. This silliness may have had its genesis in a long hike we took toward the Mill Run Reservoir. This was an especially pretty area at that time and being close to the water, we would sometimes chance upon some waterfowl. This was usually pretty standard fair, ducks and an occasional goose. But on this particular hike we stumbled upon a loon. For kids that grew up in the city, loons are big and exotic birds. Jeff saw it first and he ran down the path wildly flapping his arms screaming, "It's a loon, it's a loon, it's a loon!" We only caught a glimpse of the thing and everyone chastised Jeff for scaring it away with his jubilant cries and wild gyrations.

One summer Sunday, we decided to go for a hike above the "World Famous" Horseshoe Curve. Being from the hometown of the Curve, we could not be certain that it really was world famous, but we did come to learn that its construction in the mid-1850s was a notable historic event. For the completion of a railroad route over the Appalachian Front, the significant escarpment on the eastern edge of the Appalachian Plateau marked the conquest of a geologic barrier that, up to that point, had been overwhelmingly difficult to negotiate. The Curve is still the primary route by which rail transportation traverses the plateau and moves billions and billions of dollars-worth of goods from the east coast hubs of New York and Philadelphia to the Midwest's primary transportation hub in Chicago.

Sometime in late morning, a group of us got a ride to the foot of a creek that ran into Burgoon Run to begin the hike. Burgoon Run is one of those streams coming off the plateau that had been rendered lifeless by the acid mine drainage that resulted from decades of unregulated bituminous coal mining.

The stream we hiked along had been spared from the acid mine drainage that had killed the nearby creek. The water was crystal clear, free of the nasty "yellow boy" precipitate that stained everything that Burgoon Run's water came in contact with. When we began our hike that perfect summer day, it was more with a sense of adventure than aquatic biology curiosity. We picked this particular starting point because it always struck us as a beautiful place and an area that we had not yet explored beyond what we could see as we passed it in a car or on our bikes.

We followed the stream as far as we could and eventually came upon a path that meandered toward the top of the escarpment. I'm not sure what our plan really was but we continued wandering westward, moving further and further from home with every step we took. Eventually, we came upon the railroad tracks that had wrapped around the hillside from the Horseshoe Curve. Not too far off in the distance we spied the Gallitzin Tunnels. These tunnels, like the Curve, were built primarily by human and animal power and were dug out to take the edge off the final 100 or so feet of the escarpment that those early engineers had to scale.

While it had been a thoroughly enjoyable and educational hike, it was about the time we hit the tunnels that we realized we had once again found ourselves in a bit of a pickle. For it turned out that the

Gallitzin tunnels were nearly a dozen miles from home. To make matters worse, the nearest telephone was either another mile hike west (further yet from home) or about four miles down Sugar Run Road to the east.

Though in the broad scheme of things this was not a particularly tragic event, we were horrified to think about the worst-case scenario. It was late in the day and we feared we would run out of daylight before we figured out how to get home. While many kids with less worrisome parents would have just tried hitchhiking, we thought our parents would never again allow us to embark on such an adventure if we thumbed it home. Besides, they had managed to put the fear of God in us along those lines, always being certain to tell of us of kidnappings and gruesome murders that took place under such circumstances.

But sometimes it seems that God does lend a hand. As we walked down Sugar Run Road, we ran into a Fifth Ward boy washing his car along the creek in the shade of the trees. Though we were hard pressed to remember his name, we recognized him and, after a few minutes, he connected us with our families. Though we feared he might be a bit of a hot rod, we were relieved beyond words that we had found someone from the neighborhood who would drive us back home. We got home in one piece (without even a hint of a kidnapping) and pledged that we would never again put ourselves in such a predicament.

It was around this time that Jeff also got me interested in reading nineteenth century writer Henry David Thoreau. Though he lived more than a century before we were even born, there was something about the way he wrote, not just about nature but about the petty and materialistic way that people viewed life. For a couple aspiring naturalists, Thoreau was a neat guy.

Besides the walks with Jeff, I would sometimes hike up onto the ridge by myself very early in the morning to read. I found one spot of grass right along the trail to be especially peaceful. One morning, probably just shortly after 6:00 a.m., I heard a rustling sound in the brush. Despite the fact that my mother's fear and paranoia about so many things in life was a trait that annoyed me greatly, I immediately had a Marguerite Frederick-type reaction to the noise.

As I braced myself for a confrontation, a deer poked its head around the underbrush about ten feet from where I was sitting. The doe was as surprised to see me as I was to see her. If she could have spoken, I'm sure her reaction would have been, "Who the hell are you and what are you doing in my woods?" I sat perfectly still and she stood correspondingly motionless for a few moments. She finally leaned over and nibbled on something and then looked up again with that curious gaze. We looked at each other for what seemed like ten minutes. Then she sauntered away with the evident assurance that I did not intend to shoot her.

Though not particularly adventurous by others' standards, our hikes, birding outings, and longer bike rides continued to be a source of wonderment and excitement for us. A step up in our cycling equipment would be the next motivation to broaden our horizons even further.

Keep It Between the Ditches

"Just keep it 'tween the ditches."

— Advice to Burt Reynolds's character, Gator McKlusky
White Lightning
MGM Studios (1973)

MY OLD KENT CONVERTIBLE 24-INCH BIKE HAD SERVED ME well, dating back to those early struggles in first and second grade. By late junior high, multi-speed bikes had become the rage. Nearly unheard of among the average cycling public in the sixties, ten speeds could be purchased in nearly every department store by 1970. Some three speeds had come onto the market the previous few years and these two developments had resulted in a proliferation of the bikes that were especially appreciated in the hilly topography of a place like Central Pennsylvania.

Cousin Ed, the first to get a Stingray bike just four or five years before, was one of the first to get a ten speed, too. Other neighbor kids soon followed and I, too, longed for a replacement of my old single-speed. The son of frugal parents, I looked for the most affordable option and found a cheaper three speed at J.C. Penney's that had racing bike features like all the new ten speeds. It was gray, with a narrow racing saddle, drop handle bars, narrow tires, and "rat trap" pedals.

I would later come to realize that many such amenities were more cosmetic than functional. The gray paint covered a behemoth high-carbon steel frame and the saddle was a molded plastic imitation that was about as comfortable as a piece of granite. Though narrower than the old Kent balloon tires, the tires still rolled slowly and the rat trap pedals were a source of constant lacerations. The sharp edges of those pedals were often a source of amusement (when they hit someone else's ankles) or pain (when they hit our own).

Despite not being the same sort of machine Eddy Merckx was riding to victory in the Tour de France at the time, these bikes were still a big step up for us. No longer were the hills insurmountable obstacles and it was possible to productively pedal on downhills. This inevitably prompted us to broaden our two-wheeled explorations beyond the Fifth Ward. It was Ed that encouraged a few of us to first venture into other parts of Altoona. My first trip was out Union Avenue toward Tuckahoe Park and the tree-lined neighborhood of Llyswen. Still anxious about riding in traffic, we rode the sidewalks on most streets, necessitating that we stop and dismount at nearly every corner.

Despite that rocky first ride, this marked the first notable departure from the friendly confines of our quiet neighborhood on the Hill. That summer, I would take regular early morning bike rides across town or to the library. I would not go very far (especially compared to the miles I would ride three or four years later), but it was one of the things that built the foundation of enthusiasm for riding. Even in the city, there was something pleasant about riding through the neighborhoods before people were up and about and long before the kids were outside playing and screaming. There were lots of tree lined streets in our part of town and the birds were chirping away in them, just like they were in the woods beyond our house.

Ed and I would eventually wander further, one infamous day ending up on Sugar Run Road. This was the same neck of the woods Jeff and our crew had the hiking adventure. Much like the hike, we had a general idea where we were headed but were not quite sure where in particular we would end up. Sugar Run wound through a beautiful wooded stretch at the base of the Allegheny Front and was usually lightly traveled. Still unsure of what to do when we did have to share the road with traffic, we would scurry to the opposite side of the road when cars would come up behind us. This was not a problem when no opposing traffic was coming down the road or there was plenty of room to bail out. But, we would learn, that would not always be the case.

When one such situation presented itself six or seven miles from home, Ed took a dive into the left lane and straight into the guard rail. The incident unfolded like one of those slow motion and unstoppable disasters. As he skidded onto the gravel, he fell from the bike and slid under the wire of the guard rail, cutting open his left leg. As he careened toward the wire, it conjured up two equally horrifying visions in my mind. One was Ed tearing part of his leg off and the other was my mother tearing off my head when she found out where we were. Thankfully, I was saved from both nightmares. While Ed sustained a pretty good cut, it was superficial and the bike was still in one piece. The guardrail helped Ed "keep it between the ditches," even if just barely. We pedaled back home, relieved that Ed could pedal at all and that my mother would never be the wiser.

My Penney's three speed proved to be a big step up from the single speed tank of my youth, but I yearned for something more. Yet I could not go back to my parents so soon after talking them into the three speed and ask for a ten speed. So Mom took care of the matter in a very strange and unexpected way. One of my brother's friends was visiting our house one summer day and had ridden his AMF ten speed the half block from his place to ours. Unfortunately for him, but strangely lucky for me, he parked it in the middle of our garage. Though that would not have been an issue in many garages, it was in ours. For our garage was atop a very steep driveway and things situated just so were invisible to someone coming up the incline. My mother, always a cautious and deliberate driver, was more than surprised when she heard the crash of the bike under her car.

The bright lining to this dark cloud was made possible by our home owner's insurance. While our neighbor got a new bike, my frugal mother looked to see if the bike could be repaired. Though a bit scratched up, a new wheel and a few cosmetic repairs allowed me to get a "new" bike — one with seven more speeds. It may have first seemed like *Schadenfreude*, that I had benefitted from the misfortune of another. But when we both got new bikes, it seemed everyone came out a winner.

Our rides became longer and more adventurous that summer and the next. We were still uneasy in the traffic and tried hard to look for those out of the way places that would be a bit less nerve racking.

We became masters of finding side streets and back roads that would keep us out of harms' way. One particular ride we came to enjoy was to the Mill Run Reservoir. Less than a quarter mile of the ride was on busy highways and the last few miles wound through the woods and up the hill to the breast of the reservoir. It was a quiet out of the way place nestled in the tree-covered hollows at the base of the Allegheny Front. Though just a few miles from the city, it was nearly always deserted. Besides being a great bike ride, it was a great place to skip stones or just sit and enjoy a warm summer day.

A First Time for Everything

On the Road

"We all still buy into the cliché about road trips. That what a road trip stands for is hope. Hope. That somewhere — anywhere — is better than here. That somewhere on the road I will turn into the person I want to be. I'll turn into the person I believe I could be. That I am. And we hit the road. You and me and our whole great nation. With high hopes and no expectations for the future."

—Ira Glass
This American Life
National Public Radio
May 20, 2007

WITH THIS NEW SENSE OF ADVENTURE CAPTURING MY AT-tention, I was fascinated by the prospect of a cross-country trip when suggested by my Aunt Bernadette in the summer of 1973. Bernadette's boyfriend, Bobby Hmel, liked to travel and tinker. He combined those two hobbies and came to convert an old school bus into a camper. Though we nieces and nephews did not take Aunt Bernie to be the outdoor type, she and Bobby ended up doing a lot of camping in the converted bus. Ultimately, Bobby decided he wanted to upgrade and he bought a motor home to replace the old bus.

They decided they would break the new motor home in with a cross-country trek. They almost always took along one or more of Bernie's nieces or nephews and asked me to go on this one. The trip started out pleasantly enough and we found ourselves somewhere in Indiana by the end of the first day. I did not realize it at the time but that first day would be an indication of Bobby's propensity to pile up the miles in as short a period as possible. As my traveling experiences grew, I would come to enjoy the journey as much as the end destination. But the miles between stops were a hindrance from Bobby's perspective. Despite our differences in traveling philosophy, we shared some interests and managed to have a good time and enjoyed some laughs whenever we went anywhere together.

The laughs of the first day on the road, however, had been tempered by several unpleasant experiences. As we approached Indianapolis on I-70, Bernadette noticed that our refrigerator was not keeping things particularly cold. After a long search through the myriad of booklets and papers that came with the motor home, we dug up the Instamatic Refrigerator Owner's Manual. It sent us to a trailer court on South Franklin Road, but this turned out to be the father of the authorized repair technician. He sent us off into the Indiana countryside to find his son. The final destination was down a long and bumpy dirt road.

When we finally got there, we found a laid back 30-something man lounging in the shade in front of the dealership. After explaining our plight, he ambled over to the door of the motor home. With just a cursory look at the refrigerator, he concluded that, "Ya must gotta blackage in yer kewling system." He offered no remedy for the malady, lamenting that it would take days to get the parts. We headed back down the long dirt road, Bobby colorfully cursing out the unsympathetic service technician, resigned to be without a refrigerator for the duration of our trip.

We refused to let our refrigeration-deprived state thwart our enthusiasm initially, but it turned out to be the first in a long line of mechanical difficulties. Not long after, a new problem arose that would make the refrigerator incident seem like a minor inconvenience. As we pulled out from an intersection, a most ungodly sound came from the undercarriage. No doubt shaken loose by our adventure into rural Indiana, the exhaust system had fallen off where it connected to the manifold under the engine. Back to our bundle of owner's manuals, we were directed to a dealer not too far from where we were. Turning heads as we rumbled into the parking lot, the manager met us to see what the devil was going on. As Bobby explained our plight, the manager explained that he was "shit-out-of-luck" since the service department was ten minutes from closing up for the weekend.

Bobby, infuriated and cursing a blue streak, climbed behind the wheel, started the engine and gunned it as hard as he could. You could see the windows of the dealership rattling and the staff aghast as he gunned the engine several more times before finally pulling away to search for someone to reconnect the mess. We ultimately found the T.M. Quinn Gas Station a short distance away and Mr. Quinn reconnected everything after letting it cool down for a short while. Little did we suspect however, the fix was just a temporary one.

As we came out of church on a gloriously sunny Sunday morning in the foothills of the Rocky Mountains eight days later, it fell off again. Despite just leaving church, Bobby gave his blessings in a way quite different from the ones uttered by the priest just a few minutes before. He climbed under the motor home, tools in hand, and asked me to help him with the repairs. Showing the mechanical ineptitude from which I suffered much of my life, I was able to offer him little help, other than moral support.

Needing a laugh following the original exhaust system debacle back in Indiana, we found some entertainment in a most unsuspecting place when we stopped for 7:00 p.m. mass at Saint Rose of Lima Church in Montrose, Illinois. It was here, the furthest west I had ever been, in rural Illinois that I came to appreciate for the first time how different other parts of the country really were. This church was in the heart of farm country and the parishioners were generally pleasant, welcoming and helpful. The kid in front of us, however, set the scene for a church service that was sometimes more circus than worship. Though the young boy was alternately entertaining and annoying, it was the reader that was the greatest source of amusement. Reading two scripture verses and a responsorial in between, he had already butchered two sentences when he came across the word famine. When he pronounced it "fay mine" (and with a noticeable Midwestern drawl) it sent the three of us over the edge. We started laughing so hard we shook the pew. Our sides still hurting from the laughing we did in church, we set off to find a campground along I-70. We were happy to finally stumble upon one in Bluff City, about 45 minutes down the highway.

Beyond the cultural differences we experienced in Indiana and Illinois, the physical geography was profoundly different as well. As much as I came to enjoy seeing the country in this and subsequent trips by bike, car, and train, the charm of the Plains was frequently overcome by their indescribable boredom. This was somewhat tempered when on the bike because little details and landscapes were harder to see by car. Though much more complex geologically than most realize, much of the Plains remain a monotonous landscape to the vast majority that travel through them. To most it is just the tedious interlude between the Appalachians and the Rocky Mountains. That was certainly the case for a sixteen year old and his geologically uneducated traveling partners in 1973.

Saint Louis and the Mississippi River would finally provide a diversion from the monotony. Whether by Lewis and Clark or Bobby and Bernadette, Saint Louis, Missouri had long been identified as the "Gateway to the West." Like many other cities throughout the United States, it came to be because it was transportationally important. Setting at the confluence of the Missouri and Mississippi Rivers, this was especially true of Saint Louis.

To those who live on or near less ominous rivers, the Mississippi and Missouri would seem like the goliaths of waterways. In sheer linear miles, the Missouri/Mississippi system is among the four longest in the world. Being a massive river by nearly every measure, the Mississippi's floodplain is similarly enormous. Rather than eroding downward (like the canyon-cutting Colorado), rivers closer to sea level (like the Mississippi) wander back and forth, creating wide floodplains.

At the confluence of the continent's two largest rivers where two very broad floodplains come together, St. Louis was in a unique position not just geologically but geographically, economically, and even historically. Among its many claims to fame, it was the starting point of the famed Lewis and Clark Expedition, further cementing its claim to being a figurative and literal gateway. A formal memorial seemed appropriate and a competition was held for its design at the end of World War II. A host of challenges impeded final design and construction, but it was finally finished just seven and a half years prior to our visit.

The St. Louis Arch was not the traditional memorial in the Washington, D.C. tradition. The 630 foot tall arch is made of stainless steel and concrete and has a unique tram system that allows people to get to the top without having to scale the 1,076 steps. From the top, one could look out over a fair sized chunk of Illinois and Missouri and see many miles of the nation's two most famous rivers. While the tram system sounded like a clever innovation, it could be claustrophobic for some folks. Bernadette was not enamored by the close quarters and was especially anxious when the car made a rather abrupt jolt as it switched angles on the way to the top. The view from the observation deck was as incredible as it was advertised, though, and we concluded that the challenging trip was worth the anguish.

After a pleasant trip to the top of the Saint Louis Arch, we should have suspected that something loomed on the horizon beyond an Oklahoma sunset. Not long after skirting the fringe of the Ozark Plateau in southwest Missouri, our westward path took us back onto the Plains. This particular part of eastern Oklahoma is called the Cherokee Plain after the Native Americans that called it home. It is quintessential cowboy and Indian landscape everyone remembers from the movies—semi-arid, rolling hills more than outright flat, sandy and wind-blown. As we cruised along I-44 between Joplin and Tulsa, it seemed like an unremarkable stretch between the Gateway to the West and our first foray into Texas.

Hotter than blazes, we were happy that, at least, the air conditioning was still working. Cruising along at 60 plus we hoped to make some serious miles before dark. And then the other shoe, or more precisely the electrical system, dropped. Like a power outage during an electrical storm, everything went dead in an instant and the motor home lost all power. Bobby pulled the stalled beast to the shoulder with a cacophony of curse words soon to follow.

The frustration turned to disbelief as we sat for hours along the side of I-44 waiting for some Good Samaritan to stop and lend a helping hand. After what seemed like an eternity and many hundreds of cars and trucks, a state trooper finally passed on the opposite side of the highway and crossed over to help us out. A towing service was beckoned and another long wait ensued, followed by a long drive to Dunlap's Body Shop in Claremore, Oklahoma, just northeast of Tulsa. Interstate highway or not, the ordeal proved, among other things, that many desolate places still exist in America. It also proved that, just like the biblical story, folks are not particularly inclined to help out those in need.

Well into the evening when we finally got to Claremore, night had long before fallen on this suburb of the state's second biggest city. Dunlap's had long buttoned down for the night by the time we moseyed into town and so we were dumped at the doorstep much like an unwanted child. It was a blessing that we had been dropped off after dark, for when we awoke, we shuddered when we saw the neighborhood. The word slum may seem to be a universal term but, like ice to Eskimos, it can take on many different forms. The Southern urban variety usually differs subtly from its Northern counterpart, having larger lots to provide more room for that extra furniture and inoperable appliance that inevitably get dumped in the yard.

Not long after daylight had exposed us to the less affluent part of Claremore, the owner of the garage wandered in. While we shuddered over the neighborhood, he shuddered when he discovered the scope of our problems. The damages included ruined batteries and a host of other things far beyond my sixteen year-old mind and rudimentary understanding of electrical systems. The short story was this was going to take a while and we should make ourselves comfortable in nearby Tulsa. Having our fill of Claremore, we got a hotel and enjoyed the fair city of Tulsa, compliments of the Lifetime Motor Home Company.

Under the Neon Lights

"There are new gods growing in America, clinging to growing knots of belief: gods of credit card and freeway, of Internet and telephone, of radio and hospital and television, gods of plastic and of beeper and of neon."

—Neil Gaiman
American Gods
Harper Collins Publishers (2011)

I WOULD HAVE PREFERRED TO TAKE MY BIKE WITH ME ON the trip west but both my mother and aunt would have nothing of it. Neither Bobby nor Bernadette let any grass grow under their feet on a trip like this either. There would not be much time for leisurely bike rides. I did get to enjoy one ride in the farmlands of eastern Kansas on a warm evening. The campground rented bikes and I was able to find a Stingray that fit me. Though now a kids' bike in every embarrassing way possible, I rented it because a bike ride on a bad bike was better than no ride at all. Besides, there was no one around that would make fun of me for riding it. I rode through the campground and turned onto a farm road, the opposite direction of the major highway. The rolling road went east of the campground toward what seemed like a typical Midwestern farm.

I rode toward a barn that shared a wall with the edge of the road. As I cleared the barn I was startled by the snort and site of the biggest hog I had ever seen in the flesh. Several others were at the other end of the pen, all of them gargantuan. I had seen a few pigs from a distance on drives into the Pennsylvania countryside but I had never seen anything like this. I was certain that it would have crushed both the Stingray and its rider had it broken through the fence. I only rode a few miles that evening but my close encounter with Hogzilla and his siblings made it an eventful and memorable ride.

I can only recall one other youth-oriented leisure activity on the trip: an abbreviated game of miniature golf at a campground someplace in Colorado. The evening started out with the anticipation of a relaxing game between a fun-loving aunt and her eager nephew. The blackflies had other ideas, though, and engulfed us before we put the balls in the first hole. Though I would come to appreciate the voracity of both mosquitoes and black flies on some bike trips a few years later, this was the first time I had ever been confronted by the man-eating variety. It was our last attempt at miniature golf or, for that matter, most any other endeavors that would take us outdoors after the dinner hour.

Despite the blackflies, the Rocky Mountains were an amazing experience for me. Never having seen anything higher than the Appalachian peaks that were typically under 2,500 feet, even the Front Range was an astounding sight. After what seemed like a week crossing the Plains, the far-off Front Range and the real Rockies beyond them were almost surreal on the western horizon. The Lifetime Motor Home Express kept moving along and we sped through Rocky Mountain National Park in what surely was record time. Though the trip through the park was hastier than I would have preferred, it was still one of the most memorable parts of a very memorable adventure. Above the timberline, the snow was still piled high in early summer and the roadside cliffs seemed to drop off into oblivion. Even from the road it was possible to appreciate the majesty of the mountains and the beauty of meandering streams in the valleys. As Bobby and Bernadette hustled us through the Rockies, I was sure that I would have to return.

The trip through Rocky Mountain National Park would also mark the beginning of a rather interesting propensity: my sentimental attachment to tee shirts. Among the shirts at the park visitors' center was a dark blue shirt with bicyclists climbing up the front underneath the park's name. Not knowing at the time that the bicycle would become the dominant force in my life, I bought it for $3.99. I would wear it on bike rides many times over the next five or six years until it faded to a pastel blueish gray and eventually fell apart. I even used it for a bike cleaning rag after its days as a shirt had passed.

We had intended to travel to the west coast but the mechanical trials and tribulations of the motor home had thwarted those plans. Bobby and Bernadette decided that Las Vegas would be our turnaround point, fearing the trip over the Sierra Nevada Mountains and onto the coast could be the thing that would kick the debilitated camper over the edge. Though disappointed in not being able to make it to the Pacific Ocean, this route would take us through the Grand Canyon and onto Hoover Dam. The trip through northern Arizona would be yet another first for us, as the mountains of Southern Colorado evolve into the parched canyon lands of the Colorado Plateau.

The Rocky Mountains had seemed like a different world compared to the places I had been in my first sixteen years. But the Colorado Plateau seemed even more extraterrestrial. I realized that it became progressively drier as one moved westward away from the Gulf of Mexico, but this part of the Southwest was another order of magnitude drier than the western Plains. This was the first time I had ever been in a climate that did not typically support hardwood forest growth. So nearly every day I was introduced to yet another landscape I had only seen in pictures. Already having the feeling that I was on another planet, the sight of the Grand Canyon took me to yet another level of awe. It's not until standing on the rim of the canyon that I fully understood why they call it grand. Even though I was mostly oblivious to the details of the geology on my initial visit, it was still a most incredible experience.

The natural landscapes and geology were not the only fascinating new experiences. While not particularly interested in spending much time in the big cities, I was even less enthused to visit Las Vegas. My low expectations were confirmed once we got there. Years before gambling spread to many other parts of the country, Nevada was the only state that legally permitted gambling on a widespread basis. Both the environmental and social implications of this were, from the perspective of an innocent, nature-loving teenager, nothing short of bizarre.

Not yet of age, I was not allowed in the casinos, so I sat on the park bench out front while Bob and Bernie did some gambling inside.

The next few hours were an insightful look into the unusual world of those who don't just casually gamble, but seem to let it dominate their lives. Everything that I could see from my seat was about excess. It seemed that many of the patrons' jewelry, clothes, and cars were likely worth far more than the house I lived in back home. The town itself, with its neon lights, massive fountains, and gargantuan, gaudy buildings, was not only testimony to excesses of the people that frequented the casinos. It was a monument to the environmental excesses necessary to make such an artificial landscape in the desert. This place was built on the insatiable quest for money and a dream that one lucky day could bring riches that would last a lifetime. I had such feelings for Las Vegas and what it stood for before I got there, but was even more certain of it after only a half hour sitting on that bench.

We completed our cross-country trip in our gas-guzzling motor home in the nick of time because it was just three months later that gas prices skyrocketed. In October of 1973, Saudi Arabia instigated an oil embargo, stopping shipment of oil from the Mid-East to the United States in an effort to punish the United States for its support of Israel in the Yom Kippur War. The embargo was the newest chapter in the conflict that had been going on, quite literally, since before Jesus was a baby. For the first time in anyone's memory, Americans could not fill their gas guzzling behemoths with cheap gas.

The seeds of environmentalism had already been planted in my psyche but the oil embargo would prove to be the potent fertilizer needed to enhance it. For now, the bike was not just an interesting hobby, it was the environmentally and economically sound way to travel. I have often marveled that many enthusiastic 15-year-old bicyclists were transformed into obsessive automobile drivers (if not outright maniacs) upon the dawn of their 16th year. I'm not sure any other sport is so impacted by a birthday.

The oil embargo, though, made certain that I would not fall into that trap. The gas shortages of 1973 that followed came only eleven months after I got my license and the summer of 1973 did not call for much in the way of driving. The embargo turned things upside down for many Americans and the infamous gas lines of late 1973 and early 1974 got to be a common sight on the evening news. People would sit in line, sometimes for hours, and it was not uncommon to hear of impatient customers getting into fights over who was next in line.

Even before the shortages of 1973, I had not become addicted to the car like many sixteen-year-olds. I was not a particularly sociable kid and didn't have a girlfriend yet, so why did I really need to drive? I rode my bike everywhere I could, and when I finally figured out how to talk to them, I even took girls on rides.

I'm Eighteen

—Alice Cooper
"I'm Eighteen"
From the album *Love It to Death*
Warner Brothers Records (1971)

AS FAR AS LIFE'S LESSONS WENT, MA AND PA FREDERICK had evidently pointed me in the right general direction. Approaching my eighteenth birthday in 1974, it was clear to me that I was not nearly as confused as Alice Cooper was in his 1971 song "Eighteen." Yet I could still relate to his general premise. I sensed I had more direction than many of my classmates and friends, but in some parts of my life I was still "living in the middle of doubt."

Many of my years have been amazing adventures. But there is something extraordinary about that time in your life when you truly set off on your own and begin to focus in on a realistic vision of your future. Those times, more than many others, can be filled with anguish but are often sprinkled with serendipity. This would hold true for many things at that point in my life, but especially with matters regarding the opposite sex.

Without a big brother nor parents that paid much attention to such matters, I was poorly schooled in the finer points of dealing with young ladies. I managed to muddle through my prom and a few dates during my junior year but was never comfortable with any part of the process. Like so many other things in my life, women came a bit later than they did for many of my classmates. I had been listening to the guys talk about their escapades with the girls since I was in ninth grade. Not until the end of my junior year did the outright terror of a relationship with a girl slowly evolve into a more modest trembling fear.

The girl that finally struck my fancy was Nadine Waclo, a journalism classmate during senior year. She was cute, smart, played the piano and guitar and was just an all-around nice person. But I was such a twit with the girls and was clueless as to how to take things beyond the classroom friend level. Strangely enough, it was our senior class religious retreat that gave me the opportunity to finally break the ice with her.

It was the seventies and even in the Catholic schools, we were doing seventies kinds of things. So when it was time for a retreat, it couldn't just be a religious experience. It had to be a "Serendipity." None of us even knew what the word meant at the time, but the Religion Department hoped it would be cooler than a day of prayers or boring summaries of scripture.

Some found it a bit too touchy-feely, but I didn't think it was so bad. In retrospect, I guess I warmed to the event more than my classmates because it gave me the chance to ease into asking Nadine to go out. Father Caprio's attempt to do a hip seventies "Serendipity," turned into a real serendipity for me. It would be the beginning of my only notable courtship other than the one that led to my marriage many years later.

Nadine's family had a camper and a canoe and loved the outdoors. While my mom was making reservations at the Holiday Inn or the Fountain Motel (our favorite spot in Ocean City, Maryland), the Waclos were pulling their trailer into some National Forest campground. A single Waclo family outing would surpass the cumulative outdoor adventures of the Frederick family throughout its entire existence.

So even my choice of girlfriends would come to influence my growing interest in spending time outdoors. Nadine and I would pack up the canoe onto the roof of the Waclos' massive Mercury sedan and make the trip up Wopsononock Mountain to the lake at Prince Gallitzin State Park. Despite not having the best in cycling equipment, we would set off on bike rides as well. We had several very enjoyable rides but two unpleasant experiences are the ones that stick in my mind many years later.

One weekend we set off for the Homers Gap Reservoir, perhaps five or six miles from Nadine's house. The ride to the small lake was rather uneventful and we spent some time walking around the shore. It was that day that I saw a Tulip Poplar tree in flower for the first time and we were amazed at both the size of the tree and of the flowers. On the way home, Nadine got a flat tire. Since neither of us was carrying a patch kit or spare inner tube, we had to start walking. Not planning a long hike home when we set off, it never occurred to us there would be any possibility of darkness at the end of our trip. But such was the case as we trudged along Grandview Road, the shadows of the early evening growing longer. I recalled that one of my cousin Jeff's friends, Todd Coleman, lived on a farm along Grandview Road. Much to our relief, Todd was home when we got there and a call to one of our fathers rescued us from a dangerous nighttime walk along the curvy country road.

The other cycling moment with Nadine that vividly remains in my memory happened one summer day when we decided to ride to the Logan Valley Mall. The mall was about four miles or so from my house and most of the ride could be negotiated on quiet neighborhood side streets. While that meant traffic was light and it was easy to engage in pleasant conversation along the way, it also meant the trip had many turns, intersections, and stop signs. About a mile from the mall, in a classic Murphy's Law moment, one of us decided to turn when the other thought we should go straight. Keeping in mind that oft quoted law of physics that two objects cannot occupy the same space at the same time, Nadine and I crashed in a heap on Coleridge Avenue.

Working on the Railroad

"I've been working on the railroad, all my live long day. I've been working on the railroad just to pass the time away. Don't you hear the whistle blowing? Rise up so early in the morn."

— First published as the "Levee Song"
Carmina Princetonia— A book of Princeton University songs
(1894)

NADINE AND I WERE BOTH EXCITED TO HEAR OF A JOB PRO-gram for teenagers through the Youth Conservation Corps (YCC) that summer. Successful applicants would spend the summer working at the Allegheny Portage Railroad National Historic site about fifteen miles from home. Nadine applied and was accepted, but my mother, in her ever enduring over-protective nature, did not want me embarking on such a "dangerous" adventure. Beyond the possibility of working with my girlfriend, I thought such work would be the ideal summer job and was overwhelmed with disappointment and anger with my mother when I couldn't apply.

My disappointment was tempered, though, when I came to realize that I could visit Nadine every Wednesday evening. Though the group came from all over Pennsylvania, I ended up being the only friend that was within reasonable driving distance to make the weekly visitation. Perhaps the best news was that I could ride my bike to see her each week, too. It was a long and steep climb up the Allegheny Front from Altoona to Cresson but the ride home was a most invigorating downhill joy ride. I did not miss a Wednesday visit and made every trip on my bike when the weather permitted. We would sit at the old orphanage where her group was housed and talk or hike on the trails they had worked on the previous week.

The Allegheny Portage Railroad was part of a canal and inclined plane system that preceded the traditional railroads. Where the topography allowed, canal boats would be drawn by horses along the paths of rivers like the Juniata and Susquehanna. In the 1840s, one could board such a boat somewhere along the lower Susquehanna and take it the whole way to Hollidaysburg. West of Hollidaysburg, the passenger cars were taken off the boats and placed on wheeled cars to take them over the Allegheny Front on a series of inclined planes. A pulley system powered initially by horses and later by steam would yank the cars over the steep incline to the summit in Cresson. A grand stone traveler's rest called the Lemon House sat atop the summit and served as a way station for the weary traveler. The trip across the state took days and it was a tough trip, so these stop-overs were much appreciated by the railroad's patrons.

The railroad differed from its successor in the 1850s in that it used stone sleepers instead of wooden ties. These sleepers were massive rocks mined from the surrounding area, cut into blocks and buried in the ground so the tops were just a bit above ground level. The rails were then spiked into the stone blocks as you would spike the rails into the more traditional wooden ties. Now covered by soil and leaf litter, Nadine's group spent much of the summer digging up those rail tie sleepers so the actual path of the rail line could be seen. Though caked with soil when first dug up, a bit of cleaning would uncover the spike holes still visible in each rock. Twenty years later, the area was fully restored to its 1840s appearance (sleepers included) and a new visitors' center was built.

Though I was still disappointed that I could not have been part of that summer project on the Allegheny Portage Railroad, I became an adopted member of the group and learned much about the work they were doing and some of the natural and regional history they tried to preserve. And I got a great bike ride in to boot.

Even before Nadine set off for the YCC adventure, we both fashioned ourselves to be budding naturalists. We had gotten there by two different routes, she through a family that did lots of things outdoors and I through a curiosity of the woods that bordered our house.

These interests even spilled over into social time. One week during my visit to Cresson, we were sitting on the back porch of the orphanage talking and spied a peculiar caterpillar crawling by us. Most teenagers would have flicked it away or stepped on it but Nadine and I sat and marveled at the hairy spines on the top and sides of the insect. Neither of us had seen such a bug before and decided that we had to find out what it was. After some searching, we discovered that it was a Tussock Moth, a relative of the Gypsy Moth.

In retrospect, those rides up Cresson Mountain were even more amazing given that I was still riding the salvaged AMF bicycle that came to me through neighbor Larry Shank's misfortune. It was the typical department store bicycle — heavy and uncomfortable. Beyond the discomfort of that cheap saddle, my own stupidity would make one of the rides particularly painful. Those were the days when cut-off shorts were especially fashionable and making them really short was even better. I had a pair of checked pants that I thought would make great shorts for my weekly visit to Cresson. I took the scissors to them that Wednesday but cut them even shorter than I had intended. They ended up so short that the insides of my thighs were rubbed raw from the plastic seat by the time I got to Cresson. Many years later, I can vividly recall sitting through my visit in excruciating pain. But I was too embarrassed to tell Nadine that the insides of my thighs were on fire, fearing that she might read something else, terribly inappropriate, into the comment.

That fall following the Allegheny Portage adventure I went camping with her family to Allegheny National Forest. It was yet another trip that excited me about the outdoors in a way I had not yet experienced. It was on that trip that I came to realize how incredibly dark the sky can become when one is far from the light pollution of an urbanized area. On clear nights, overwhelming starlight dominates the otherwise dark sky in a way that can be seen only in the absence of city lights. Having lived in the city for my entire eighteen years, the nearest streetlight was never far away and it was difficult to experience such a sky. Even though the Waclos were prepared with such accoutrements,

Nadine and I embarked on an after-dark stroll without a flashlight, evidently looking for that romantic ambience. It must have been a new moon because just a few hundred yards from our campsite, we found ourselves in a clearing, the only light coming from the abundant stars. Somehow finding a boulder in the darkness, we sat in the damp, chilly October air talking and looking at the stars. Maybe we really didn't need that flashlight after all, I thought to myself.

A few weeks later, her family set off for a weekend camping trip to Prince Gallitzin Park. I was excited to ride my bike the 25 miles to the park but was disappointed when I awoke to a dank October day. Intent on pursuing the adventure and visiting my girlfriend, I would parade to our thermometer every ten or fifteen minutes, promising myself that I would set off when the temperature surpassed 45 degrees. It never did and it became the first time that I missed a ride that could not be postponed to a later date. I decided that, if it was humanly possible, I would never let that happen again. Four years later, on a snowy July day in the Grand Teton Mountains, I would have a chance to follow-up on that pledge. But that's a story for another chapter.

A Dark and Stormy Night

"It was a dark and stormy night; the rain fell in torrents—except at occasional intervals, when it was checked by a violent gust of wind which swept up the streets."

—English author Edward Bulwer-Lytton
From the novel *Paul Clifford*
(A man who leads a dual life as a criminal and a gentleman)
(1830)

AS THE FALL TRIMESTER DREW TO AN END, A GROUP OF friends and classmates planned a backpacking trip on the Mid-State Trail. I had hiked a great deal but had not done an overnight trip and was eager to do so. The trip was to begin at the trailhead near Spruce Creek and go on as far as we could walk in several days. Jeff Colledge was organizing the outing and Nadine was planning to join the group, so I was even more thrilled to be part of such an adventure. Though my mother had conceded to allow me to do more and more on the bike, I was shattered when she told me I couldn't go on the hike. I begged, implored, and even groveled, to no avail.

The trimester ended in mid-November and that meant the weather was shadowed in uncertainty. November in Pennsylvania can present relatively pleasant autumn weather, sometimes even into the sixties, or bring the worst of early winter. The adventurers had been lulled into a false sense of security and climatic optimism, thanks to an unseasonably warm October. From October 5th to November 6th all but five days were above 55 degrees and most of the nights were mild by October standards.

As it progressed further into November, the climatic odds began to catch up with our aspiring hikers. While the trip started on one of those pleasant days, it would end up in a much different meteorological place. At bedtime, a night or two into the hike, I took a gander at the thermometer outside our kitchen window and was shocked to see it already hovering near the freezing mark. As I crawled into bed, snow began to fall and the wind whistled through the spruce trees outside my window. Part of me was consoled that I had not made the trip, but another part of me was worried about my friends.

The nasty weather subsided a bit as the hike neared its final destination. I was eager for their return to hear how they had weathered the storm. Strangely, nobody really wanted to talk about too many of the details. Finally, after some coaxing, Jeff and Nadine shared the unholy story. While not as bad as the Donner Party's nightmare 128 years before in the Sierra, there were some eerie parallels. As the afternoon wore on that fateful day, the group feared the worst. The temperature had dropped and the skies had turned an ugly gray. It was the ugly gray that usually forebode late autumn snow. Nightfall was coming quite early by this point in November and as late afternoon crept upon them, it was already unbearably cold and nearly dark. They had a difficult time fathoming how cold their night would be if the temperature continued to plummet. To complicate matters, the hikers were as far away from a town as one could get in this part of Pennsylvania.

Keeping in mind the old adage that desperate times call for desperate measures, the group decided that sleeping outside simply was not an option on that night. In what seemed like an act of divine intervention, they stumbled upon a small cabin just a short distance from the trail. Could they talk the owners into some sort of shelter for the night? Since hunting season did not begin until the following week, the cabin was empty. That also meant that it was locked. Exploring every option to get into the structure, they finally concluded that the only way in was by breaking and entering. They carefully broke one of the windows on the front door and left themselves in.

It was unlikely there was a more law-abiding group of college aged kids in the entire country, making their crime that much more traumatic. They were so overcome with guilt that they decided they had to repair the window the best they could and leave money to pay for the final repair. The edge was taken off their anxiety when they were able to build a warming fire, assuring not only that they would not die of hypothermia, but they would actually be the most comfortable criminals in Centre County, Pennsylvania.

I would not realize it at the time, but the infamous backpacking adventure of November 1974 would be indicative of the sorts of thrills and tribulations that would beset us on all sorts of outdoor adventures on foot, on our bikes, and even in automobiles. With all the adventure and overwhelming natural beauty we experienced on such trips, we also had difficult times, unexpected glitches, and physically demanding ordeals. Despite the less-than-ideal conditions on the Mid-State Trail those frigid November days, I still felt cheated that I missed that one.

As that early winter weather turned even colder, our attention turned to our time off over Christmas, a holiday that was always particularly momentous at the Fredericks'. Even well into our teenage and high school years, we looked forward to "Santa's" visit each Christmas Eve. And he always came. Somehow or other he knew when we would be going off to Midnight Mass and would have all our gifts neatly arranged in the shadows when we wandered back home shortly after 1:00 a.m.

Though not permitted to open anything until Christmas morning (it was the tradition), we would always try to discretely sneak a peek when we passed through the living room. Having the prime spot near the bottom of the steps (another tradition), I had the chance to see more than my siblings. On that Christmas Eve of 1974, it was hard to miss the new bike. Still holding on to that childlike excitement, I had a hard time going to sleep thinking about that new bike setting at the bottom of the steps.

As I walked down the hallway from my bedroom, I saw it. While I had told "Santa" that I wanted a racing bike with a lugged frame, I knew little more about what I might get. Not that I would have really known at that point anyway. It was a Concord Aztec and Saint Nick managed to find it in my favorite color to boot. The burnt orange bike seemed to glisten as it sat there among the many other gifts. Concords, it turned out, were not particularly noteworthy bikes and this one weighed in at a robust 32 pounds. But I didn't realize that at the time and I could not have cared less. I had stepped up and that was all I cared about at that moment.

The Concords were made by a Japanese company, Kawahara Bicycles, who also made bikes for Puch and Schwinn, among others. Americans were buying bundles of bikes in the late seventies and Kawahara was making as many as they could to fill the demand. They were shipping them across the Pacific in 707s to fill the orders in a timely fashion. The Concords were mass produced, mid-priced bikes, but to me, it seemed like the top of the line.

Three dozen years later, as we found ourselves cleaning out our childhood home, I realized that the Concord was still hanging up in the garage. Perhaps more amazingly, among the thousands of pictures we went through was a picture of my brother Gerard, Nadine, and me from that Christmas Day 1974. My new backpack was over my shoulders and Nadine was holding onto the handlebars of the new bike. In what might be described as a Twilight Zone moment, we were standing on the very spot that Dad had taken the stereo-optic picture of me with my new tricycle exactly seventeen years before.

Though the winter of '74-'75 was a mild one, I didn't ride a great deal until the weather broke in late February. After all, bicycling was not a winter sport to me in those days and basketball kept me busy. My excitement for the sport got another nudge, though, when I found out that one of the physical education classes in the spring trimester was bicycling.

After a childhood of athletic mediocrity, I had become obsessed with basketball in high school and played every chance I got. I went from being among the worst in my seventh-grade gym class to among the best non-varsity players by the end of high school. Though not a great player by any standard, I was a different person from the twit that missed 25 foul shots in my junior high gym class. I certainly could have never played for my varsity high school team, but I played in the YMCA Church League. The league had been around for decades and was always a very competitive one that included many of the kids that had been good grade school and junior high players. I didn't play much in tenth or eleventh grade but saw more action my senior year. I came off the bench in one memorable game to score six points to spark a come-from-behind win over Todd Coleman's church team, Good Shepard. (Yes, that's the same Todd Coleman that had rescued Nadine and me from certain death the previous summer.) It was really the first time that I had publicly distinguished myself in any kind of athletic event and the very modest accomplishment came after four years of very hard work.

For some reason, I thought that I might be able to do the same thing on my bicycle. I'm still not sure what could have possibly possessed me to think that I could pull off such a feat. Despite a couple well played basketball games in a YMCA league, there was still little reason to think that I had an athletic bone in my entire body. With a new bike and a cycling gym class on the horizon, I decided, seemingly against all odds, that I would be a bicyclist.

From Journalism to Geography

"Mathematics was hard, dull work. Geography pleased me more."

—Naturalist John James Audubon
(1785—1851)

BEYOND THE PHYSICAL PART OF THE BICYCLING, THE BIKE would impact other parts of my life. It even influenced my choice of majors in school. One late night toward the end of my freshman year, I sat in our basement family room struggling mightily over an English paper. Try as I might, the words would not come and a sickening feeling overwhelmed me. If I were to continue on as a Journalism major, I would be cursed, not just to a night of anguish, but to a life of writer's block in the ominous shadow of impending deadlines. Soon after, I would explore my other major options.

Though I had not consciously sensed the link between the bike and the Geography at that early stage of both endeavors, the connections were simmering on the back burner. The bike presented a unique lens by which to observe the natural and man-made world. It was slow enough to see what was difficult to see from a car or plane but fast enough to cover much more ground than one ever could by foot.

My first Geography classes coincided closely with that first cycling physical education class and both used topographic maps extensively. Our cycling instructor had assembled a collection of those maps that went from Altoona to State College and they spilled from his office wall onto the adjacent offices in the old Ivy Hall. I would study those maps every chance I got, looking for the lightly traveled roads that I had not yet explored. The United States Geologic Survey (USGS) topographic maps were amazing publications, showing incomprehensible detail and managing to portray three dimensions on a flat sheet of paper through the miracle of contour lines.

Though still smarting from my first collegiate 'C' in a Spanish class I did not now even need, I was excited about the prospect of a course of study that was all about the environment. I hadn't a clue what this meant on the job front in a few years but it still seemed like a good idea. While it all turned out for the best, it was also sad that I walked away from the writing all together at that point in my life. It made me wonder how many aspiring writers were unable to get by one of those early spells of writer's block and turned around before they got very far down the author's trail. It also made me wonder how many found their way back, as I had, many years later.

While I was fascinated by the prospects of my new major, I was also anticipating my first collegiate physical education class in the spring of 1975. For someone that nearly flunked gym one marking period five years earlier, this was an interesting turnaround. It was the first time the cycling physical education class had been offered at Penn State Altoona. So untraditional was the class, it was not actually taught by the Physical Education instructor. Rather, a Philosophy professor by the name of Roddy Gerraughty was the teacher. Roddy loved to ride. He was the first to get me truly excited about the next level of cycling and helped me better appreciate the difference that good equipment could make. While a far sight better than the old tank I had been riding, the Concord Aztec that I had gotten for Christmas was still a beast. At more than 30 pounds, it was nearly ten pounds heavier than even an entry level racing bike at the time. Though Roddy had helped me understand how and why the equipment mattered, financial limitations would force me to labor along with the Concord. Despite the weight, it would serve me well for the next year. It became the machine on which I would accomplish a number of firsts.

Roddy also taught me you had to ride even when you didn't want to. For it was not possible to be a well-conditioned cyclist in Pennsylvania unless you went out in the cold and wet weather of a typical spring. Trouble was, this cold weather riding was even more unpleasant if one didn't dress properly. In that first spring, it seemed like I never did.

I over-dressed. I under-dressed. I wore cotton and got soaked with sweat. I wore baggy stuff and flapped around in the wind. It was trial and error to figure it all out and, for me, it was mostly error. I rode on many unpleasant days, but I was seldom comfortable.

I was a bit intimidated at first, too. Jeff Lovell was one of my classmates and had ridden across the country the summer before. He rode a lighter bike and had the build of an endurance athlete, unusually long and lean. I hoped that he would not embarrass me when the day of the final ride arrived. But as the term passed, I realized that I was among the better riders in the class. I put in the miles, cold weather or warm. Though I never expected to be the first one to complete it, by the end of the spring I thought I could at least ride the final 100-mile ride at the end of the term. By then, my motivation to complete the ride went far beyond the 'A' I would get in the class.

So while others my age had become preoccupied with exploring new physiological experiences of another sort (and a bit more promiscuous), I was contemplating my first journey into glycogen debt. Problem was that I had no idea what glycogen debt was. It could have been an accounting term for all I knew.

A few years later, I would have laughed hysterically at my appearance the morning of the big ride. We started very early in the morning and the weather was cool. I was typically over-dressed again. But I had learned something about clothes and planned for the warmup that seemed so likely. Having no bike bag, I opted for a cloth backpack to carry my extra stuff.

The morning of May 10th finally dawned and I set off from home in my cutoff shorts, a sweatshirt, Keds sneakers, and a small backpack with an advertisement for Razzles bubble gum plastered across the back. I thought it seemed utilitarian at the time but in retrospect it looked damned stupid and was dreadfully uncomfortable. Not coincidently, it was the last time in my life I ever wore a backpack on anything but a short commute.

A few miles into the ride we climbed Brush Mountain. While the Appalachians are not in the same league with the world's younger and larger mountains, the climbs are still demanding. This was especially so for a neophyte on a bike weighing nearly three dozen pounds. Just to make it a little more challenging, the good Lord added some fog. But not just any fog. It was more like someone had thrown a damp white sheet over us. I wasn't sure at that stage if it was the mountain that would kill me or if some motorist blinded by the fog would run me over first. It was so thick that I needed wipers to clear the water that kept condensing on my glasses.

That first climb scattered the riders far and wide. Besides the class members, Roddy had invited other cyclists from the area to join us and there were dozens of riders of widely varied abilities. Like so many Pennsylvania mountains, the painful struggle of the ascent is amply rewarded with a thrilling descent. This one is especially rewarding because of its length and the pleasant woodland through which it passes. A more gradual downgrade follows the initially steep decline. This translates into a fast paced ten miles that ends at an incredible limestone arch called, of all things, Arch Springs.

The foggy early morning turned into a glorious spring day. The bliss of a brisk descent, perfect weather, and the naivety that it would be all downhill lulled us into the false sense of security. The valley into which our descent deposited us was wall to wall limestone, full of sinkholes and an occasional cave. Quite appropriately, this one long ago became known as Sinking Valley. It is a textbook karst landscape of holes and cavities that form when water dissolves, rather than physically wearing away the calcium carbonate rock.

This limestone also makes great agricultural soil, so a ride through such topography can also be a ride through Pennsylvania's most scenic farmland. Unfortunately, the sinkholes of this landscape have a dark side. For they make great garbage pits into which farmers often dumped anything they didn't want, including the proverbial kitchen sink. Undetectable from the road itself, even those trash dumps hidden in the deep dark recesses of the valley couldn't spoil this perfect spring morning.

The Man of Steel

"Yes, it's Superman, strange visitor from another planet, with powers and abilities far beyond those of mortal men!"

—Announcer Jackson Beck
Adventures of Superman radio series
(1940-1951)

THE NEXT PART OF THE RIDE, IN RETROSPECT, TURNED OUT to be a life changing experience, for it was here that I first came to meet the real "Man of Steel." A bunch of us had formed a group that benefitted from each other's company, both socially and aerodynamically. Though I understood the benefits, this was the first time I had experienced such a profound push from the aerodynamic efficiency of riding in a large group. We were buzzing along at an uncommonly high speed with a lot less effort than usual. At the same time, we talked about the ride, the countryside, and what brought us to this place on an early May morning.

Through it all, one rider stood out above all the others. He was a tall, lanky guy on a Schwinn Paramount. The skin on his face was leathery and his arms and legs were already well tanned though it was still early in the season. His long legs straddled the large framed bike and his pedal stroke seemed effortless though he seemed to be riding a bigger gear than anyone else. He took much longer turns at the front of the pack, doing an inordinate amount of work compared to the rest of us.

I was excited, and somewhat surprised, to be with this group of riders. Besides this mystery man, it included Jeff Lovell, the cross-country rider from my cycling class. Though I might have had the heaviest bike in the group and one of only a few without toe clips, I managed to hang on. As we rode on, word quietly swept through the group that this mystery man was a guy by the name of Steel. The way he was riding, I thought the "Steel" part was a nickname he had earned for his riding style, but it turned out his real name was Ken Steel. In an almost reverent manner, the details went through the crowd that he rode thousands of miles every year and had been across the coun-try three times — all by himself. Despite being in his mid-thirties, nobody in Altoona could keep up with him on a long ride. I was, at first, amazed that I was riding with this guy. But my sense of accom-plishment quickly turned to panic when I realized we had more than 60 miles to get home.

Roddy Gerraughty had planned a lunch of sandwiches and fruit for us at the halfway point of the ride, north of State College. Just as importantly, we also had a chance to rest the tired legs and sore butts. It was perhaps the sore butt that was the most painful part of those first 50 miles. I realized that my bike was not just heavy, but had a most uncomfortable saddle — something closer to a plastic covered rock rather than an actual seat.

The ride southward back toward Altoona was along Route 550, a beautiful but hilly road that took us through more farm country. As we should have deduced from the morning ride, the wind was in our face heading back home. Under the best of circumstances, the second half of a long ride is tough. Add the fast pace of the first 50 miles to the hills and wind and this was lining up to have all the ingredients of an unpleasant ending.

By this time, Ken Steel and a few others had ridden ahead. As we came close to the crossroads near Frogtown, the bodies began to drop. Jeff Lovell started to have bad muscle cramps. Now this was, it turned out, an event that both horrified and excited me. The horrified feeling overcame me because I was sure I was destined to collapse if the star of our class, a cross-country rider, had fallen apart. Yet, as I rode away from him it struck me that I, too, could complete a cross-country tour. Though the thought of such an adventure had crossed my mind, this was the first time that I seriously thought I was capable of doing it.

A couple of us rode with Jeff to the old country market in Warriors Mark where we all tried to recharge with massive quantities of food and drink. Just before we got to the crossroads, we saw three riders in black cycling shorts and racing jerseys charging up the hill behind us. I later came to learn that it was Jim Deen, Dave Most, and a third rider from the Nittany Velo Club, the racing team from State College. They sort of snickered as they rode by us, no doubt commenting on my fashionable Razzles backpack. As they sprinted up the hill past us, it struck me that I had a long way to go to ride at that next level.

I was tired at that point, but Jeff and a few others were really laboring. We would later come to learn the physiological term for this debilitated state; we were entering the mind-altering state of glycogen debt. My delight in out-riding Jeff Lovell only lasted about a dozen miles though, for glycogen debt caught up with me somewhere just north of Tyrone. I later realized that many people never experience this zapping loss of energy even once in their life. But endurance athletes may suffer through it many times. Marathon runners call it the wall, bikers often call it the bonk.

Glycogen debt happens when the body begins to run out of the carbohydrate based energy from your glycogen stores. This very efficient energy metabolism begins to fade as the miles go by. When it does, the body begins looking for other energy and starts to metabolize proteins and fats, much less efficient energy sources. At the same time, deficiencies of potassium can cause muscle cramps. Proper hydration and high carbohydrate foods can stem the tide, but inexperienced riders don't usually realize that.

I mistakenly thought that a 100-mile ride would be just like stringing five 20 mile rides together. That incremental approach may have seemed like a logical bite-sized strategy for this mouthful of a ride. But the limits of carbohydrate metabolism would ultimately shoot that theory squarely in my sore backside somewhere in the middle of the fourth 20 mile segment. The ten miles between Tyrone and Bellwood would be ten of the longest miles of my life, a seemingly unending series of hills that must have taken nearly an hour to conquer. The prospect of finishing helped make the next few miles a bit less painful, but we were hammered with one more disappointment when we got back to the Altoona campus. In order to get an even 100 miles, we had to do one final three-mile loop west of the campus and Mr. Gerraughty told us we would not get our century patch from the League of American Wheelmen unless we did the loop. I had ridden from home and back on top of the official 100 miles and ended up with 105 miles on that May day. Needless to say, I was one tired puppy. I got home, ate and drank a bunch more, and collapsed fast asleep on the living room floor.

I rode several times that week in cycling class and decided that I should ride the 50 miles to Warriors Mark that next Saturday. I set off by myself in early morning and finished the ride without much trouble. Just a year before, such a ride would have seemed overwhelming, but after the 100-mile marathon of the week before, this ride was a cakewalk. This surely was the first sign that I had been inflicted with the bug. Those next few weeks, I would ride whenever I could and as far as time would allow. After the school year ended, Mr. Gerraughty would call and ask me to ride with him. Ken Steel and others from the bike club eventually hooked up with us and the disease became well entrenched. Somehow, I had managed to get by the summer of 1975 without a full-time summer job. Though I would still help in my mother's grocery store, I had only one true obligation that summer—riding that 32-pound bike every chance I had.

In mid-summer, a local road race was organized and I thought it was worth exploring. The race began along Mill Run Creek on the western edge of Altoona. We went south to Eldorado and up the Allegheny Front by way of the nasty climb on Sugar Run Road, finally descending Route 36 into Altoona. I went out on the course several times in the preceding weeks riding as hard as I could. One day, with my head down to the handlebars in an attempt to improve my aerodynamic profile, I ran over an animal for the first time near the town of Coupon, a chipmunk that tried to beat me across Buckhorn Road. I was sure this was a sign of how fast I had become, for surely only the fastest of riders ever ran over anything alive.

On race day, the day after Independence Day, I would come to realize that this was not the indicator of excellence that I believed it to be. Even before we began the climb up Sugar Run, I found out how really slow I was. Dave Most, one of those that had passed us like we were standing still on that century ride earlier in the spring, gave us a safety sermon before we began. Hoping to avoid the carnage likely to occur with a bunch of neophyte riders, he reminded us that few races were won in the first 100 meters. Though my future riding partners John Bradley and Ken Steel would finish second and third (far ahead of me) the seasoned racer from State College overwhelmed all the locals. But all the news was not bad for me, for I finished in the middle of the field, just well enough to give me the motivation to continue.

Though the riders from the racing club were much better than most of us from Altoona, it was also easy to see that they had much better bikes than most of us. This would help give rise to another symptom of my growing bike affliction: a new-found preoccupation with the equipment. Though a gradual process, every improvement brought the revelation that what I had been riding before was woefully inadequate. A new seat demonstrated how truly dreadful the old one had been. The comfort and efficiency of toe clips made me wonder why I had ever doubted their merits.

I was further fascinated by the prospect of my cousin, Brian Weakland, striking off on his own cross-country trip that same summer. He was beginning a reporter's job with the newspaper in State College later in the summer and planned to write a series of articles on the trip for the paper. It was the year before the national Bicentennial, but Brian had sold the paper on the idea this could be a celebration of the event, even if it was a year early. Brian and I had more than a few things in common. We were both the nonathletic sort when we were young and had discovered the bike in our late teens. Our parents felt that doing well in school was the highest priority and were not particularly interested in whether or not we participated in sports. Neither of our fathers was particularly athletic. Though Brian's dad, my Great Uncle Fred, would live to be 100, he was not an athlete in any traditional sense. He was a tiny man that struggled his entire life to keep his weight much above 100 pounds.

Riding cross-country at that time was probably something only a few hundred Americans attempted each year. For most, the physical, mental, and time demands of such an ordeal meant that it would be a once in a lifetime opportunity. For some strange reason, Brian and I shared the vision. But completing it alone, at least it seemed to me, required a higher level of insanity. To further testify to his unusual approach to the trip, he decided not just to ride solo but to take the southwest to northeast route. Such a route would take him through the Sonora Desert at the hottest time of the year. I suppose he didn't want anyone to speculate that he was taking the easy way out.

His reports back east were a source of curiosity to the entire Weakland family, and his newspaper articles were greatly anticipated. The stories were of particular interest to me and inspired me to ride even more often. At some point, it was suggested I might hook up with Brian for the last leg of his trip from Altoona to the East coast. Brian had developed cyclists' palsy, that horrible, numbing and often painful feeling at the base of the hands and wrists that comes from riding a hundred miles, day after day. With that in mind, Brian was especially happy to have someone join him for a few days at the end of that very long journey.

I went with his mom and dad to Pittsburgh to meet him and give him a day or two off the bike in the hopes the discomfort in his hands would fade. My bike was already packed and I was raring to go. I installed a rear rack on the bike and had recently gotten toe clips. But I was still wearing cutoffs and those white leather sneakers, confirming once again that ignorance really is bliss. Ill equipped or not, I was ready to begin my first real tour on two wheels.

Headed for the Coast

A Random Act of Kindness

"No act of kindness, however small, is ever wasted."

—Aesop
Sixth Century B.C.

AFTER BRIAN TOOK A COUPLE DAYS OFF THE BIKE, WE SET off for his sister's house in State College. Since it was only about 40 miles from Altoona, we left late in the day and got there for supper. As we neared State College, Brian took us on the unfinished portion of US 322. Though only a mile or so, I was freaked out to ride on a paved road completely absent of traffic. Before the days of any sort of bike ways in Pennsylvania, closed roads like this one brought a unique experience to riders that were accustomed to battling traffic. Being unfinished, though, the road really did not have any connection to any other road. We had to climb down a steep hill to a dirt road to ultimately get to his sister's place. Though a rather minor adventure, it was the first of many that my bike touring would bring me.

The next morning we set off for Harrisburg, where we intended to stay with another relative, my mom's sister Mary Jean and her husband Bobby. We rode to Lewistown and then onto old US 322 that ran along the Juniata River. About seven miles east of Lewistown the route went to four lanes while the old road continued through the villages and towns that grew up along the river. This was the first time that I fully appreciated what author William Least Heat-Moon would call Blue Highways, those little roads that showed up as tiny blue lines on the old maps.

As the limited access highway buzzed around these old communities, the old road meandered quietly through the farms and towns of Central Pennsylvania. Beyond the charm of such a route, they were flat whenever the highway followed the path of a river, as US 322 did. The towns and the interesting people one meets are where the really funny experiences and insightful conversations occur. While I had sensed this from my trip with my Aunt Bernadette a few years before, it was not until this trip to the East Coast that I fully appreciated what a fascinating experience such a trip could be.

One such story came to pass on that first full day of the ride when we pulled into Thompsontown. PA 333 intersects US 322 on the main street in Thompsontown and right on that corner sets a little ice cream and sandwich shop. It was a typically hot July day in Pennsylvania and we were mighty parched by the time we got to the crossroads. My thirst was magnified by yet another in my growing lists of blunders of cycling inexperience. I had bought an insulated water bottle with the hopes of always having cold water within my grasp, even on the hottest of days. What I forgot to consider was the possibility that I would run out of water first. For these insulated bottles sacrificed capacity for insulation and the things held only about two thirds what the standard bottles held. I quickly came to learn that warm water was much better than no water at all. It would be the last long trip I took that insulated bottle.

Since the establishment sold sandwiches, we decided it would be a good place to grab a bite and fill up our bottles. Now a full-fledged vegetarian, I had my standard cheese sub. A tall, pleasantly plump young lady waited on us but seemed preoccupied as she shuffled back and forth from the kitchen to the counter where Brian and I sat. We surmised that she and the boss had a bit of a tense relationship. As we finished, we asked if she would be so kind as to fill our bottles for the next leg of our trip. She gazed at us with a look of panic as if to say, "Oh, how could you ask this of me? The boss will surely be annoyed." But she did not speak the words; she simply continued that terribly troubled look.

Then, with what was surely her most defiant act of independence in some time, she looked over her shoulder toward the kitchen and whispered, "What the hell, give me your bottles." We thanked her profusely, but quietly, so the boss would not realize what revolutionary act had just occurred. Brian and I sipped the water in the ensuing miles with a special reverence in respect of the courageous gesture of the repressed waitress. I passed that crossroads on the four-lane road many, many times in the next 30 years and seldom did I go by that I didn't smile as I recalled the tiny act of kindness in Thompsontown.

The ride along the Juniata River was an incredibly beautiful one through one of the prettiest parts of South Central Pennsylvania. The weather was perfect and we even had a bit of a tail wind. But as the Juniata met the Susquehanna near Clarks Ferry, our pleasant ride was destined to take a very unpleasant turn.

Brian and I had looked at the map and were uncertain as to which route along the Susquehanna River would be easier. Unlike the path along the Juniata, there was no less-traveled alternative route along the Susquehanna, only the major roads. We ultimately decided that US 11/15 would surely be preferable to the highly-traveled US 322 on the east side of the river. In this case, though, it turned out that the answer to the question was none of the above, for one road was as bad as the other. US 11/15 was a narrow, congested mess with loads of truck traffic that was especially harrowing late in the day. It was one of those small handful of times that I truly wondered if I would live to tell the tale.

As if the road and traffic were not bad enough, several miles down the river the skies opened up on us. We came upon a school and raced up the driveway. It turned out to be Susquenita High School and we found a portico to duck under at one of the side entrances. Despite lots of water falling from the sky, I was thirsty, having again emptied my dreadfully inadequate water bottle. Though in the midst of summer vacation and apparently deserted, we thought we'd try the door in the hope that we would find a water fountain. In what would be the lone serendipity of our ride along the Susquehanna, the door opened and a fountain was a short walk away. I drank until I couldn't drink any more.

We walked back outside to survey the weather situation and were disappointed to see the rain still falling. After sitting under the portico for what seemed like hours, the rain finally began to let up and we walked back toward the school doorway to fill up our bottles before we set off. Much to our chagrin, the door had locked when we exited the building a short time before. A custodian's oversight had given us sustenance in our time of need and our own stupidity left us high and dry again. Once more, I found myself with this terrific insulated water bottle — still well insulated but very empty. Now I knew exactly what the Ancient Mariner meant when he spoke that oft repeated phrase, "Water, water everywhere nor any drop to drink."

One's appreciation of the natural landscape is usually enhanced by experiencing it on a bike, rather than a car. You're going fast enough to cover a significant distance but slow enough to see things that whiz by in the car. Under normal circumstances, the Susquehanna Valley is one of those truly remarkable landscapes that should be an incredible cycling experience. But when one must hang on for dear life with every massive truck and speeding car that passes by, it's challenging to appreciate the scenery.

The reason the Pennsylvania Canal and later the Pennsylvania Railroad followed this route in the middle of the nineteenth century is because the Juniata and Susquehanna Valleys carved the path of least resistance. It is only where larger rivers, like the Susquehanna, cut through the mountains that one can perpendicularly cross the ridges. This would indicate that the river has been around throughout the folding and the subsequent erosion of the rocks. By contrast, if you were to draw a straight line from Altoona to Harrisburg (the western most and eastern most Pennsylvania cities in the Appalachian Ridge and Valley), the trip would be a seemingly never-ending series of mountain ascents and descents. I would later bicycle over a number of those mountains, rather than through the water gaps. Needless to say, the mountains are a difficult endeavor and the miles pass much more slowly.

Rather than struggle over the mountains, we chose this route through the water gaps of the Susquehanna River. Unfortunately, the proliferation of the automobile meant that thousands of cars do the same every day. With them, came not just the traffic, but the visual blight of the highway as well. Some parts of these two river routes had more blight than they did pleasant scenery. The dilapidated buildings, junked cars, billboards, and shopping plazas at the end of massive expanses of paved parking lots turned an otherwise spectacular landscape into the ugliest of places. And the closer you looked at some of it, the worse it got.

The blight spilled over into our other senses as well. While the noise from the traffic came as no surprise, the smells were enough to choke you, too. The car and truck exhaust was bad enough, but Brian and I added yet another page to the book of olfactory unpleasantness. Parched and down on water (again), we stopped at an old diner and Brian got a can of pop (as we Western Pennsylvanians called it) from the machine in front of the greasy spoon. We sat down and began to partake when we were overwhelmed by the aroma of dog doo. Tucked away on the side of the place was a dog pen that had not been cleaned out perhaps since dogs were first domesticated. We drank our pop quickly and dashed back into the traffic.

But like all bad experiences, this too would pass and we finally cruised into my Aunt Mary Jean and Uncle Bob's, just in time for supper. I remember my Aunt Mary Jean as a remarkably even-tempered woman who smiled much more than she frowned. It always meant that any visit with her family was a pleasant one. On this day of frustration, their cordiality and tasty home cooking was just what the doctor ordered.

A Blue Eagle

"The best-laid plans of mice and men
Often go awry
And leave us naught but grief and pain
For promised joy."

—"To a Mouse"
Robert Burns (1759-1796)

IF THE TRIP INTO HARRISBURG WAS TO BE A TRYING EXPE-rience, it seemed certain that a trek into the most densely populated part of the state toward Philadelphia would be even more hair-raising. Brian chose his routes with care, hoping to avoid the worst roads and traffic but the US 11/15 experience proved that the best laid plans of mice and men do indeed go awry. The early part of that next day passed without incident, as we found our way through the countryside east of Harrisburg and through Lebanon and Berks Counties. Though parts of this area have been overwhelmed by suburban sprawl in the ensuing years, its character was still distinctly rural in the mid-seventies. This made for pleasant riding with lighter traffic.

The Ridge and Valley section of the Appalachians ends near Harrisburg and the hilly (but not mountainous) Piedmont begins. Those hills (as well as the Piedmont south into Alabama) can be pesky obstacles that make for a tiring ride as the miles pile up. I recall one such hill near Reading, Pennsylvania that was a long, steep climb that confronted us at the peak of the heat on that afternoon. After climbing for five or six exhausting minutes, we finally came to the top to find a graveyard before us. Brian speculated the cemetery was surely located here because it was easier to carry the bodies of the cyclists that perished on the climb to their eventual resting place.

We survived that climb and a bunch of others and arrived in Boyertown around supper time. We had gone nearly 80 miles and we were both famished. Those were the days of fading downtowns and Boyertown was experiencing the same loss of business that downtowns all over were experiencing. A semblance of a business district hung on and a cute restaurant on the main street was still open when we wandered into town. Brian and I were among a small handful of guests and the waitress was fascinated by the nature and scope of our endeavor. Only about a half year into my vegetarianism, I was genuinely excited to see eggplant parmigiana on the menu. I would not realize it at the time, but that meal would be a common thread on several other memorable days in the saddle as varied and distant as Idaho Springs, Idaho and Boyertown, Pennsylvania. We ate well at the quaint little place and it was a good thing, for it sustained us through a most rigorous final 25 miles that would end in the dark as well as in disagreement.

Though I would remember Boyertown for its eggplant, it was most famous for its long history of transportation related business endeavors that dated back to horse and buggy days. In 1872, Jeremiah Sweinhart had opened a new carriage factory near the Mount Pleasant seminary for the manufacture of carriages, buggies, spring wagons, and sleighs. His factory was the forerunner to the Boyertown Body and Equipment Company that would make ambulances during wartime and other box trucks for decades afterward. When I realized Boyertown's dominance in that marketplace, I began to notice how many delivery trucks of all sorts had the Boyertown logo. Each time one passed me on a ride I would think back to a tasty meal on a quiet summer evening in 1975.

We decided we would ride another 20 miles or so and try to find a motel close to Norristown. As it happened, this would be my first painful lesson in how ill fortune and bad decisions are magnified when you're traveling by bicycle. When something goes wrong on a car trip, the next town, the next lodging opportunity, or the next repair shop is never much more than fifteen minutes away. That same ride on a bike may be an hour or more down the road.

The first lesson along these lines came to be known as the Blue Eagle Incident. Brian was lagging a little bit behind me on the hills as dusk was approaching. As I climbed out of the valley carved by Skippack Creek on US 422 a few miles west of Norristown, I spied the Blue Eagle Motel on the right. Unjustifiably fearing it might belong to the Fleabag Inn chain of motels, I passed it and charged up the hill, thinking that one motel would surely be followed by several others.

But alas, the next few miles clicked by without any sign of another place. As darkness kept inching closer, I stopped to discuss our situation with Brian. We always got along with each other, but he was ready to choke me at that particular moment. Even after the stop, we had to pedal up and down several more hills before finally finding a place in Norristown. Many years later, we would still fondly recall the Blue Eagle Incident. It was such a memorable event it even gave rise to a new verb in the Frederick/Weakland Dictionary. Whenever one of us would be confronted with a difficult decision on where to stop or which way to go, the other would inevitably warn his traveling partner, "Just don't Blue Eagle me!"

The next morning, we walked over to a restaurant next to the motel. Both of us being baseball fans, we were amused by the baseball theme as well as its name, Home Plate. I ordered pancakes and eggs and Brian got something similar — nothing extraordinary or challenging to prepare. The Blue Eagle Incident forgiven, we were fairly-well rested and eager to begin our final day in the saddle.

But the waitress had other ideas. We waited, and waited, and waited some more. Brian glanced down at the place mat, scratched his head and concluded that it surely was a misprint.

"A misprint?" I inquired.

"Yeah, there's an extra p."

Now I was really confused. "An extra p?"

"Yeah, it should read Home Late, not Home Plate."

A Cyclist's Vision of Heaven and Hell

"To appreciate heaven well 'tis good for a man to have some fifteen minutes of hell."

—"Gone with a Handsomer Man"
Poet Will Carleton
Farm Ballads (1873)

CYCLING AND LIFE REALLY ARE FUNNY AND FULL OF UNEX-pected turns. On this day, we would ride through both heaven and hell within a few hours of each other. Our Home Late culinary experience delayed us enough to throw us into the peak of rush hour, which in suburban Philadelphia and Trenton is more like rush half day. We somehow managed, I suppose through some good route planning, to get through the Philadelphia area with less difficulty than we feared. Though not a pleasant ride in the country, we survived unscathed.

But the same could not be said for the Trenton part of the trip. The traffic was atrocious and the roads not well-suited for bicycles. Brian had concluded, and my later experiences would clearly confirm, that the further east you go in the United States, the more impatient and rude the drivers become. Trenton was certainly the exclamation point to that premise. We decided one of our visions of hell was cycling through Trenton for all eternity. To make matters worse, we were confronted with the infamous New Jersey traffic circles as we crossed the Delaware River. I am told circles are supposed to reduce the number of potential points of conflict at an intersection while allowing traffic to continue moving. But they can be particularly hair-raising for cyclists. Besides the traffic volume, bicycles become invisible to many motorists, both by choice and by accident. As we entered one of the circles, an elderly woman edged out, completely ignored Brian and ran right into the back of his bike, knocking him to the street. I saw the whole thing, seemingly in slow motion, and could not imagine he was not hurt. Much to my relief, he jumped up from the pavement. When he got to his feet, he threw his sunglasses at the car. It was perhaps the angriest I had ever seen Brian, one of the most even-tempered individuals I've ever known.

The old woman was pretty shook up, too. One of us, if not both, asked her what the hell she was looking at, finding it especially difficult to garner much concern for her anxiety. I recall thinking at the time that she had acted as if we would vaporize as she drove through us. After all, she was in a car and we didn't even belong in her circle. After we realized Brian was not injured, our attention turned to his bike. At first, things looked pretty bad. His fender and rear wheel were both bent, the wheel so badly that it was hitting the frame. With visions of lawsuits and insurance increases dancing in her head, the lady implored Brian to let her pay for all the repairs. At the bike shop, we were relieved to find out the damage was all reparable and we could be out of Trenton in fairly short order. When the accident happened, I feared Brian's cross-country adventure would end a few dozen miles from the east coast, but a mixture of good fortune and determination would not allow such an injustice to occur.

The first few miles after leaving the bike shop were as insane as the trip through the middle of Trenton. The traffic was worse than it was on US 11/15 going into Harrisburg, and the drivers were twice as crazy and impatient. When we finally got through that mess, it struck us that we were on the Coastal Plain of New Jersey, a flat and sandy landscape like nowhere in Pennsylvania. Having lived in a place where it was difficult to go four or five miles without running into a hill or mountain, this was a new kind of riding for me.

The Atlantic Coastal Plain is new rock and soil (as rock and soil go) on the edge of very old rock and landscapes to the west. The brisk ride over the pancake-flat roads with wide berms was a stark contrast to the hills and narrow roads we had struggled over just a day earlier in eastern Pennsylvania. Beyond the anticipation of reaching the end, we welcomed the cycling friendly road and topography. It is no coincidence that our ride that day passed many produce stands selling watermelons and cantaloupes, for those fruits love sandy, well drained soils. These were the days when regional agricultural markets were still vibrant and a large portion of your fresh produce came from the part of the country in which you lived. In this case, it was often just a few feet off the road.

While the end of the trip was a noteworthy and a special time for me, I could not fathom what must have been going through Brian's mind. Though a fairly quiet person, he talked to me about the trip enough so that I knew what a challenging experience it had been for him. I, like many others, had also read the stories in his diary in the State College newspaper. But I felt particularly privileged to have been part of the trip, even if for only four days. I, more than anyone, could empathize.

I sensed then, and fully realized when I completed my own cross-country trip a few years later, part of what you feel is relief. Under the best of circumstances, rides of such lengths are trying—mentally and physically. Day after day in the same boring landscape of the Great Plains, unbearable traffic in the cities, the fear that some nut might do something to you, lousy weather, sore hands and saddle sores, all tax your limits. But for Brian it rose to another level, riding alone for most of the trip and simmering through the desert heat. I learned many lessons in those four days with Brian and only a few of them actually had much to do with the bike. Such an endeavor takes persistence, patience, and a mental toughness that is not often called upon in everyday life. I would later come to understand that it could be a rite of passage; one much more noteworthy than college graduation or your first real job.

Brian's mother and father, Aunt Margie and Uncle Fred as I had always called them, drove to the beach to meet us and give us a ride home. Like my own mom and dad, Brian's parents were very protective, perhaps even more than my own. They had worried about him for much of the trip and were especially concerned when he developed hand numbness toward the end of the trek. Though for different reasons than Brian, they too were breathing a big sigh of relief as they watched their son dip his wheel in the Atlantic Ocean, just five weeks after doing the same in the Pacific.

Recovered from his cross-country adventure, Brian asked me to go with him on an overnight camping trip late in August. It was my first bicycle camping experience and, not surprisingly, included several painful lessons on how not to camp. The ride was a beautiful one on a warm August day and ended in the similarly spectacular Bald Eagle State Park. A manmade lake sat in the middle of the park, and the campground was situated on the eastern shore. Being late in the summer, the crowd was sparse and the park quiet. A year later, when I moved to State College for my junior year at Penn State, this part of Centre County would come to be one of my favorite places to bicycle.

After supper, Brian and I set up his tent and, shortly after nightfall, crawled in for a pleasant night's sleep. The cicadas, one of the indicators of the impending autumn weather and almost deafening by late August, transformed the quiet afternoon into a (pleasantly) noisy early evening. Cicadas can drown out many urban sounds when they are at their peak, so in a place like this it's difficult to hear much of anything else at all. Our trip, up to this point, had been nothing short of idyllic. But that would change soon enough.

The longer nights of late summer and early fall tend to make for more foggy mornings than mid-summer, and the dew can be heavy. Having grown up in Central Pennsylvania, I suppose Brian and I expected dew on the grass but were quite surprised when it crept into other places as well. Sometime in the middle of the night we awoke to rain. But this rain was on the inside of the tent, not the outside. Our respiration had conspired with the moisture laden air outside to cover the inside of the tent with droplets of water. When enough of the water accumulated on the inside it started to rain down upon us and our sleeping bags. It leaked through the seams of the tent as well, making the uncomfortable situation even worse. By sunrise, the inside of the tent looked as if someone had sprayed the entire thing from top to bottom with a hose and nearly everything inside the tent was soaked. Needless to say, we got very little sleep after the interior deluge started in mid-morning.

Half asleep and fully discouraged, we got up and futilely tried to dry everything out. As we sat in front of the nearby general store in Howard eating our breakfast, still soggy and chilled, we concluded one night was enough and decided to head home.

Later in August, Jeff Colledge and I rode from Altoona to State College. It was a warm day and by the time we got to the village of Franklinville about fifteen miles from our destination, we were thirsty and short on water. We came to a stream across from the old church in Franklinville where President Jimmy Carter attended services when he came to Spruce Creek to fish. While I had grown suspicious of drinking out of streams and springs, Jeff saw the bucolic and peaceful setting as assurance this would be a safe source of water to quench his thirst. After drinking heartily, and returning to the highway, we saw three cows trudging through the very creek from which Jeff had just partaken. A distressed look came over his face and I could not help but chuckle.

On our return trip, we stopped at Colerain State Park in Spruce Creek and decided a dip in the creek would be a relief from the very hot and humid afternoon. A small rock dam had been built in the creek to make a pool that was well-suited for the weary and warm cyclist. The sun filtered through the trees on the shores of Spruce Creek and the swim was a welcome respite from the oppressive heat. We laid in the pool made by the dam for a long time. Yes, we concluded, this was the life and we could easily spend the rest of our summer vacation in that very spot.

The week that school started, Jeff's brother Tom and I rode our bikes back to State College to visit Jeff. He was rooming with two college friends in their new apartment. Tom and I had a great ride over the same country roads through Huntingdon and Centre Counties that Jeff and I traversed a week or two before. But like the adventure to Bald Eagle State Park, the pleasant trip was destined to end in a much less pleasant way than it began. Being the first weekend away from home, his roommates decided they would take advantage of their newly acquired freedom and have a few beers. But a few turned into a whole bunch and when the two of them staggered in sometime around 1:00 a.m., they were well plastered. What transpired after that was a marathon of puking, groaning, and swearing that they would never drink again. I'm not sure what time the ordeal finally ended, but for the second cycling trip in a row, I couldn't get even half a night's sleep. Not surprisingly, the 45-mile ride home the next morning took much longer than the northbound trip the day before. The ordeal confirmed little good could come from the excessive consumption of alcoholic beverages, and it reinforced my annoyance with our collegiate classmates' preoccupation with partying. I didn't attend a party in four years of college and had no regrets that I didn't. A bike ride seemed a much more worthwhile use of my time.

Discovering Unexpected Connections

"Creating a new theory is not like destroying an old barn and erecting a skyscraper in its place. It is rather like climbing a mountain, gaining new and wider views, discovering unexpected connections between our starting points and its rich environment. But the point from which we started out still exists and can be seen, although it appears smaller and forms a tiny part of our broad view gained the mastery of the obstacles on our adventurous way up."

—Albert Einstein (1879-1955)

THE MILES STARTED TO PILE UP IN 1975, RIDING AT LEAST 500 miles each month from May to September. Ken Steel and Roddy Gerraughty would instill in me the importance of the miles, both from a conditioning and competitive standpoint. Like runners, bicyclists love to compare their training logs and 1975 began a lifelong competition with my cycling friends (and foes) to accumulate the most miles. Ken, of course, would be the barometer by which all other cyclists in our parts would measure themselves. Ken was single, had three full days a week off work as a city fireman, and had a generous vacation package that gave him plenty of time to ride. Free time in the station house also gave him a bunch of time to work on his bike. Over the next few years especially, Ken would drag a few of us out on the most extraordinary rides. In that first year or so, I was horribly intimidated to join him and a few of the older riders that frequently accompanied him.

While I would ride with Brian Weakland or Ken once in a while, many rides were solo endeavors. These could be especially interesting adventures, too, as I discovered things and unknown places not very far from home. An unseasonably warm late October weekend took me to the village of Blue Knob atop the Allegheny Front in southern Blair County. The quiet, tree-lined road climbed steadily westward up the escarpment, ending with a hairpin curve and a sharp ascent to the summit where the back road met the more heavily traveled Route 164.

The Appalachian Highlands stretch from southeastern New York to Birmingham, Alabama and the western portion is divided into two sections: the folded Ridge and Valley Province and the uplifted Appalachian Plateau. The boundary between the folded mountains and the less deformed plateau is an escarpment (not truly a mountain geologically). In Pennsylvania, it is known as the Allegheny Front and generally marks the border separating Centre, Blair and Bedford Counties from coal country in Clearfield, Cambria and Somerset Counties to the west. Several dozen roads climbed up the escarpment in Blair and Bedford counties, including this one up to Blue Knob, and I would become intimately familiar with each of them the next few years.

I also came to realize that there were few places in America where we can see a more definitive cultural and political boundary than the one created by the Appalachian Front in south central Pennsylvania. To the east, we find a politically conservative region that seldom elects a Democrat to any public office. The rich soils of the limestone valleys are excellent agricultural lands. A high percentage of church-goers are Protestants.

West of the front, the coal mines and steel mills attracted immigrants from European countries who were known for mining and related skills well-suited to the economic base of this region. These folks tended to be slightly more liberal in their political leanings, and Republicans had long been in the minority in public office. A much higher portion of them were Roman Catholic. Small coal towns, many of them company towns, are still scattered across these western counties. Even the smallest of them had their own Catholic Church. Many had two different ethnic churches that still offered Sunday mass in the native European tongue well into the Twentieth Century.

Never particularly affluent places, these coal towns became even more economically depressed as the coal industry faded and what was left of the industry became more mechanized. Though the countryside of this region could be very scenic, riding through the towns themselves could be depressing. Run down old houses and trailers often sat right next to boney piles, the ugly mountains of coal mining waste that came from decades of unregulated coal strip mining.

Most roads climbed the first part of the Allegheny Front steadily. Thanks to the miracle of differential erosion, somewhere toward the top of the incline it always pitched up sharply. Though you didn't notice the steeper slope of the very hard Rockwell Sandstone in a car, you always knew when you hit it on the bike. The steep climb was transformed into the ungodly.

This sharp change in slope confounded the Pennsylvania Railroad in the 1840s and 1850s and has challenged road builders since the first paved roads were built a half century later. Even today, these slopes are the most challenging to keep clear of snow and ice and are still occasionally closed during the most severe winter weather events. The steep slopes also have thin, unproductive soils, making it a difficult place to build much of anything. For both practical and environmental reasons, the slopes usually remain tree covered. Its stream valleys are also easy to dam, making the Allegheny Front well-suited for public water supply reservoirs. The highlands above the reservoirs make ideal watersheds, as long as they are not fouled by acid mine drainage from coal mines on the plateau.

Living at the base of the Allegheny Front my entire life, rides up the escarpment made up a disproportionate share of the miles I would pile up over the years. That kind of topography would either make you a good climber or push you toward some other, less painful sport. Though I would not realize it until several years later, the slight build that had cursed all my other athletic endeavors would be an asset when it came to climbing these mountains and hills on a bike. Cycling was an oddity in the world of sports, actually rewarding those that were otherwise viewed by typical jocks to be emaciated twerps.

It's Cold Outside

The Choir
Written by Dan Klawon
Canadian-American Records (1966)

AFTER SOME GREAT AUTUMN RIDES, I WAS PARTICULARLY unhappy to see winter arrive. For the first time in my life, a cold or snowy winter was not something to look forward to. Bicycling is one of those handful of sports that is profoundly impacted by inclement weather, and a late spring is a big setback to anyone with racing aspirations. In an unfortunate coincidence, the winters during my college years were especially snowy and cold. It was tough to get out even when a warm day would sneak in. The city streets would remain sloppy from the melting snow much longer than highways in the country. December 1975 started out warmer than usual, but that came to an abrupt end in the middle of the month. An eight week stretch that ended on my sister's birthday on February 10th saw only two days go over 40 degrees. The low dipped to zero or below eight times, about a half dozen times more than it does in an average winter.

I was obsessed with living lightly from an environmental standpoint, so I rode my bike and walked everywhere I could. There was nearly always a car at home if I needed one but I almost never took it to school. In four years at Penn State, I never even bought a parking permit. I walked to school if the roads were not clear enough to bicycle. It was nearly three miles one way, so in a winter like the one of 1975-1976, 100 walking miles in a month would not be unusual. The days before affordable electronic music players, the walks could be long and boring if you didn't have company.

Most days, especially my sophomore year, were solo walks. During my freshman year, Jeff Colledge and I would walk together when our schedules were similar. In an effort to keep my edge on the bike, I also started to run that fall and winter when the days became too short or cold to ride. So when I needed a physical education class, a physical conditioning class sounded like a great fit. Being the dead of winter, most days we would run in the gym. It turned out that only one classmate, Frank Galosi, could keep up. Frank took several environmental classes with me and hailed from Ehrenfeld, Pennsylvania, an old coal town between Altoona and Johnstown. Ehrenfeld was also home to Charles Buchinski, better known by his stage name Charles Bronson. But the town was also infamous for having a ringside seat for the Johnstown Flood of 1889. While some backwash from the flood waters found its way up the tributary, Ehrenfeld was spared from the worst of the flood. Whether by car or bicycle, I could not help but recall the flood and Frank and Bronson's common roots every time I would pass through.

Frank and I would run together every day, talking and laughing as we lapped our slower and less-fit classmates. When test day came, I was determined to be the best in the class. I pulled away from Frank and took top honors, seemingly assuring myself of an A in the class. I would be foiled, though, as the second half of the semester was a personal defense unit. In an effort to challenge the person with the highest grade in the class, the instructor gave me the most difficult of all defense scenarios for the final test—disarming a female classmate armed with a pistol. As I attempted to chop her arm with my hand, I chopped her instead squarely in the left breast. In a real life confrontation, she would have presumably shot me dead. Beyond the mortification I experienced as the entire class laughed hysterically, I watched my certain A vaporize into a disappointing B.

I longed for the warmer days of spring and was thrilled when the cold weather broke on February 25th as abruptly as it began in mid-December. We would get eleven straight days above 55 degrees, most of them warm enough to wear shorts on our rides. Term break between winter and spring terms came the same time the warm weather erupted, turning my early February hell into a late February heaven.

Denny Page, a friend of my cousin Jeff, who lived a few blocks from us, got a new bike (a fire engine red Motobecane) at the end of February and he was eager to test it out. He picked up his new bike in State College on one of the warmest of those days and planned to meet me about half way between there and home at Colerain State Park near Spruce Creek. We got to the park sometime in mid-afternoon and decided to hike up the mountain to Indian Lookout, a breathtaking mountain top vista, but a demanding hike. It was another one of those things that seemed like a great idea at the time but would seem less prudent later in the day.

The lookout is perched on the edge of a rock outcrop and cliff that resulted from the exposure of a very hard rock strata of Bald Eagle Sandstone. This formation is only exposed on that side of the ridge, making such a cliff impossible on the opposite side of the mountain. The scope of the resulting cliff was much more than what it may have seemed to the casual hiker. In the early seventies, a girl that lived just a few blocks away from us fell to her death when she plummeted down the cliff during a hike with some friends. Just a teenager and only a few years older than I, her accident would come to mind every time I passed the outcrop, even from the highway in the valley below. Not one that was comfortable in high places anyway, I was particularly careful whenever I hiked to the lookout. The view was breathtaking but the prospect of falling to your death was unnerving.

After taking in the view from the mountain with Denny, we hiked back down the trail and climbed on our bikes. It was about 25 miles back to Altoona and Denny was whipped even before we began the demanding final climb. More than once, we questioned our judgment on taking the hike, particularly as night began to fall. As we made the climb up Kettle Road, a tough climb even when fresh, we came to realize we could not possibly make it home before dark. Even though it had been an incredibly warm day for that time of the year, it was still the last week of February, bringing not only an early sunset but a rapid cool down once the sun dropped behind the mountains. So beyond fearing we would be hit by someone in the dark, we were also freezing.

Mom wasn't particularly happy when I came through the door

a good half hour after darkness had fallen and I was annoyed with myself for planning things so poorly. It would be the sort of thing I would look back on and declare that I would never let such a thing happen again. Yet a year later to the week, I repeated the same folly on the same road. Indeed, those that fail to remember history are doomed to repeat it.

Moving on Up

To the Head of the Class

"I always wanted to be somebody...If I've made it, it's half because I was game to take a wicked amount of punishment along the way, and half because there were an awful lot of people who cared enough to help me."

—Althea Gibson
Tennis Champion
July 31, 2001

RODDY GERRAUGHTY AGAIN OFFERED THE CYCLING PHYSical education class in the spring of 1976. With the bittersweet physical conditioning and personal defense course experience still fresh in my mind, I was excited to begin the cycling class upon the return to school in early March. Given that I would not have to disarm a female classmate in cycling class, the chances of poking a girl in the chest this trimester seemed much less likely.

After some serious winter and early spring training, it also seemed likely that I would be at the head of my class. I was looking around for an affordable bike upgrade but would not find one until early in the summer. I was destined to struggle along with the mid-priced tank I had ridden the year before. I had finally realized the previous summer that toe clips would make a difference but the 32-pound machine was still an impediment.

It was a typical up and down early spring in Central Pennsylvania. The last week of February and first week of March were unseasonably warm, followed immediately by two weeks of the most miserable spring weather this part of the country can experience. Only eight days over a month stretch were dry and seven of those had below average temperatures. I have always hated to ride in the cold and this spell seemed even worse because it had been preceded by such unseasonably warm weather.

I still had not figured out how to dress for the cold, frequently being overdressed on many cool days and underdressed on cold ones. I was similarly clueless on the wicking abilities of some fabrics and would often wear cotton on cold days. I would end up getting soaked with sweat on the uphills and then risk hypothermia on the descents. My feet and fingers were always cold when the temperature dipped below 50 degrees. Consequently, I looked for the shortest ride possible on those days, and Roddy would poke fun at me for being a wimp.

In mid-April, the weather roller coaster went back up, temperatures on a few days near record-breaking levels. It hit 90 degrees on April 19th and our depression turned to glee. I never complain about the heat and if the thought crosses my mind, I simply think of the January alternative. Though still laboring with a bike that was far from ideal, the warm weather got me excited about riding again, and I was able to talk a few classmates in joining me for longer and challenging rides. An old high school classmate and fellow Earth and Mineral Science student, Bruce Rossbach, was in my cycling class. After some coaxing, he agreed to tackle the climb to Wopsononock Lookout with me one of those glorious days in April.

Though in good shape and possessing the slightly built frame that enabled him to be a good climber, the Wopsy ascent would be more than Bruce bargained for. I crested the climb several minutes before Bruce and had time to catch my breath and have a drink of water. Nearly falling off the bike as he finally finished the horrible climb, I could see there was an urge to curse me but no breath left to do so. After a couple minutes, he finally recovered enough to complete a full sentence. The sweat still dripping off his forehead onto the lens of his glasses, he peered over the top to see me more clearly. "You must be nuts," he quietly concluded in his typical mild-mannered way.

The day of the 1976 Penn State spring football intrasquad game (a strangely momentous event in Central Pennsylvania each spring), we set off for our 100-mile ride. Unlike the previous year, the day was cool and a brisk west wind made for slow going on parts of the trip. Roddy had altered the course a bit and designed a figure-eight route, rather than the loop we rode the year before. This sent us over the wind-blown stretch of still-bare farm fields between Seven Stars and Warriors Mark, not just once but twice. Though much better prepared physically than the year before, the cool and persistent wind made for a tough ride.

Though I was not sporting the Razzles canvas backpack I took the year before, I was still handicapped by the cumbersome Concord bicycle I had been riding for a year and a half. Riding more and more with riders that had better equipment, I came, first hand, to better understand the advantages of higher quality bikes and components. As I struggled to pull my 32-pound bike across three counties that blustery spring day, I did not realize that was soon to change.

A few weeks after our gym class ride, I found out that Dave Berry, an occasional riding companion and manager of one of the two bike shops in town, had ordered a new Schwinn Paramount. He asked me later if I would be interested in buying his Raleigh International. While the International was not the highest end bike Raleigh made, it was a gargantuan step up from what I was riding. Perhaps most importantly, it was half the price of a new Paramount.

Before committing to the purchase, Dave asked me if I wanted to take it for a test ride to be sure it was a good fit. With the unbridled excitement of a little boy getting a new toy, I rode my old bike across town to Dave's house to pick up the new bike the morning of a big group ride. As he wheeled the machine toward me, its champagne-colored frame and chrome lug work glistened in the early morning sunlight. Dave was a meticulous caretaker of his bicycles and he had managed to keep this one looking like new. Though my initial excitement centered on a better performing bike, I was surprisingly excited about the appearance of the machine once I saw it. I had long before lost interest in fancy cars but could not help but admire the craftsmanship of this two-wheeled masterpiece before me.

High-end framesets of the time were either made of Columbus or Reynolds tubing. This one was Reynolds 531, referring to the proportions of manganese, carbon, and molybdenum in the alloy steel tubing. (The amount of carbon was actually about half the amount implied by the 531 label but 5-1.5-1 just did not roll off the tongue like 531.) The tubing was introduced in 1935 by Reynolds Cycle Technology of Birmingham, England and was the state-of-the art for more than 40 years. Cheaper bikes, like my old Concord, were made of high-carbon steel. The department store tanks that I had ridden in high school had an even lower quality and heavier frame. Though reliable and easy to bend back into shape when damaged, the high-carbon frames were not just heavy, but less responsive. I could not have imagined just how much until I climbed upon the Raleigh on that June morning. The bike seemed to explode forward when you stood up for an acceleration.

To further add to the day's adventure, Ken had promised to take us over a few roads to which several of us had never ventured. I would come to learn that this was a red flag bigger than the stars and stripes flying over the Capitol. For anytime Ken would talk about someplace we had never been before, visions of ungodly climbs, obscure and remote locales, or a gravel pathway would come to mind. Similarly, when he suggested a climb was a "small ridge," as opposed to "big climb," you could rest assured it was still a substantial ascent. Such was the case of Ribot Ridge, a rise that separated two valleys between the towns of Petersburg and Huntingdon. Ken ended up being correct in his geologic assessment of the climb, for this was not the typical sandstone ridge that characterized the true mountains in most of Pennsylvania. But that did not change the topographic profile that took us up sharply over what also seemed like a mountain-sized distance. After cresting the climb, we dropped down toward Route 26 and noticed some gathering rain clouds. As we rode north toward the village of Donation, the skies opened up on us. Years later I would read Ken's account of the weather event in his journal and was struck by his insight. It so happened that a low-pressure system had passed over us, and Ken had noted the southerly winds had turned northerly as the low passed by.

I had not known of his observations on that day until I read them in his journal more than 30 years later, but they matched the historical weather maps perfectly. It was the first of many times that Ken would note such an event or explain some natural phenomena on a ride, hike, or ski trip. I would not know it at the time, but this impressive knowledge of the natural world was mostly self-taught. Despite no formal education beyond high school, Ken might have been the most knowledgeable natural scientist I had known.

We made it to a store and Texaco gas station in Donation before we got too wet. The elderly and jovial proprietor welcomed us, likely deducing that a long stop with a big bunch of hungry and thirsty bicyclists would be good for business. The store was an old style wood frame building with a covered porch out front, providing a dry spot to refuel the tanks and watch the progress of the rainstorm.

This was one of the first times I had ridden with Tom Baldwin, a 30-something school teacher and bachelor. He was a slow but steady rider and always seemed to be delighted just to be on the bike. His dry sense of humor would make me chuckle many times over the years. On this day, it would be his incessant optimism that would be the source of amusement. The rain at first seemed like a passing shower, and Tom would optimistically peer into the sky every five minutes or so and declare he could see clearing on the horizon. After the third or fourth declaration, we realized that Tom's thoughts were based more on hope than meteorology. "Yep, yep, it's definitely letting up." The fact that we put any credence in his prediction was testimony to the premise that hope springs eternal, especially in rain-soaked bicyclists 30 miles from home.

After more than an hour of Tom's dreadfully inaccurate prognostications, we started to discuss our other options. It was the sort of hard driving rain that made riding home in the shower impractical. I was especially opposed to that possibility given that my immaculate new bike would be slopped up on my maiden voyage. As we discussed our rescue options, the group confessed to a history of rescues over the previous year. Roddy, especially, had no reservations in calling his wife when the weather or the ride overwhelmed him. Even many years later, people would joke that we should "call Mary Ellen" if a ride became too arduous, even when Roddy wasn't with us.

The most humorous of the tales, though, was from a trip the previous June, just before the big race up Sugar Run Road. Looking for that big training ride prior to the race, Ken took Dave Berry, Gary Kephart, and John Bradley on a marathon into southern Bedford County. As so often happened, the group blindly followed Ken with little concept of where they would end up. Some hours into the ride, they stopped for food and drink in Hyndman at the foot of the Appalachian Front. Already feeling the effects of a long ride, Dave was less than excited when they began the long climb towards Berlin (Pennsylvania, not Germany).

Somewhere on the climb, the last straw was placed on the camel's back. When Dave finally stopped breathing heavily, he declared he was calling home. (Since Roddy wasn't on this trek, it wouldn't have been polite to call Mary Ellen.) The storekeeper in Berlin graciously let Dave make the collect long-distance call to his wife. Though they had never met before, Dave and the storekeeper realized they had a mutual friend down the road in Meyersdale and Dave and Gary pedaled a few more miles to visit with the friend. Sharon eventually rescued them but it took her nearly two hours to make the trip and find them in the deep, dark recesses of southern Somerset County. She found Dave and Gary resting in the comfort of the friend's house in Myersdale. Ken and John ended up with a ride just under 150 miles.

So, a year later, Dave was unfazed by the possibility of calling home. By stark contrast, Ken Steel took such desperate measures only when there was no other choice. On this day, our options were also complicated by the size of the group, making an automobile rescue impractical. We decided that my father's van was the only choice we had. When Dad arrived, Ken, Gary, and Tom all decided to wait it out and ride home. Tom was not about to let all that optimism go to waste. But the threat of rain persisted through the rest of the afternoon and Gary and Ken left Tom in Neffs Mills, 30 miles from home, hoping to beat the next shower back to Altoona. Many hours and raindrops after our morning departure, Tom crept back to his home in Bellwood alone, still convinced it was just a brief passing shower.

That Tuesday, Ken invited John Bradley and me on a long training ride in preparation for the upcoming state championship road race. Though I had a real bike and was getting stronger, I was still intimidated by Ken and John. They were in a class by themselves among riders in Blair County, and I just did not think it was possible to keep up with them on the long, intense ride they had planned for that day. Using my work responsibilities as justification, I let them know that I could only ride from the departure point in Sinking Valley to State College. Their 116-mile ride turned out to be a gut-wrencher that even troubled John. John fell ill near Petersburg and Ken rode ahead to get the car, rescuing him at the top of the long hill near the village of Water Street.

As good as these two were, their foray into the 100-mile race with the big boys at the end of the month fell short as well. John dropped out after ten laps of the 4.4 mile circuit and Ken called it a day a lap later when race leader John Bare of State College lapped him. Ken was encouraged he had covered the 46 hilly miles at 21 miles per hour but was depressed the leader covered an entire additional lap in the same time. John Bare, however, was a bigger legend than Ken Steel (and much younger, too). Bare rode for a nationally-known sponsored club, the Century Road Club of America, and had experienced success in United States Cycling Federation (USCF) races as well as the collegiate races during his days at Penn State. On top of his incredible cardiovascular conditioning, his classroom smarts carried over to the race course, making him perhaps the greatest bike racer to ride the roads of that part of Pennsylvania. Bare was polishing off an impressive racing career just as I was starting mine, and our paths crossed a few times, but I don't recall ever being in an event with him. Sometime the next year, Penn State racing team members were exchanging some equipment and I ended up with John's old racing helmet. His name and the abbreviation for his club, CRCA, were printed in marker on the inside of the helmet.

Helmets in those days were helmets in the loosest sense of the term and we seldom wore one unless we were required to do so in a race. Bell had begun to manufacture and sell hard shell helmets but hard core racers made fun of the bulky white monstrosities. "Real racers" wore "hair nets" a series of thin padded straps covered in leather. I never fell while wearing one, but it's hard to imagine they offered much protection at all. We were young and foolish, though, and wore what we thought was fashionable and cool. Bare's hair net was especially skimpy and I thought it was a particularly great helmet for time trials, where we looked for every edge to shave a few more seconds off our time. I would wear it many times over the next three or four seasons, safety and good sense be damned. Thirty years later, much to the chagrin of my wife, I still had the helmet in my box of old parts and accessories. She thought it another in a long list of silly articles that I refused to part with; I saw it as a revered relic.

Riding Across Penn's Woods

"Patience and diligence, like faith, remove mountains."

—William Penn

THE AMERICAN BICENTENNIAL WAS BEING CELEBRATED IN 1976 and Fred Long, a good friend of Ken Steel's and active in the local historical society, had organized a six-day cross-state ride to commemorate it. Fred Long was a "Born Again" bicyclist that had long ago fallen away from a sport of his youth, only to find it again following a heart attack later in life. He used the nation's 200th birthday as an opportunity to combine his two avocations. Though the rider list had folks from all over, there was a distinct local flavor to the group of about two dozen. We drove to Indiana, Pennsylvania the first morning to begin the ride. I rode my new Raleigh, eager to give it another test on the demanding up and down route through Indiana and Cambria Counties. I didn't know most of the riders when we began and was eager to show that my new bike and I were ready for the challenge. Though such moves are usually reserved for races rather than tours, the result was a solo breakaway.

Just a few miles from Indiana, I found myself riding alone and in the zone. I kept looking back, certain there had to be someone else that could keep up but they never materialized. Ken was behind me, but as he usually did on a ride such as this, was shepherding the less powerful riders along the route and providing a history lesson or two as well. In an effort to avoid the busy roads and the always dangerous coal truck traffic this part of the state was notorious for, Fred had mapped out a rather circuitous route back home to Altoona.

Though the complicated route required frequent consultation of the map Fred provided us, it was otherwise difficult to complain. The ride was beautiful, I felt great, the weather was perfect, and the roads were lightly traveled, just as Fred had hoped.

Given the historic focus of the trip, Fred also tried to follow the Kittanning Trail as much as possible through this part of the state. The Kittanning Trail was an American Indian trail that had been an important connection between Pittsburgh and Lancaster. The eastern end of the trail was near Frankstown, just east of present day Altoona, and the western terminus was in Kittanning along the Allegheny River north of Pittsburgh. It was most active as an Indian trail from 1721 to 1781, but was not such a peaceful one after 1737. Native American uprisings became much more frequent following the infamous "Walking Purchase" of that year.

The purchase had undermined the positive relations built by William Penn. Penn, a devout Quaker, had felt strongly that relations with the Indians should be fair and peaceful. But after his death, colonial leaders claimed that they possessed a 50-year-old deed that said the Lenape would sell a parcel of land north of the junction of the Lehigh and Delaware Rivers that stretched "as far west as a man could walk in a day and a half." Always looking for an edge, fair and ethical or not, the colonial officials found the three fastest runners in the colony to "walk" the prepared trail northwest. Seventy miles later, the frantic pace of the "walk" left only one of the three runners still standing. One runner actually died the beginning of the second day.[1]

The repercussions of the massive loss of territory were felt far and wide and were a major contributor to unrest, even at the other end of the colony. Still, some positive relationships persisted and one of the most notable in Western Pennsylvania was Hart's Sleeping Place along the Kittanning Trail. Trader John Hart was granted a license to establish a trading post there in 1744, in a part of the colony that had been closed to white settlers. Despite the unrest in much of the rest of Pennsylvania, Hart's Sleeping Place became a popular trading post and way station for both whites and Native Americans.[2]

In a strange coincidence, my mother's family originated from that part of Cambria County and many ancestors, including my Fourth

Great Grandfather John Weakland, were buried in the cemetery at Hart's Sleeping Place. Yet on that warm summer day in 1976, with my nose to the handlebars, I was oblivious to both the regional and personal history that was nearby. The historical markers along the way might have been of interest to the rest of the group, but I never noticed them nor the tombstones of my ancestors. I had spent so much of the day off the front, several riders wondered if I had even done the ride when they saw me the next morning.

That next day we were to ride from Altoona to the town of Orbisonia in southern Huntingdon County. I had hooked up with Ken Steel and several young riders who were able to keep pace with us. Andy Johnson and Bobby Faith both lived in Sinking Valley and met us as we passed near their homes. They rode the quiet country roads in the valley whenever they could, still enthralled by the youthful exuberance that bicycling often instills. Still not sixteen, they had not yet been torn from their bikes by the powerful pull of a driver's license.

Keeping a brisk pace, we got to Orbisonia shortly after lunch. Our only notable stop had been the quaint Swigert Automobile Museum just east of Huntingdon. While at first pleased by our incredibly swift ride, we realized we were stuck in this little town for the rest of the day without much to do. Knowing now what I know about Ken Steel, I can't believe he didn't suggest we go another 25 miles or so down the road and back, just to get us a 100-mile ride.

Instead, we shopped at the Orbisonia IGA market and wandered a short piece down the road to neighboring Rockhill to see the historic narrow gauge East Broad Top Railroad. The railroad had been built in 1872 to haul coal from the Broad Top coal fields and was still active 80 years later. That the railroad still existed in 1976 was a bit of an oddity, for few of them survived the scrap dealers' salvage efforts of the 1940s and 1950s. The railroad had, in fact, been purchased by scrap dealer Nick Kovalchick after its last run in 1956. But a nostalgic excursion to commemorate the bicentennials of Orbisonia and Rockhill in 1960 convinced Kovalchick and the community that the historic line might have a future as a tourist attraction. [3]

Orbisonia and Rockhill would be part of another oddity that we would come to learn of that afternoon as well. Orbisonia was a "dry" town, while Rockhill, its liberal next door neighbor, allowed alcohol-selling establishments. The community watering holes, often more common than the churches in rural Pennsylvania, were conspicuous by their absence in Orbisonia. Locals even joked about it, laughing that Orbisonia's prohibition of drinking establishments didn't mean much if you could walk down the street a short piece across the invisible municipal boundary to quench your thirst.

As the afternoon passed, more and more of the riders trickled in and we got acquainted with those we had not seen much of so far. The three younger riders and I were particularly proud of our ride, and the group seemed to hold us in high esteem, especially when they found out we had ridden with the iconic Ken Steel.

After a good and sober night's sleep in the Orbisonia Methodist Church, we set off for Carlisle. These were new roads to almost all the group, and there was a sense of excitement that comes with such new adventures. This part of Pennsylvania is a series of agricultural valleys and tree covered sandstone ridges, and the roads are quiet and frequently car-free. Typically moving through this part of the state in a car, the Pennsylvania Turnpike smooths out the otherwise jagged profile with interstate grading and a series of tunnels that go through, rather than over, the mountains.

The steepness and length of the climbs in this region cannot be fully appreciated until they are conquered under one's own power. It also makes one appreciate the cleverness of the highway engineers that built the nation's first limited access highway four decades before. Though we had been challenged by a number of ascents over the first few days, the two that climbed over Tuscarora and Timmons Mountains were as overwhelming as any I had ever tackled. Convinced that I would need the rear rack on my old, heavier bike, I rode it from Altoona instead of my new Raleigh. About half way up the first ungodly climb, I regretted the decision. I survived the ordeal, though, and we arrived at Dickinson College in Carlisle in mid-afternoon and found our way to the dormitory we were staying at that night.

Carlisle has its own historical notoriety, being among other things home to the U.S. Army War College. The college was established in 1904, but the barracks of the college date back to the American

Revolution. Beyond the War College, the town center also remained vibrant, the oldest buildings surviving both the Civil War and the plagues of urban renewal a century later.

The next morning, we awoke to the first unpleasant weather of the trip, a steady rain brought by a passing cold front that stretched from Canada to the Gulf. Though the temperature remained warm enough to still ride in shorts, it was a soggy morning. A half inch of rain would fall in many places that day, but we had no choice but to ride through it in order to stay on schedule. We rode out of town on US Route 11 and quickly came to realize the suburbs of Carlisle had not been as fortunate as downtown in holding on to their 19th Century charm. Route 11 was one truck stop, fast food joint, and motel after another, and the traffic was similarly uninviting to a group of cyclists.

Not far from the busy turnpike interchange, I came upon a truck stop and saw one of our riding companions stretched out in front on the ground. The doctor that had joined the ride looked to be attending to him. I thought it only considerate to stop and inquire as to their well-being and began to slow as I neared the driveway. As soon as I touched my brakes, I fell to the pavement and slid headfirst up Route 11. With heavy truck traffic all around, visions of semi-tractor trailers running me over immediately flashed through my mind. I gathered myself as quickly as I could in the hopes of avoiding the carnage. Several other riders in our group repeated my mistake and the single fallen rider soon gave rise to four.

It did not take long for us to figure out that diesel and oil had washed down the driveway of the truck stop and onto the road. The inch and a quarter bike tires might have rolled over the hazard had we kept moving and kept them straight, but as soon as we touched the brakes, we were on the pavement. We were able to warn the subsequent riders but the four of us that fell found ourselves scratched up and covered with petroleum by-products. I had on an old sleeveless basketball shirt and a pair of cut-off blue jeans held up by my favorite leather belt. It was my good fortune the belts of the day were very wide and adorned with massive metal buckles. This one had four small metal protrusions that stuck out from the rest of the buckle and it was these on which I slid when I hit the pavement. I burned four little holes in my basketball shirt but was saved from having abrasions all over my stomach and chest.

Seeing the conditions created by the truck stop as a negligent act that could have resulted in serious injury or worse, several of us stormed into the establishment to protest the situation. Bleeding, covered with an oily residue, and carrying our damaged bikes, it was hard for them to deny that something was amiss. When someone mentioned possible legal action, the manager quickly asked how he could make things right. We told him that compensation for our ruined clothes and damaged components would take the edge off, and he agreed to pay for whatever had been damaged.

Though torn and tattered a bit, the rain cleared later in the morning and we continued eastward toward our destination, the American Youth Hostel in Denver, Pennsylvania. Denver was on the northern edge of Lancaster County, an area well known for its rich farmland and notable population of Amish and Old Order Mennonites. Like suburban Carlisle, development pressures had already been felt in much of Lancaster County by 1976, but Denver had still managed to preserve its small-town atmosphere and agricultural character. The ride the next morning went through more of that classic farmland. Ideally, we would have shared the roadway with Mennonite horses and buggies, but one stretch near the town of Blue Ball more resembled rush hour in the city.

As we got closer to Valley Forge, the struggles with traffic became more frequent, but Fred Long had still managed to plan a route that would get us all to the National Park in one piece. As that region would grow over the next three decades, it would be more and more difficult to find similar safe passage. This was suburban Philadelphia and the exodus from the city would be profound from 1960 to 2000. Mass transit never kept up, and the perceived solution was to build more highways. And just like Kevin Costner's *Field of Dreams*, if you build it they will come. In this case it was cars, not baseball players, that would come.

Valley Forge National Historic Park would be an oasis of relative calm in the ever-growing suburbs northwest of Philadelphia. The thing that made it attractive to George Washington, its close proximity to (but separation from) the City of Brotherly Love, would make it attractive to commuters two centuries later. In 1976, its transition year from a state to a national park, the typical peace and tranquility of the park was not quite so peaceful or tranquil. The Bicentennial celebration was a big deal and the park was jammed with visitors the day we arrived, just a few weeks before the actual anniversary of July 4th.

Only possessing a modest interest in history at the time, Valley Forge was not as exciting as it was to the real history buffs in the crowd. What happened there, though, was considered to be one of those watershed events in the American Revolution. Badly beaten in the previous autumn at Brandywine and Germantown, Washington's troops retreated to Valley Forge to regroup in December 1777. Out of sight and out of mind of the British, they took the opportunity to train and strategize. Valley Forge is well known today because of the great suffering endured there, but the Continental Army came out of Valley Forge a better disciplined and trained army. Despite the loss of 2,000 men to disease and the harsh winter weather, the surviving 10,000 soldiers were better trained and more confident.

Ken, a history buff among his many other interests, was sorry to miss the final day's ride to Valley Forge due to work obligations. He rode to Lancaster and caught the train to Altoona. He had been the consummate mentor and ride leader during the tour, serving as a guide, naturalist, historian, and mechanic. We all missed him the last day.

The following Saturday, he invited Tom Baldwin and me on an 80-mile ride over two mountains. While Tom started out with us, he didn't last long. Ken noted in his journal that, "We lost Tom somewhere in Tyrone," barely 20 miles from home. His entry made it sound like he was a set of keys and we had simply misplaced him.

On large group rides, like the tour across the state, Ken would take even the slowest rider under his wing, but smaller groups or rides with tight time lines were quite different. If Ken was sure you knew where you were (which was not always something you could be sure of on one of his rides), he would not hesitate to ride on with the faster riders. Consequently, regular riding partners were prepared to fend for themselves if the ride got away from them. Tom Baldwin knew this feeling more than anyone.

After we left Tom wandering around Tyrone, we kept a blistering pace, climbing over Bald Eagle Mountain and riding on toward Huntingdon to assault two climbs I had yet to experience. The first was over the mountain between Huntingdon and Williamsburg, one that typically took Ken about 22 minutes to ascend. The east side was the more evenly sloped side of the ridge, with several long straight sections where the road goes on forever. The other side passed through several different rock strata, the slopes varied depending on the hardness of the rocks. A series of hairpin turns were necessary to climb that side of the mountain.

As we caught our breath before beginning the descent, Ken warned me of the impending crazy ride. Somewhat matter-of-factly at first, he went on to tell me he was in a horrible automobile accident on the mountain when he was just nineteen years old. He, his mother, and grandmother started down the mountain only to realize they had lost their brakes. While it might have been possible to survive such a disaster on the more consistently sloped eastern side of the mountain, it would have been impossible on the western slope and all its hairpin turns. Ken recalled his mom made it through one or two of the turns but could not make it through the next one. They all initially survived the accident, but Ken's grandmother died a few days later, evidently having suffered internal injuries. Ken's mom ended up with a limp she carried to her grave, and Ken experienced some serious facial injuries and broken teeth. As I plummeted through the hairpin turns a few minutes after Ken told the somber story, I wondered how Ken ever lived to tell the tale.

I Don't Eat Animals

—Melanie Safka
From the Album *Leftover Wine*
Buddha Records (1970)

IT'S STRANGE HOW RANDOM EVENTS, SEEMINGLY UNRELATed, can converge to change your life. Or maybe it isn't as strange as it seems. Perhaps your loves, passions, and talents pull you toward those things.

Near the end of my junior year in high school, I started to pay closer attention to what I was eating. Having spent my entire childhood as a junk food junkie, I came to realize there were a dozen reasons to turn over a new leaf. My initial motivation, of all things, was driven by a concern over my complexion, suspecting, as we did at the time, that chocolate, cola, and other sugar laden foods contributed to acne. I had also come to appreciate the other health issues connected with high fat, low fiber diets. Even as a young child, I had been repulsed by the appearance of arteries in roast beef or the skin of a chicken. When I realized it wasn't particularly healthy for you either, cutting back on meat wasn't a difficult thing to do.

Ken Steel had influenced me on this front, too. While he ate meat, he ate it infrequently and usually only if he killed it himself. Ken was a hunter and fisherman and he didn't do it just for the sport of it. In all the years that I rode, hiked, and cross-country skied with him, I only ever saw him eat store-bought flesh one time—a can of sardines at a campground in the middle of nowhere in Idaho. He ate next to no refined sugar, but bundles of vegetables of every sort, wheat germ, brewers' yeast, and a host of other natural foods along those lines. I realized that part of the reason he was the incredible athlete he was, even in his late thirties, was because he took care of himself and ate an incredibly healthy diet.

Yet it wasn't just the health issues alone that pushed me toward this profound change in the way I ate. In late winter of my freshman year in college, civil rights activist turned political activist Dick Gregory spoke at Penn State Altoona. Though he spoke of Kennedy assassination conspiracies, it was his discussion of the world food problem that most interested me.

"Food is the new bomb, the new military," Gregory said. "Now that the superpowers can no longer rape the Third World and undeveloped countries, we still have control of the breadbaskets. We get the image that India cannot produce enough grain to feed its people. India produces enough grain for its people and enough to export," he said, "but rats eat 60 percent of it. I don't hear anybody say get rid of the rats, they say get rid of the people." [4]

Gregory ran from Detroit to Washington the year before to raise awareness about the world food crisis. He had also gone on long-term fasts, contending that such fasts cleansed the digestive system. While a few of his ideas on fasting seemed extreme, his basic premise stuck with me. Our eating habits were bad for us, often bad for the country, and usually bad for the world's poor as well. The local paper had downplayed the worthwhile commentary on the world food problem and chose, instead, to write about the sensational assassination theories.

Though the newspaper account did not give the issue the ink it deserved, my reading and several of my upper level Geography classes the next few years would reinforce Gregory's contention. Beef was a particularly inefficient way to produce food, especially if grain-fed. In a world having a tough time feeding itself, it seemed silly to be using ten pounds of grain to make a pound of edible beef, especially if it wasn't particularly good for you.

To make matters worse, some in the cattle industry were beginning to deforest tropical rainforests in the hopes they could grow animal feed and graze cattle on the cleared land. It was cattle production that would become the most common reason to chop down tropical rainforests. Our preoccupation with beef and pork would also contribute to an insatiable appetite for chemical fertilizer to grow the grain and soybeans that fed the cows and pigs. This would drive the world-wide demand, and hence the price, for fertilizer upward, making it more difficult for Third World countries to buy what they needed for food crops.

Before I even understood the world-wide implications of eating too much meat, I had decided I was going to quit eating it. Already paying closer attention to what I was eating, Dick Gregory's talk had cemented my decision to become a vegetarian. I decided that an incremental approach would be easier, and sometime in the summer of 1974, I stopped eating hotdogs and pork. A few months later, I quit eating beef and steak. That was easy, though, since I was never particularly enthralled by cow. Hamburger, I suppose because it was hard to recognize as a cow, was more palatable to me. I gave it its own phase-out date a little while later. I recall eating one final hamburger from the Burger Chef in downtown Altoona that had just added a buffet line with all the trimmings. I covered the burger with lettuce, tomato, and special sauce. Though it tasted good, I decided it would be my last.

I phased out chicken a couple months later and ate my last turkey dinner on Christmas Day 1974. At each milestone, I felt the satisfaction of moving closer to a dietary ideal, one that would be healthier and make me a better bike rider. It did not at all seem coincidental that my bike riding had reached a new level and that I could consistently ride with the best riders.

The bike, what I ate, the food I grew, and the things I was studying in school all seemed to converge in my life at once and it was a most miraculous time. It was a time that changed my life and would build the foundation for a host of fascinating things yet to come.

When I was still in high school, I had begun playing Sunday morning softball with a diverse group of guys that lived at my end of town. By 1976, I was frequently torn by indecision as to whether I should play or go for a bike ride whenever Ken would beckon. Even though my baseball and softball skills had greatly improved since the days of playing in the yard of my childhood friend Jerry Hirt, I was still not a great ballplayer by any stretch of the imagination. But this was a laid-back bunch and these were not formal teams. A couple of the senior players would pick up players from the pool that would show up each Sunday.

And when I say senior players, I mean senior. My great Uncle Scoop, then well into his sixties, usually pitched. (Scoop's real name was Cyril, though he seldom ever confessed that to anyone.) Vince Farabaugh, my old elementary and high school church league basketball coach, Skip Cole, and Bill Hunter, fixtures in left field and third base, were closing in on retirement. Mitt Corbett was among a group that clearly had been great players when they were younger and could still hit and field despite being in their forties.

It was a wildly diverse group, too. Though many in the group had their roots in Saint Leo's Catholic Church and had been acquainted for a long time, the group came from various backgrounds. Mitt and Jimmy Miller were African American. A Jewish businessman and his son from the other side of town would play once or twice a month. An Italian man and his two sons from Mount Carmel Church, the Italian American parish across town, came frequently. And an incredibly athletic, mentally handicapped kid that lived across from my grandparents rarely missed a Sunday. The group ranged in age from a bunch of us in our teens to Uncle Scoop in his late sixties. There were many father/son teams that came each week, too.

It was truly a cross-section of the community, and the camaraderie that arose from the group was astounding. Beyond a stern warning from one of the old timers when you made an error or a base running mistake, you never heard an ill word. Usually, though, the coaching advice came in the form of sarcastic comment rather than a critical evaluation. The result was that we laughed much more often than we frowned.

Scoop, especially, took the games seriously, and he would freely offer his input. Some of the guys were especially funny, Don Gibbons being among the most jovial. Don, my Uncle Bob Gibbon's brother, loved baseball but had become a bit paunchy as he aged. He usually ended up pitching, as he was not particularly mobile anymore. Standing out there with a chaw of tobacco that the Pirates old second baseman Bill Mazeroski would have been proud of, he was a humorous site to begin with. But he always managed to say something that would make us chuckle every Sunday.

After someone made a particularly bone-headed play one week, Don peered out to the player and declared, "I'm afraid we can't keep you anymore, son."

"What do you mean," the offending teammate responded.

"We're sending you down," Don explained.

"Sending me down?"

Don elaborated further. "Yep, we're sending you back to Spindley City."

"Where the hell is Spindley City?" the confused teammate queried.

"Up the hill from Amsbry," Don replied, as if that would help. "It's our farm team. We just can't keep you here anymore if you're going to play like that," Don concluded, still stone-cold serious on the outside. By this point, the entire bunch was cracking up, including the offending player. It turned out that Spindley City was a crossroads up the mountain, near the town of Ashville where some of Don's clan still lived. Certainly, if the Westfall Sunday softball crew were to have a farm team, it would have had to be in a place like Spindley City. Indeed spindly, but clearly not a city, I would pass the turnoff for the little village many times when I rode my bike through that neck of the woods. I thought of Don's demotion announcement and smiled every time I passed.

We played for many years at Westfall Park, not much more than a half mile from my house. Coincidentally, Westfall was west of my house and on the west end of Altoona and helped me remember compass directions, not just in my youth, but even into my young adulthood. Westfall did not get its name, however, from its location but rather from the family that donated the land for a park. Unfortunately, the field was a stone pit with no grass to be found within fair territory. The stones provided an unwelcome challenge, bringing a new dimension to the term "bad hop." I was not a Gold Glove winner to begin with, and the hops that could result from the ball hitting one of the millions of stones made me that much worse. The stones lay on a field of hard-packed clay. It got so dusty during a summer dry spell that our white socks would take on a pale yellow cast by the time the doubleheader ended. Later on, I would find out that even this had an interesting geology connection. For it so happened the underlying rock throughout this entire part of town at the base of the Appalachian Front was made of a yellowish shale. Beyond making for poor clay soil that cursed everyone trying to garden or grow a decent lawn, it also made Westfall the stony, dusty, hard-packed clay field it was. But while we complained every time a bad hop made us look bad, we kept going back every week because we loved to play and loved to laugh about things like Spindley City.

As much as I loved playing softball, the bike eventually became the stronger draw, and as 1976 faded into 1977, the softball occupied fewer and fewer Sundays. Beyond the enjoyment, the bicycling became part of the healthy lifestyle I was finding more important. Besides, I came to realize I could be a much better bike rider than I was a softball player. While evidently blessed with superior cardiovascular capacity for cycling, the eye-hand coordination I needed to be a good softball player was clearly lacking. My sister would come to explain it was a good thing the cranks on the bike went only one direction, for if eye-hand coordination were an important part of cycling, I would be doomed to fail.

One of the Sunday rides I missed to play softball the last week of July turned out to be more eventful than normal. Ken was leading a demanding ride into Cambria County, which coincidently passed by Spindley City. Somewhere between Ebensburg and Portage, near the Eastern Continental Divide, the group confronted a hair-raising descent. Roddy Gerraughty and Dave Berry were especially daring and brisk descenders, so the ride was likely to be even more spirited than usual. It ended up being a bit more spirited than John Bradley would have liked, though, as he was surprised by a hairpin turn and crashed and slid under the wire guard rails and into a two-foot-wide maple tree. He anticipated the turn and began to brake but could not slow enough and sustained some nasty road rash on his left shoulder and knee. Most importantly, he later joked, the bike was undamaged. The shoulder could heal, he reasoned, but the frame of his new black Schwinn Paramount was a different matter.

His spill gave me pause and hammered home how dangerous the

sport could be. While I had come to tolerate the pain of training, I was not fond of the longer-lasting pain that accompanied such tumbles. I would witness many awful falls over the years and experience a few of them myself. This instilled a fear of falling in me that would affect the way I raced. I seldom felt comfortable in a large field of riders, especially in the particularly tight quarters of a criterium, and it would result in me falling off the back of more than a few races over the years that would follow.

The summer of 1976 was especially fascinating because I was introduced to a new road or place nearly every week. I stumbled onto many of them and looked for others. Ken's introductions to new places always seemed to have a bit of extra spice sprinkled on top that made them especially memorable experiences. The first Thursday of August was one such unforgettable ride. Roddy; Andy Johnson, who had joined us on the cross-state ride; and I joined Ken for another ride into previously unexplored territory. In a typical Ken understatement, he told us we were going on a ride to Lake Raystown. But like so many other rides over those years, the devil was in the details.

We rode 25 miles south into the farm country of Morrisons Cove and then over Fredericksburg Mountain. Fredericksburg Mountain climbed through the same geology as Williamsburg Mountain, which we had ridden down a few weeks before. Like a large portion of the ridges in the Appalachians, mountains on opposite sides of the valley usually mirrored images of each other. One side climbs through several strata of different rocks, resulting in different slopes and numerous switchbacks. Only one kind of rock, usually Tuscarora Sandstone, is exposed at the surface on the opposite side of the mountain. The Huntingdon County side of both Fredericksburg and Williamsburg mountains consequently had fewer switchbacks and changes in slope. Hair-raising as it might have been, it was possible to approach the 55 mile per hour speed limit on the fastest part of the descents.

After the thrilling descent, we went north to the town of Entriken and across the lake. Raystown Lake had become the largest man-made lake in Pennsylvania after the completion of the dam by the United States Army Corp of Engineers just three years before. A much smaller lake had occupied the valley for more than 60 years, but the Corp of

Engineers would design and build a dam that was much higher than its predecessor. The lake was named after the Raystown Branch of the Juniata River, one of three major tributaries of the Juniata River. The configuration of the Appalachian Ridge and Valley made the Juniata and its tributaries a maze of waterways that ultimately came together near Huntingdon, Pennsylvania. A classic trellised drainage system, creeks and rivers on opposite sides of a ridge or hill could flow parallel for many miles before meeting. Since roads most frequently follow stream valleys, bicyclists could be similarly stranded on the wrong side of a mountain for long spells if there were no water gaps cutting through the mountain.

Lake Raystown itself came to be, in part, because the river meandered through this steep-sided valley, facilitating the formation of a very long lake, similar in some ways to large man-made lakes out west, like Lake Powell on the Colorado. This was to be the classic multi-purpose dam, providing flood control, recreation, and hydroelectric power. Geography Professor Dr. Greg Knight would teach me that multi-purpose dams like these were myths. The uses were contradictory, some needing water to be stored, others necessitating it be released. In the case of Lake Raystown, whole villages were destroyed as well. With the new dam being 136 feet higher than the old one built in 1907, towns along the river and old lake were inundated. The most famous of these is the town of Aitch, where several buildings and the main street remain in a watery grave.

The ride ended up being 100 miles for me, but this would be a relatively short ride for Ken. It came on the heels of a long July road trip through the Pacific Northwest and Northern Rocky Mountains. Beyond the demanding topography, Ken piled up ungodly miles on the trip, riding over 140 miles on several days. His first day, from Spokane, Washington, to Lozeau, Montana, covered 163 miles. The mileage he accumulated on his annual long tours was mindboggling, but they instilled an urge in all of us to embark on such adventures, too. With the anticipation of similarly experiencing incredible landscapes beyond our own backyards, Brian Weakland and I set off for the Blue Ridge Mountains the next week.

The Blue Ridge Mountains of Virginia

"In the Blue Ridge Mountains of Virginia,
On the trail of the lonesome pine—"

—Lyrics by Ballard MacDonald
Music by Harry Carrol
1913

THE WEEK BEFORE THE ONLY BIKE RACE OF THE YEAR IN Blair County, Brian Weakland and I decided to explore the Skyline Drive through Shenandoah National Park in the Blue Ridge of Virginia. Besides being an interesting and scenic touring adventure, I thought the ride would be a great tune-up for the following week's race. Hoping to spend as much time as we could in the national park, we decided to drive a few hours south into Virginia to begin our ride.

In the first of a long line of unpleasant occurrences, it began to cloud up as we unloaded the bikes from the car. The pleasant summer day turned into a cool and dank late afternoon. We planned to take US Route 11 south toward Front Royal, Virginia, where the Skyline Drive began. Only a few blocks after we began our ride, Route 11 (unbeknownst to us) made a turn. We missed it and wandered nearly three miles into the West Virginia countryside before we realized what we had done.

The light rain continued off and on for much of the next 30 miles, and daylight faded as we approached Winchester. We had seen dozens of signs for a motel called Echo Village long before we got to Winchester but didn't come upon it until we finally got to Kernstown, many miles after the first sign. Though the signs would have hinted at the fact this was not a five-star establishment, it really did not seem to be important to us at the time. We were wet, tired, and happy just to have someplace to shower and collapse. Why pay a bundle to do that anyway?

As we entered the lobby, we were overwhelmed by what was perhaps the biggest collection of motivational religious signs and bible quotations ever assembled by an individual motel. In a spirit of Christian generosity, they offered us a room for $7.50, a very frugal charge even by 1976 standards. We soon came to learn, though, you usually do get what you pay for. We assessed that the rooms had last been redecorated during the early years of the Eisenhower administration, and if operable showers had ever been in the rooms, they were long ago disconnected.

Another more contemporary Republican president was in that week's news. Gerald Ford was in the process of winning the contentious nomination over Ronald Reagan, and Brian and I watched some of the convention on the small black and white television. It wasn't as if we had any choice. Echo Village's spartan accommodations were limited to begin with; the selection of television stations was miniscule. And since the conventions were covered gavel to gavel on all three major networks, nothing else was on.

After ample blessings were showered upon us by our holy innkeepers the next morning, we set off toward Skyline Drive. We hoped to make it to the campground at Big Meadows, about halfway through the 100-mile roadway in Shenandoah National Park. At twice the distance of any other ride Brian had been on in 1976, it would have been a tough ride even if it was flat. But Skyline Drive is anything but flat.

The Blue Ridge boasts some of the oldest rocks visible at the surface anywhere in the country and several of the highest peaks in the Eastern United States. The granite that made up the base of the Blue Ridge is dated at more than a billion years old. Though the Blue Ridge fades as it progresses into Pennsylvania, it is a dominant geologic feature south of the Mason-Dixon Line and continues as part of the Great Smoky Mountains at its southern end. More notably from a cyclist's perspective, the erosion resistant rocks in Virginia and North

Carolina made for higher mountains and steeper climbs than what we were used to in Central Pennsylvania. At the top of one ascent, clearly exhausted, Brian characterized the climbs as "demanding," in perhaps the understatement of the week.

Late in the day, we pulled into the Skyland Visitor Center on the western face of the mountains and were overjoyed to find there was a restaurant there. As an added bonus, it overlooked the picturesque valley below. The scenery had been incredible throughout the ride, but the view (and the food) from the Skyland restaurant seemed to bring the day to a very pleasant end. A tasty vegetarian platter made me particularly happy. But while hope springs eternal, unexpected realities often thwart such optimism. We dilly-dallied at Skyland longer than we should have and then found ourselves confronted by a nasty climb to our end destination. We arrived there at dusk and watched the deer grazing for a while in the appropriately named Big Meadows.

When we got to the ranger station, we were panic-stricken to find out the campground was full. We explained to the ranger that we had no choice but to stay there for the night; it was nearly dark and the nearest alternative provisions were many miles away. He said they sometimes had a few spots set aside for hikers or bikers that wandered in at some late hour, and he eventually found us a spot, albeit one in an obscure corner of the campground.

One seldom sleeps well on a picnic table, but a chilly night, made even cooler by our high elevation, made it even more difficult. I slept poorly and Brian said he felt as if he had hardly slept at all. Though exhausted, we were looking forward to more downhills the following day than what we struggled through on Monday. I had begun my first detailed cycling journal on the trip and wrote of that first day's ride that it "seemed like it was 75% uphill." The trip had gone from 595 feet to 3,680 feet above sea level and back up and down many times.

The first 55 miles of the next day turned out to be the most enjoyable miles of the trip, as we passed through beautiful scenery and went more downhill than up. At the end of Skyline Drive, we took Virginia Route 250 west toward the city of Staunton. After the initial descent off the Blue Ridge, the ride went figuratively downhill as well.

The road surface was terrible and most of the route was one annoying hill after another. After two days on the truck-free national park road, the trucks and heavy car traffic on Route 250 seemed intolerable.

We had initially thought we would ride back and forth on Skyline Drive. But we reconsidered when we surmised that a ride on US Route 11 through the Shenandoah River Valley would be an easier ride. After all, we reasoned, it was flat and the rural nature of the valley would make for a pretty ride. Even after the dreadful fifteen miles to Staunton, we remained optimistic about the ride north because we were confident Route 11 would be a much better road. Coupled with a good night's sleep at the Econo Lodge in Staunton, we were looking forward to a pleasant ride in this scenic and historic part of Virginia. Staunton was one of those rare middle-sized cities that had been able to hold onto many of their historic buildings in the face of the misguided urban renewal of the seventies. Their downtown remained vibrant when most other cities of similar size had succumbed to the exodus of business and people.

When we turned north on US 11, we were disappointed to find a brisk wind blowing in our face, a northerly wind cursing us following the passage of the cool front. Though Interstate 81 was just east of Route 11, a great deal of local traffic still used the old highway. In our pre-ride planning, Ken Steel had assured us that Route 11 was "flat and all the traffic rides on the interstate." Nothing could have been further from the truth.

The traffic and wind were discouraging enough, but the inhospitable natives added insult to injury. More often than not, we were treated rudely by both drivers and those we ran into off the highway. Parched and frustrated, we decided to stop for some food and drink at what appeared to be a quaint country store just off the highway. In a scene reminiscent of the old *Petticoat Junction* television show, a small group of locals were sitting around a small table in the middle of the store chewing the fat. They were not nearly as friendly as old Sam Drucker, though, their only words to us being what we owed them.

We sat down in front of the store to partake of our lunch, downtrodden and disillusioned. Our foray into the charming countryside of Virginia seemed more like a trip into a strange and forbidden land.

Short of Rod Serling himself walking up to us, the next incident made us feel like we were in the *Twilight Zone*.

It was actually his car we heard first. The sound of a sports car coming north on Route 11 grew louder until we finally saw it come over the small hill south of the store. The car came to a screeching halt right in front of us and a young driver dressed in something out of *Saturday Night Fever* jumped from the car. I could not pinpoint his accent, but it was clear that he was not a native-born American, let alone a Virginian.

"You gentlemen looking for a gift for your girlfriends?" Before we had a chance to answer, he continued, "Got anything you could want." Like a scene from a movie, he pulled up his sleeve to display seven or eight wristwatches from wrist to elbow. Overwhelmed with disbelief and amusement, Brian and I had still not offered much of a response.

"Wouldn't your girlfriend love beautiful new watch? She think you great boyfriend."

Having neither girlfriends nor an interest in a hot watch, Brian and I looked at each other, trying to hold back the hysterical laughter that was bubbling up within us. "No, thanks just the same."

"You missing great chance to make her happy," he responded in broken English in one last attempt to sway us.

"No, thanks anyway," Brian answered as the traveling salesman hopped back into his still running car and sped off. Brian and I finally let the laughter burst forth as he went out of sight in search of his next prospective customer. Though the watch incident gave us a hearty chuckle, it could not overcome our frustration with the wind or the traffic, and we concluded we just wanted to get back to the car. We decided we would try hitching a ride as far north as we could. Ah, but the best laid plans of mice and men…

After nearly three hours of sticking our thumbs out, we finally found a friendly pickup truck driver that was willing to give us a lift. Had we just persevered and ridden through the wind for those three hours, we would have likely covered twice as much ground as what we did by truck. The kind gentleman dropped us off in New Market, Virginia, cutting only 20 miles off our ride. Frustrated even more, we resolved to plow forward and get as far as we could by the day's end. Sometime close to 7:00 p.m., we found ourselves between another rock and hard place. We had passed up the town of Strasburg, deciding the choice of lodging in Front Royal would be better. But the road between the two towns was hilly, and we were exhausted long before we got to that point. While less than ten miles, that stretch seemed to go for hours and the battle to beat the darkness made a bad situation worse. When we finally saw the overly-commercialized Front Royal from the top of the hill a few miles away, many of the town's lights were already shining in the twilight. We found a motel as dusk was turning to nighttime, ending the most trying day of riding of my cycling life.

Eager to get home, we rode the 45 miles into Martinsburg, West Virginia the next morning at a brisk pace and got back to Altoona in early afternoon. Driving home, we concluded Shenandoah National Park was perhaps an anomaly, not only geologically and naturally but culturally as well. The Park Service had purchased 450 farmsteads from the mid-twenties to the mid-thirties, in effect creating an island of parkland in the midst of rural Virginia. Though there was broad support for the park, some landowners were unhappy. As a concession, some were allowed to occupy their land for a few years. By 1938, the last of the original landowners had officially vacated the parkland. But a secret list of 43 occupants had been allowed to stay until they died; the last of them, Annie Lee Bradley Shenk, was still in the park when we went through in 1976. She died three years later at the age of 92, more than three decades after her husband, and nearly 40 years after the park was supposed to be vacated.[5]

Marathon Rides and Giant Hemlocks

"It is not so much for its beauty that the forest makes a claim upon men's hearts, as for that subtle something, that quality of air that emanation from old trees, that so wonderfully changes and renews a weary spirit."

—Robert Louis Stevenson

WHILE THE VIRGINIA RIDE HAD BEEN DEMANDING AND GOOD preparation for the race the following week, the struggles of that ride made me realize I was still far from being a great bike racer. Coming off his long trip out west, I could not fathom beating Ken Steel, with those kinds of miles under his belt. The race was on a hot and calm day, the sort of day that generates sweat even before you get on the bike. Hoping that I could stay close to the front of the race for a while, I tried to get a spot on the frontline of racers as we were instructed to line up. I was in the lead group of riders when we went around the first corner a few blocks from the starting line.

As we made our first notable climb just outside of Altoona, I stayed in my big chain ring and muscled up the hill. I had to pinch myself when I realized I was the only one still with Ken and John Bradley. Even though I was still riding in my Keds sneakers, I was matching the two cycling heroes stroke for stroke up the first few hills. When we got to the Horseshoe Curve and the turnaround, we had what seemed like an insurmountable lead over the rest of the field. I also realized that Ken and John probably couldn't drop me on the return trip since it was mostly downhill.

At that time, the race did not go up the steepest part of the Allegheny

Front but instead turned back toward Altoona before the worst part of the climb. We worked together to stay in front of the other racers on the way back down, and it was a mad sprint to the finish line when we turned the last corner a few hundred yards from the line on Beale Avenue. I popped into one of my biggest gears and gave it everything I had. John Bradley held me off at the line but I outsprinted Ken to take second place. I might have been just a tad disappointed to be that close and not win, but to be in that company was triumph enough. While I was ecstatic, I also felt funny. Though it always felt good to beat a rival (that you oftentimes disliked at least a little), it felt strange to beat a good friend. I almost felt guilty to have beaten Ken, who had done so much to help me get where I was. He had spent the previous two years waiting for me and I repaid him by outsprinting him in the only race in Blair County.

If Ken felt slighted, he didn't show it. Perhaps he reasoned that, at age 39, he was proud to be with his much younger rivals at the finish. Showing little disappointment, he asked a few of us if we wanted to go for another ride since the day was still young. We set off for the town of Portage, climbing the steep incline that we avoided in the race. I never finished the ride, though, as I flatted and had to hitchhike back, since I had left my pump and spare tire at home for the race. I counted my lucky stars the flat had not happened 20 miles earlier, costing me the chance to do well in the race.

Despite the flat tire to end the week and the frustrations we experienced on our Virginia trip, it had still been quite a week of cycling. The 360 miles was the biggest mileage week of my life, I had experienced some incredible riding (and geology) on the Skyline Drive, and I had my best race result ever. Yet I felt like I had only scratched the surface. There was so much more to see, so much more to learn, and so many more races to ride.

The week before school began, Ken put together several rides that would make my high mileage total for August go even higher. He organized a ride with Tom Baldwin and a Penn State classmate of mine, Kevin Williams, that Tuesday. Excited to get out for another ride or two before surrendering to the school year, we eagerly accepted Ken's invitation. But I was destined to more tough luck, as I broke my first spoke climbing the hellacious Locke Mountain between Williamsburg and Hollidaysburg. I got my third flat of the week on the ride, thanks to a tiny, nearly invisible sliver of glass stuck in my rear tire.

All this ill fortune would not deter me though, and I was resolute that I would ride every mile possible. Though my mechanically cursed ride (on the heels of a difficult trip) should have caused me to throw my hands up in despair, I excitedly joined Ken on a planned 125-mile ride down into the deep, dark recesses of Bedford County a few days later. In what turned out to be a blessing in disguise, a stubborn thunderstorm cut 20 miles off the ride. Stranded at the supermarket in Bedford, we were tempted to call Ken's dad to rescue us, but after two hours, the sun came out and we pressed on. Though shorter than we planned, the ride was still a tough 105 miles.

Ken asked John Bradley, Gary Kephart, and me to join him on a long ride northeast of State College that Sunday. In the Ken Steel tradition, every aspect of the ride was wildly understated. A "little more than 100 miles" turned out to be 125, a "couple of gravel stretches" ended up being several climbs over lose stone, and a peek at some of the scenery necessitated a half-mile hike. The ride and the hike were worth the effort, though, as Ken's troop through the woods in Alan Seeger Natural Area took us into a virgin stand of hemlocks. Pennsylvania's state tree and the finest needled tree of all the conifers that grow in the Northeast, the hemlock would become my favorite tree. The one that Ken always showed people was five feet in diameter and likely one of the oldest living things in this part of the United States.

The 125 miles was my longest ride ever at that point in my fledgling cycling career and prompted us to talk about other long rides we had been on. As usual, Ken was able to top everyone. A few summers before, he had done a 24-hour marathon race in upstate New York and rode more than twice as many miles as we did that day. Held the weekend closest to the summer solstice, daylight riding could be done from just after 5:00 a.m. until 9:00 p.m. That meant there was still considerable riding in the dark, a challenge from several different perspectives.

Ken had ridden well into the night and said the first few hours were not as bad as he might have feared. But with the monotony of the short nighttime loop, the ungodly amount of time in the saddle, and the lack of sleep conspiring against him, he knew he needed to stop for a while. The leading contenders, he found out, were taking very short breaks, some sleeping just an hour or so to take the edge off their overwhelming fatigue. While Ken didn't think he could win the event, he had aspirations to do well. So he decided his break would be a short one as well. His good intentions were confronted by the reality of his own exhaustion, and he woke up nearly four hours later. Still, he did well by our and his standards, covering more than 300 miles. As we ate and drank on the front porch of the store in McAlevey's Fort, we decided we should go to the event together the next year. I actually sent for the information on the race, but our foray into the ultra-marathon cycling world went no further than the talk we had on that August afternoon.

Even though that 300-mile day never came to pass, August 1976 was proving to be my biggest mileage month ever. I was just short of 1,300 miles after completing those long rides during the last week. Still needing about 40 miles to pass the threshold, I went for two rides on the last day of August. A classmate and friend of my brother Gerard, Steve Lawruk, joined me for a ride to Canoe Creek State Park to put me over the top. Steve was just fifteen and was riding a heavy department store bike, not dissimilar to the one I had been riding just a few years before. When he survived two rides to Canoe Creek the last week of August, I fully realized just how well he could ride. Though he still had that tank of a bike, he rode on longer and longer rides the next summer. He eventually won his age division of the race to the Horseshoe Curve in 1977 before fading from the sport to pursue his first athletic love, basketball. I realized then cycling was contagious and, just as Ken had passed it onto me, I had done the same for Steve.

Good Times, Bad Times

—John Bonham, John Paul Jones, and Jimmy Page
"Good Times, Bad Times"
From their first album *Led Zeppelin*
Atlantic Records (1969)

I WOULD BE LEAVING HOME FOR THE FIRST TIME IN September 1976 and moving 40 miles down the road to the University Park campus of Penn State for the last two years of college. I was sharing an apartment with Brian Weakland, now working for the newspaper in State College. Our apartment was about the same distance from campus as my parents' house was from the Altoona Campus I had attended the two previous years.

Stricken by my cycling obsession as I was, I informed my mother of my school transportation plans.

"Mom, I'm going to ride my bike to school whenever I can."

"I guess that would be okay. You've been riding it to school for the last two years," she calmly responded.

"This first week, I'll have to leave in the late afternoon on Labor Day to get there before dark," I explained.

Assuming at first that riding to school meant I would be going from my apartment to campus each day, Mom was somewhat shocked when she realized what my statement really meant.

"That's a long trip!" she said as she began her testimony as to why I should make the trip by car.

"I've made it many times before," I retorted.

"How are you going to get your clothes and food down there?" as she continued to make her case.

"Brian said he would take it down." Brian's family lived only four blocks from me and he came home almost every weekend. I had planned all this out and was prepared for everything my mother could throw at me.

"How will you get home?" she continued.

"I'll ride home after class on Saturday morning." And before she could ask the question, I answered it. "Brian will bring home my clothes and books."

Though Mom might not have been crazy about the twice weekly ride, she had, by this time, come to a passive resignation this was the teenage obsession she would have to deal with. Labor Day was a pleasant day, but a brisk wind and some rough roads would slow the 40-mile ride to two hours and fifteen minutes. The fact I was keeping track of times in my journal spoke volumes as to how serious I had become about all this.

I had worked up a good appetite, and as usual, ate everything that wasn't nailed to the table. I came to realize that riding a thousand miles a month had the additional benefit of allowing me to eat gargantuan amounts of food with little concern over gaining weight.

A week or two into the fall trimester, I discovered the Dandelion Market natural food store a few blocks off campus. For the aspiring health food devotee, this was an amazing discovery. I had never seen anything like it before. Beyond the incomprehensible selection of natural foods, most sold in bulk, I was overcome by almost everything else about the market—the old fashioned appearance of the store, the hippy-style attire of the staff, even the smell. It was intoxicating.

I came upon a granola recipe posted on the wall and decided I'd give it a try. I gathered what I needed, stuck it all in my backpack, and pedaled home, quite a few pounds heavier than I started out that morning. But like many other of my early cooking and baking efforts, my attempt at making granola did not go so well, the uncooked barley I added giving it a gravel-like texture. A peanut butter banana cake made from scratch a few weeks later, like the granola, smelled scrumptious as it baked but ended up mostly inedible. So dense was the cake, I feared had I dropped it from a height of even two feet, it would have cracked the kitchen counter upon impact. It more resembled an adobe brick than a cake.

As the autumn turned to early winter, my kitchen talents improved and I figured out how to plan my complementary amino acids, too. Of the 20 amino acids that build proteins, only 11 are synthesized by the human body. The other nine must come from your diet. Meat and fish have complete proteins, containing all nine essential amino acids, but they are found in varying amounts in other foods. So it's important for non-meat eaters to make sure they're getting their essential amino acids. One must make up for those that are missing from one food with something else that does have the amino acid. If a vegetarian doesn't pay attention to these building blocks, they will not get enough protein.

I learned grains like rice were higher in methionine (which is missing from beans and other legumes) while peas and beans contain lysine (which is not abundant in rice and many other grains). One of my favorite meals featuring those complementary amino acids was cornbread and bean soup. Both my Granny Weakland and my Aunt Madeline would have the meal once or twice a month. When they came to know I had converted to vegetarianism, they were certain to invite me to their home whenever they had the meal. If the weather was fit, I'd hop on the bike and ride to their houses to enjoy the vegetarian treat. Many decades after their deaths, I could still vividly recall sitting in my aunt's immaculate kitchen or joining my grandparents at the tiny table in the corner of their kitchen enjoying soup and pone.

After those first few rough cooking experiences at school, as the fall and winter progressed, things went much more smoothly in the kitchen. That is, with one tiny exception. As I prepared to set off one winter evening for a film session on campus, I decided to cook up some beans for the next evening's supper. Somehow, in my rush to get ready for my long walk to campus, I forgot about the beans. Realizing what I had done part way through the session, I nervously sat through the rest of the films. The moment the last one ended, I exploded out of the classroom and ran the three miles back to my apartment, hoping I had not burned down the building. When I got to the side of the building, I was relieved to see that it was still standing but sickened to see Brian was back. I sprinted up the steps and was welcomed by the pungent odor of burnt beans and the similarly pungent look on Brian's face. Despite the cold, single digit night outside, Brian had the windows open and the fans going on high to air out the apartment. An incredibly even-tempered person, Brian seldom got mad at me for anything and we hardly ever had even a mild confrontation during all our time together. But like the Blue Eagle Motel incident of the previous summer (when I passed up a motel on our way to the east coast), Brian found it difficult to muster much patience for my mistake that night.

While my cooking came along (burnt beans aside), my classwork was a struggle the entire term. A Saturday morning math class and a required statistics class made for a very long week. Much to my chagrin, even one of the classes in my major was painful. Assuming that every geography class I took would be enjoyable, I was especially frustrated when my first one at University Park seemed to be more about economics than geography. The transition to living away from home had not been difficult; it was the frustration of the worst class schedule I had ever had that was making me crazy. The bike and my rock and roll collection were the only things that kept me sane.

One particularly trying afternoon, I sat on the old swivel chair in the living room of our apartment, struggling with industrial location theory and chi square charts, when the Led Zeppelin song "Good Times, Bad Times" came up on the stereo. While I had been able to personally relate to lyrics in music once in a great while, this one resonated like no other song ever had. It was as if Led Zep had written the song for me personally. As I sat on the chair, overwhelmed by schoolwork I did not enjoy and saw no point in studying, away from home for the first time in my life, and with no prospect of any romance, I was as melancholy as I had ever been. These really were not, as it turned out, traumatic events, but they were as difficult a time as I had ever experienced. The line in the middle of the song, "I know what it means to be alone, I sure do wish I was at home," convinced me that the subtitle of "Good Times, Bad Times" should have been the "Ballad of John Frederick."

The anxiety and mental anguish even haunted me when I was able to get out on the bike. As I rode out Whitehall Road one pleasant afternoon in late September, I caught myself mumbling "the coefficient of spatial variation" to myself. The economic geography term ran through my mind over and over again like some horrid advertising jingle that follows you long after you've turned off the television. No matter how hard I tried, the term would not leave my mind.

The first couple weeks of September were otherwise pleasant and the bike distracted me from the awful school experience. Since I was cursed to have a Saturday morning class, I could not ride my bike back to Altoona until after class each Saturday. The first or second weekend I was there, a perfect September morning welcomed me as I began the ride home. It had crossed my mind that Penn State had a home football game that day, but the traffic ramifications of that escaped me, that is, until I hit the traffic a couple miles from my apartment. When I got to Route 45, I was overwhelmed by the number of cars going the other direction. It was the first time I had ever seen a rural road with nearly bumper-to-bumper traffic.

While early September weather was as nice as it could be, it didn't last. The weather gods would drive me back to the brink, as rain and cold prevented me from riding fifteen days over the next three weeks. After a beautiful week of early autumn weather that started on October 11th, the weather turned foul again and the cycling season came to an early end with an unpleasant two week stretch of rain, cold, and earlier sunsets. (Daylight Savings Time ended the first week of October in those years.) A balmy Friday and Saturday the last weekend of October was the only respite to the dreadfully miserable autumn weather that was the precursor to a similarly rotten winter. My ride home from State College to Altoona that weekend would be the last ride over 35 miles I could embark upon for four months.

One of the few rides of any significance I endured during that stretch happened on November 21st, the Sunday before Thanksgiving. Ken called a bunch of us and asked if we wanted to brave the weather and ride to the Horseshoe Curve and on up the steep escarpment to Gallitzin and Coupon. It was only in the mid-forties when we started in early afternoon. When we got to the Horseshoe Curve, two riders in the group decided enough was enough and turned around. Four of us struggled on with Ken, too proud to give up before making the climb into Cambria County. On top of the mountain, it was in the upper thirties, and the clouds began to look more and more threatening. The ride down the mountain was so cold I could not feel my toes or fingertips. When it began to flurry partway down the descent, I knew my commitment had reached a new level. I wasn't sure at that moment, though, whether that meant I was committed to being a great cyclist or that I should simply *be* committed.

Let It Snow

—Lyrics by Sammy Cahn
(1945)

THE UNPLEASANT AUTUMN HAMMERED HOME THE FACT I had to have some way to keep riding when the weather did not cooperate. So I told Santa Claus I wanted a set of rollers. Before the days of the resistance trainers, everyone in the eighties and beyond would use rollers. Rollers were three rotating drums powered by the back wheel going over two of the six inch drums, simulating a ride on the road. Or such was the theory...

Though I'm not quite sure how he got them down the chimney, Santa brought me a set for Christmas. As soon as I could get away from the Christmas Day family obligations, I took them to the basement and set them up. They were only about two feet wide, so it gave the rider little margin for error. I set them up in a doorway so I would have something to lean on, but it did not matter. I felt as if I was going to fly off the apparatus on nearly every revolution of the pedals. I was determined that I would master them, though, and after some anxious moments, I figured it out. I rode ten miles that first day and didn't miss a day of riding through my entire Christmas vacation. The weather outside was frightful, but I was going to get my miles in regardless.

In what would become a brutal stretch of particularly cold and snowy winters in the Northeast, the winter of 1976-1977 was another frustrating one for someone trying to become a better cyclist. January was as cold a month as I would experience in my entire life. Only once, the last Saturday of the month, would the mercury creep over the freezing mark, and the low temperature dipped below zero eight times. The high on January 18th never got above zero. Between the cold weather and my schoolwork, I couldn't log even a hundred miles.

I'm still not sure how he got them down the chimney, but Santa Claus brought me a set of rollers for Christmas 1977. I decided if I was serious about racing for Penn State and riding across the country, I had to put some miles on even during a cold Pennsylvania winter. Photo by Marguerite Frederick.

Thankfully, my winter term class schedule brought a refreshing about-face to the dreadful courses I suffered through the previous term. A forestry class and two geography classes that focused on cultural ecology restored the enthusiasm for my schoolwork. The two geography teachers, Dr. Greg Knight and visiting professor Gary Klee, approached their classes in very different ways.

Klee was in the early stages of his teaching career and began a long tenure at San Jose State the academic year following his stint at University Park. Klee's class was actually entitled "Cultural Geography" and as such could have focused on the sometimes dry trivia of economic, agricultural, religious, and uniquely cultural details of various peoples and regions. Instead, he chose to look at the world through the eyes of an environmental geographer and tried to convey that different societies used (and sometimes abused) their environments in vastly different ways. He also stressed industrial societies like ours consumed resources in a most unsustainable way and our lives would be wildly different without the tools and technologies we usually took for granted. To hammer this home, we had to do a "failed technology" project in which we made something using only human energy and without any modern technology or materials. I made a bird feeder out of a broken tree branch and the head of two sunflowers. Proving Klee's point, it was indeed difficult to make without using any tools. I sanded the tree branch into the shape I needed with a piece of sandstone, seemingly taking forever to do so.

Dr. Knight was in the first few years of a distinguished four decade-long tenure at Penn State. His emphasis was similar to Klee's, examining man's profound impact on the natural environment, but his approach was different. He laid out the fundamentals of what he called "Environmental Dynamics" and followed that with discussions on our sense of place and how we perceived our environment. His lecture topics flowed one into another, seemingly without interruption, and I tried to follow that same approach when I became an Earth Science teacher a year and half later. Like almost all effective teachers, he also managed to engage and entertain. Going to those classes was something I wanted to do rather than an obligation I had to tolerate.

After the frustration of the brutally cold late fall and winter, I decided I needed to hit the rollers as often as I could. I rode a hundred miles indoors in February with the hope of being ready to hit the road when it finally warmed up. The frigid weather finally broke the second week of February, but it was short-lived. We went back into the deep freeze for another ten days in the middle of the month. Despite the time on the rollers, it simply was not possible to replicate the real road miles. I walked the nearly five-mile round trip to school almost every day, and Brian and I would run around the indoor track on campus in the evening when we had time. But by the end of February, I had a very bad case of cabin fever.

Finally, as spring term break began, the long, cold winter weather broke and I was able to get out three out of four days at the end of the month. On the last Wednesday of February, I tackled the onerous climb of Wopsononock Mountain, my first road ride since Thanksgiving Day. Snow still covered the north facing slopes of the winding road up the Appalachian Front. It was a chilly descent, but I was so delighted to be outside I really didn't care I was cold.

That Saturday Ken asked Roddy Gerraughty and me to venture toward Martinsburg and the flat farm country south of Altoona. Ken had noted in his journal that his garden soil had finally thawed, but it was warm only by comparison to the frigid winter that had just ended. Yet we persevered through the chilly spring air, turning north when we got to Martinsburg and following the rich limestone valley to Williamsburg. Ken decided to tackle the three-mile climb toward Huntingdon, but Roddy and I feared the additional 20 miles might make it difficult to get back before dark. Nightfall was still coming early the last week of February, and we were cold and tired besides. Though Ken ended up beating the darkness back home, Roddy and I did not regret our decision. A week and a half later, I would not exhibit such good sense.

It turned downright hot on March 9th, the first day over 70 in nearly five months, and it prompted Ken to plan a hundred-mile ride. Without thinking about the ramifications, I excitedly accepted the invitation. It was a glorious late winter day that more resembled the ninth of June than the ninth of March. The early parts of the ride went perfectly. Since it was a Wednesday, all of Ken's other riding partners were working, so it was just the two of us. With the exception of the steepest climbs, I was able to keep up, and we seemed to breeze through the first part of the ride.

A few dozen miles into the ride, Ken developed a slow leak in his front tire. We stopped in Petersburg at the old-style country store and gas station on the main street to refuel and change the tire. Like the typical gas stations of the first half of the 1900s, the gas pumps were under a roof that was connected to the main building. It was one of those charming vestiges of an earlier time that were much more likely to survive in the country or a small town like Petersburg.

Ken had begun riding tubular tires the prior summer and this complicated the tire repair efforts. Tubulars, or "sew-ups," were the high-performance tires of choice in the late seventies. They could be inflated to higher pressures because the tire was actually sewn around the tube. But it also meant the tire had to be glued to the rim. The rim cement was a nasty adhesive that would stick to everything and would inevitably get all over the rim. Trying to repair one on the road was particularly difficult since there was no time to let the glue get even slightly tacky. The glue would ooze onto the tire and rim even more after it was inflated. Ken had all of those things conspiring against him that day, and it took him 45 minutes to make the repair and clean up the mess. At the time, I was relishing the rest. By the end of the day, I would wish I had some of that time back.

We finally started back up the valley a bit before one. Though I still had some things to learn about the details of the geology we were passing through at the time, the ride was yet another lesson in the intricacies of Pennsylvania's Ridge and Valley topography. We had climbed over a sandstone ridge (Brush Mountain), into a limestone valley (Sinking Valley), through the Little Juniata River gap into the shale Stone Valley, and would go over yet another sandstone ridge (Stone Mountain). That was just the first half of the ride. The second big climb started at Greenwood Furnace State Park and ascended through a hemlock-covered mountainside that was green even while the rest of the landscape was still suffering from the defoliation of winter.

Rather than the geology lesson, it was the beautiful scenery I would enjoy that day. Even when we fell into Big Valley, the ride continued to be scenic as the mountain forestland faded into Amish farmland. Big Valley was a wide limestone valley full of rich farmland well-suited for the small-farm economy of the Amish and Mennonites. I had not realized their enclaves, for which Lancaster County was so well known, had spread into this part of Pennsylvania on such an extensive scale. As my adult years passed, they bought more and more farmland closer to my hometown.

We stopped at the general store near the bottom of the mountain in the town of Belleville. Like the store and gas station in Petersburg, it was a remnant of an earlier time, a corner store that sold groceries and dry goods long before convenience stores or Walmarts. Belleville was the cultural and economic center of the Big Valley and our lunch break was a lesson in the sociology of rural communities of a by-gone time. For all intents and purposes, the Big Valley Amish still lived in the 19th Century in those days. Their houses had no electricity, they owned no phones, they worked their fields with horse-drawn plows, and they traveled in horse and buggies. Though there were many "English" that lived in the community, it was the Amish families walking, working, and riding their buggies through town that caught the attention of this young "English" boy from the city. Besides the physical challenge that attracted me to bicycling, it was this incredible natural and aesthetic experience that drew me to the sport. Without realizing it, I had wandered into the study of Geography beyond my classroom experience.

On that March day, I would also learn several lessons (a few with their roots in Geography) that were on the painful side. The same bicycle that had brought ecstasy and fascination in the morning would bring misery and fright through the afternoon and early evening. As we turned south toward Huntingdon, it was quickly apparent why the first part of the ride had been so swift; we had been pushed along by a robust southwesterly wind that was now blowing in our faces. This meteorological reality and my lack of training miles came back to haunt me in an unpleasant way.

The most persistently windy days in Pennsylvania come in the spring. It's not uncommon to have a 50-degree day following a half foot snowfall at this time in February and early March. These wildly different air masses are reflected in tight air pressure gradients that bring high winds. The bigger the difference between the air pressures in two air masses, the faster the wind blows. This was one such day, and it was not enjoyable riding into that wind, especially having already ridden 50 miles, climbed two mountains, and gone up and down countless hills. I struggled to keep up with Ken as we trudged southward. In Allensville, he stopped and instructed me to get behind him and draft on his wheel into the village of Mill Creek. About 200 yards after setting off, he had already opened a gap that I could not bridge, his good intentions blown away in the stiff wind.

We crawled into Huntingdon just before 4:00 p.m. and I realized even Ken was starting to feel the effects of the long ride. We stopped at the IGA supermarket to refuel and realized we now had another problem confronting us. It was, after all, still early March, and sunset was around 6:00 p.m. Two nasty climbs (one of them over gravel) and more than 30 miles lay ahead and we had less than two hours to complete the trip. We could not expect to average much more than fifteen miles per hour even if we went nonstop and enjoyed a more beneficial wind.

It was dusk by the time we hit Sickles Corner, a crossroads ten miles and a mountain climb from my house. By the time we got to the top of the mountain near the Kettle Reservoir, it was dark, and every time a car came near me, I had to pull over onto the berm of the road. Once into town, I wandered through the side streets to avoid the traffic, and it took even longer than normal to travel the last few miles. I tried to be nonchalant when I pedaled up my driveway long after night had fallen. Not having learned anything from my ride with Denny Page the previous February, I got home even later than I had twelve months before. My mother was not quite as infuriated as I might have feared, particularly after I reassured her that I had gone out of my way to negotiate the safest path home.

A Time for Firsts

"Minor things can become moments of great revelation when encountered for the first time."

—Margot Fonteyn
English Dancer/Ballerina
1919-1991

TWO DAYS LATER, I RODE TO STATE COLLEGE AND BACK, logging just short of 200 miles in three days. I feared this warm weather might not last, and I intended to take advantage of it. After a spell of inevitable cold, the warm weather finally returned the last three days of the month with some record-breaking heat. It coincided with some lighter classwork, so I set off to explore some new roads. I climbed the sandstone ridge that separated the Nittany Valley from the Bald Eagle Valley.

For many people, and certainly for me, the late teenage years are a time for firsts. My firsts, like so many other things in my life, were often different from more traditional teenagers. My first ride on a new road was often something I could vividly recall many decades later. On that unusually hot March morning, I enjoyed a beautiful day and just such an incredible ride. It was, perhaps, only the second or third time that I found myself in the "zone," that almost super-human feeling that I could ride with anyone and make any climb. I had never done the climb over the mountain toward Port Matilda before and was surprised the top came so soon. The valley is narrow there and the climb toward Phillipsburg began soon after the previous descent ended. I was somewhat apprehensive to venture up the road since it carried considerable truck traffic, even in the mid-seventies. Since it was the middle of a weekday, a Tuesday, the traffic was light. A passing lane began just a short distance from town, and my apprehension about the road quickly faded. Years later, it would be one of those rides I wished I would have timed, for I could not imagine that many humans had ever climbed that mountain as briskly as I did that perfect afternoon. The ride back down was similarly incredible. The wind blew through my hair (which was longer than it had ever been), and my bike was going faster than it had ever gone. A new route, a new experience, brought a new high.

On the heels of this natural high, I thought of legendary basketball star Bill Russell. When discussing drug abuse in the National Basketball Association in particular and the country in general, the old Boston Celtic center said he preferred to see life go by at the speed it was intended. I thought that sound advice and came to realize life could provide its share of natural highs if one simply sought them out. On this day, I confirmed the only rush I needed was the one the bike provided.

I did a 50-mile ride over Tussey Mountain to McAlevey's Fort, down the valley, and back up over the mountain the next day. The eastern anticlinal side of the mountain was a long rigorous climb, especially after 40 miles, but the descent into Pine Grove Mills quickly helped me forget the pain. The warmer weather continued through the end of the week, and I took off for Altoona after my last class on Friday.

Then it happened again. The fickle and dreadfully inconsistent Pennsylvania spring weather reared its ugly head yet again, and it snowed three days the next week. Though it would be winter's last stand, it was most unwelcome. The next week, the warm weather returned, and I rode from home back to school on Monday morning. Having enjoyed the ride over Tussey Mountain two weeks before, I decided to go through Stone Valley and over that gut-wrenching climb again. I followed that up with a fifty-mile ride on Tuesday and made plans for another long ride on Wednesday since I didn't have class until mid-afternoon.

I awoke to one of those spring days sliced from the edge of heaven, inhaled some of my homemade granola, and set off eastward.

Climbing Tussey Mountain yet again, I went onto Lewistown and south along the Juniata River. Just northeast of McVeytown, I passed a farmer loading his hogs for market. Much to my shock, I was again confronted by Hogzilla, the monstrous sized hog that I had first met on a bike ride in the Midwest. My amusement over the hog (that was bigger than a Harley) was short-lived though, for it was here I realized I had made a dire miscalculation. Though the geographer part of me should have known this, not having topographic map sheets of this part of the state, I missed one little detail. There was an extra mountain that stood about 2,400 feet above sea level between where I was and where I needed to be.

I had already been shaving it close, but I was now panic stricken that I could not get back to State College in time for class. I climbed Jacks Mountain east of McVeytown as fast as I could and flew down the other side into Belleville. The climb up Stone Mountain began just outside Belleville, and I still had more than 20 miles just to get back to my apartment. As I dragged my now exhausted body up the long, winding climb over Tussey Mountain, I realized I was about to miss my first class in three years of college. While many college students took pride in being able to skip classes without flunking out, I feared I would miss something really important. I got back to my apartment just about the time my class was ending, overcome with guilt. It soon passed, though, when I rationalized that it had been for a noble cause. When others had missed class, it was because of all night drunken binges, one night stands, and a dozen other shallow or mindless things. I had done it for a good reason and, if I was lucky, my professor, Dr. Cecil Goodwin, wouldn't even miss me.

Though I was busy with schoolwork, I was able to ride back and forth between Altoona and State College five times in the next few weeks, despite some rainy days. My obsession had gone to yet another level. I became downright angry when the weather or schoolwork kept me off the bike. I had little other life beyond the schoolwork, the bicycle and my vegetable garden. By May of 1977, I had gone a year and a half without a date, and unbeknownst to me at the time, it would be more than another year until I would go out again. Yet most of the time, that didn't seem to matter, since I was so tied up with my bike and all that went with it. Bicycling, I realized, was a time-consuming sport, and it took a commitment of many hours every week to do it well.

Most days, I found myself on familiar roads, but I was still exploring new places a few times a month. Being in State College most of the week, I had to do this exploring on my own, rather than depending on Ken to lead the adventure. The next new experience came the first week of May when I set off north on an incredibly beautiful Friday afternoon.

State College sits in the Nittany Valley just southwest of the famous Mount Nittany, the namesakes of nearly everything Penn State. Nittany Mountain splits the valley into two and my ride would take me up the one and down the other. Mount Nittany itself is the tip of a synclinal mountain, somewhat of a geologic contradiction — down warped rock strata that sits higher than the surrounding landscape. If we think of the Appalachian Ridge and Valley as something akin to a wrinkled sheet, the wrinkles here are complicated. From a cycling standpoint, it meant plenty of climbing and awesome scenery. Much of the woodland was hardwood forests, but many of the stream valleys and shaded north facing slopes were covered by hemlocks, the Pennsylvania State Tree. The fine needles of the Eastern Hemlock made for a unique tree unlike any other in this part of the United States.

The next few weeks coincided with the end of the school year and the miles were much fewer and further between. But taking classes in my major, my spring trimester had been genuinely enjoyable and it took the edge off the hectic final two weeks. A class on alternative energy systems and an environmental geology course weren't just interesting to me, they fit into the lifestyle to which I aspired. The final project for my Low Energy Living class was on organic gardening and farming, and I didn't have to look much further than my own experiences for many of the topics in the research paper. The geology class included extensive field study work, giving me a chance to see things that can never be fully appreciated unless seen in person. We visited a toxic chemical site along Spring Creek (where the pesticide Kepone had been dumped) and the petrochemical smell was still conspicuous. Tours of the university's sewage treatment plant and the county landfill in the village of Snowshoe were two more sensory experiences which were difficult to erase from my olfactory memory bank.

It was Dr. Fred Wernstedt's Climatology class that particularly fascinated me. Though the subject was already of interest to me, Wernstedt's teaching style and enthusiasm enhanced my intellectual curiosity even more. I came to realize climate, and not just soils, landforms, and water resources, drove how we used our environment, where we lived, and how we made a living. Climate became another part of the puzzle I would try to piece together as I bicycled and traveled across the country.

Much as I might have enjoyed it, I looked forward to the end of school so I could roll up some real mileage. I rode 650 miles over the next two weeks, including my first ride with Ken since early March. Infamous for building two or three roads going to the same place, Pennsylvania consequently often offered a less heavily traveled highway option for cyclists. Such was the case for the trip from the town of Newry to the village of Blue Knob atop the Allegheny Front. While one of the routes was more heavily traveled, one could ride for long spells on the other two without seeing a soul. I went for rides to Blue Knob on two consecutive days after school ended — a pair of 70 mile rides, one solo and the other with Ken and Roddy by way of Portage and Beaverdale. Though both rides included many of the same roads, the same tree-lined beauty and challenging climbs, they were stark contrasts to each other. One was a ride of quiet solitude through Pennsylvania's hardwood forests. The other was an adventure with the two people that had ignited the fires of enthusiasm for the sport that had come to be the dominant thing in my life. The two rides reflected my attitude toward life in general. I could have a great time with others but was also very happy to ride through much of my life with only the road as my companion.

New Explorations

When the Levee Breaks...

—Original Lyrics by Memphis Minnie (1929)
"When the Levee Breaks"
From the album Led Zeppelin IV
Atlantic Records (1971)

AT THIS POINT IN 1977, ONLY JOHN BRADLEY, GARY KEPHART and I would venture out on the epic marathons with Ken, so it came as no surprise that when we set off that Sunday morning, the four of us were the only ones that showed. Like was so often the case in those first couple years riding with Ken, he gave us only a vague notion of where we were headed. I knew Johnstown was on the route and that he planned to go beyond there as well, but we knew little else.

Given that we were heading off on a very long ride, I thought a second bottle would come in handy and had attached a handlebar-mount bottle cage, a throwback to what some racers used back in the fifties and sixties. What seemed like a good idea was not. The cage lasted less than an hour, cracking and falling off before we got to the town of Portage. I had no way of knowing at the time, but before the day would end, that second bottle would have come in handy.

As we approached Johnstown, John Bradley had a bit more hair-raising experience. As we plummeted down the descent into the infamous valley in which Johnstown was situated, John flatted at 45 miles per hour. Thanks to John's practice of using plenty of rim cement on his tubular tires, his back tire stayed on the rim. He was able to come to a safe stop, but not before a few anxious moments. Though the hill gave John a bit of a scare, it gave me my first image of the drop-off from the bluff into the floodplain that is Johnstown, Pennsylvania.

I had ridden down the incline in a bus on the four lane Johnstown Expressway many times going back and forth to basketball games. It was a much different sensation on a bike, looking over the edge of the steep hillside, the entire city laid out in front of you.

Once in Johnstown, we continued going west along the oft-flooded Conemaugh River. Johnstown is similar in layout to Pittsburgh, the Little Conemaugh meeting the Stoney Creek River at the Point where Johnstown's (aptly named) Point Stadium sits next to the river. The Conemaugh's gorge is a narrow one and would be prone to flooding on its own because of that. The fact that Stony Creek and its sizable watershed also ends up in this narrow valley makes Johnstown the closest thing to a topographic drain as you'll find. Though we had no way of knowing on this pleasant, late May day, just eight weeks later, Johnstown would experience yet another massive flood.

The 88th anniversary of the worst of Johnstown's floods was just two days after our ride through town. The horrid flood of 1889 is the most infamous of the floods that have cursed the western Pennsylvania community. It killed over 2,000 people and destroyed much of Johnstown and a number of other towns along the Conemaugh River. It was not, however, an Act of God, as floods are so often described, but rather an act of human stupidity and greed. While the rain had been heavy indeed and was making life less pleasant in and around Johnstown, it was the failure of the South Fork Dam that was the root cause of the disaster and the reason it became the worst of the Johnstown floods.

The dam formed Lake Conemaugh and was part of an exclusive (if not somewhat secretive) country resort and fishing club. Construction of the dam had begun nearly 50 years before the flood to provide a constant source of water for the Pennsylvania Canal, the cross-state transportation route that was the predecessor to the Pennsylvania Railroad (PRR). The dam and lake was abandoned by the Commonwealth of Pennsylvania, who had built it, after the canal system became obsolete. It was, in turn, sold to the PRR and then to a group of steel and coal industry magnates led by Henry Clay Frick. While the original dam was constructed with great care and the best engineering practices of the day, the sound construction was undermined by the subsequent owners, the South Fork Fishing and Hunting Club. In the decade or so prior to the flood, the top of the dam had been removed to facilitate the construction of a road, a fish screen (that also trapped debris during high water) was installed, and several iron drain pipes had been removed and sold for scrap. The dam had become prone to leaks as well and was usually patched with mud and straw.

A storm that would bring the wrath of hell upon Johnstown had come across Colorado, Kansas, and Missouri before turning suddenly northeastward near Chattanooga, Tennessee, on May 29, 1889. The storm was moisture starved when it began in the intermountain west, but blossomed as it drew moisture from the Gulf of Mexico and the Atlantic Ocean. It hardly rained at all in Colorado and only about an inch fell in Missouri. As it took its left turn in Tennessee, the influence of the Gulf and the strong southerly upper winds kicked in, as Louisville, Kentucky picked up three inches on May 30th. As the storm moved toward Pennsylvania, a second low pressure system formed over Southern Virginia. The bucket (or more accurately, the barrel) for the Perfect Storm had been filled. After the first low hit western Pennsylvania, the second low came northward, providing the knockout blow. Harrisburg got eight inches according to the War Department's records. (The War Department filled the role of the yet-to-be established National Weather Service in those days.) Rainfall totals from most of the rest of the storm-torn region are missing from the charts on the historic weather map of May 31st; the totals were literally off the charts. Some have estimated the worst flooded regions got close to a foot.[6]

President of the South Fork Fishing and Hunting Club Elias Unger pulled together a group of men to try and hold things together, but it was all for naught. Try as they might, the dam continued to deteriorate as the day passed and more rain fell. Unger sent engineer John Parke to the town of South Fork twice to telegraph downstream communities that the dam's collapse appeared imminent, but the warnings went unheeded. People had heard these warnings before and the dam had always held. In a classic "cry wolf" moment, most people ignored the warnings, despite the ungodly amount of rain that had fallen.

A bit after 3:00 p.m., the dam began to crumble. By 4:00 p.m. the dam was gone, the lake was empty and 20 million gallons of water was rushing down the valley of the Little Conemaugh. As it carved its incomprehensible path of destruction, it picked up a similarly incomprehensible amount of debris. And this wasn't just any debris; both the size and the volume of the material defied description. It really didn't look like water by the time it hit Johnstown, as one witness said it looked more like "a huge hill rolling over and over." So powerful was the wall of water that it washed away buildings and picked up train engines.

As we dropped into Johnstown 88 years later, and just 51 days before its next major flood, we wondered why anyone would have stayed. Though surrounded on its bluffs by two affluent suburban communities, Richland on one side and Westmont on the other, much of inner city Johnstown was not pretty. Beyond being flood prone, the city's steel mills had closed, leaving unemployment, poverty, and vacated mills. The mills were not very attractive when they were still operating and were even less so when abandoned. Like river cities all across America, Johnstown came to be because it was on a river. In the early days, it provided water for people and industry, river transportation, and a place to dump what it didn't want or need. As years passed, the floodplains were also recognized as the paths of least resistance to build railroads and highways through this rugged topography. It seemed an unwise place to build and live in 1977, but it was a very logical place to settle a century before.

In an effort to control the frequent flooding, the Army Corps of Engineers built an extensive (and very ugly) system of concrete flood-control walls, and we would ride by and over them as we traversed the city. The flood control walls usually did what they were designed to do. Unfortunately, they couldn't hold back the worst that Mother Nature could offer, as would be demonstrated later in the summer of 1977.

Our ride remained in the Conemaugh River gorge, as we followed State Route 56 downstream through a narrow valley surrounded on both sides by steep, tree-covered slopes. Despite the frequently obscured view, Seward was easy to spot in the skyline, the cooling towers of its coal fired power plant a conspicuous marker of the town. At New Florence (a nice little town but not to be mistaken for its Italian namesake) we left the Conemaugh Valley and struggled through the classic up and down topography of the badly-eroded Appalachian Plateaus. As the road leveled out near Ligonier, it struck me that we were very far from home and not yet on our return route. Ken had taken me on some long rides, but this looked like it would be an order of magnitude beyond anything I had done before.

It would have been quite a ride had we turned back homeward at that point, but Ken wanted to take us through Linn Run State Park. To do that, he told us as we approached the park, we would have to not only leave the pavement, but also climb Laurel Mountain. It was a beautiful ride over the tree covered mountain, but I missed much of it because I was intently watching the road surface in an effort to avoid the bigger stones that could puncture one of my tires.

Laurel Mountain was not a mountain in the strictest sense of the term. Rather, it was a gentle uplift (an anticline in geology terms) that was actually part of the Appalachian Plateau. From a cyclist's perspective especially, these bumps in the plateau region were topographic mountains for sure, even if they were not geologically. Being up-folded features in a plateau, these ridges could be among the highest elevations in the Appalachian system. Snow comes early and hangs on until early spring most years.

On this May afternoon, snow was the farthest thing from our minds. The dusty ride over the gravel park road magnified our already parched state and we began looking for a watering hole as we wandered back into civilization. The nation, however, was still struggling with oil shortages and it prompted a ban on Sunday sales of gasoline. Particularly in this part of the state, most small gas stations doubled as country stores, meaning that very few places were open on this Sunday afternoon. This was a source of amusement at first, as we chuckled about the irony of it all. Here we were, a group of adult men out on the road trying to liberate ourselves from the tyranny of the internal combustion engine, unable to get a drink of water or a banana because all the gas stations were closed.

Our initial amusement, however, turned to dismay and then to panic as we realized we hadn't eaten in hours and had little water. It was true that we weren't in a life-threatening situation, but the prospect of the bonk and an unpleasant 50 miles back to Altoona was a real possibility. After a long ride through the woods over the gravel roads, we went through the town of Jenners, but the only gas station and store we could find was closed. Unable to find anything else, we started north on US 219, a four-lane limited access highway that had very little along its rural exits south of Johnstown. Already whipped, out of water, and well into glycogen debt, we tried working together as we moved northward. After Route 219 crosses Stoneycreek River, it climbs out of the floodplain in a steady, seemingly endless ascent. A relatively straight section of road for this part of Pennsylvania, the entire climb seemed to be laid out in front of us. Tired as I was, I started to pull away from Ken, John, and Gary.

Though we were good friends and got along with each other, if we had the chance to beat the others into submission on a climb, we would jump at the opportunity. (Thirty years later, not to forget rides like this one, Gary got to return the favor on a ride into Clearfield County.) Even the road was straight for much of the climb; by the time I got to the top, no one was in sight down the hill. Finally, after a few minutes, I saw John struggling up the climb, and not far behind him came Gary. Having recently surpassed his fortieth birthday, Ken would trail behind on a climb now and again to one of us younger riders. To trail two of us was unusual; to finish behind three of us was unheard of.

We waited a long time and when we finally saw Ken, he was struggling just to turn the pedals. When he finally reached us resting on the overpass at the interchange for Eisenhower Boulevard, he nearly collapsed. Below us to the east was a dairy store, a respite to the dry, foodless expanse over which we had struggled since leaving Ligonier many hours before.

"What do you want to do, Ken, continue on or go down to the store?" I asked our elder statesman.

"Well," he began in that deep voice of his, "we can go down there, or I could collapse and fall off this damn bridge."

Had I counted how many times I heard Ken curse over the course of our friendship, I would have had most of my ten fingers left over after adding all of them up. It made the already comical situation that much funnier. But Ken wasn't done making us laugh on this stop. We staggered into the store and began to grab up everything that looked even remotely appetizing. When Ken walked out, we wondered what he was going to do with all of it.

"Ken, is some of that for me, or are you taking some of it home?" Gary wondered. We were especially struck by the massive ball of cheese he had among his pile of grub. "That would stop me up something awful," Gary continued as he made the face that might have come from a cheese-induced constipation. Now heartily laughing, we all agreed some sort of gastrointestinal distress seemed inevitable. Not to be proven wrong, Ken took out his pocketknife and methodically cut up his cheese into bite-sized chunks. He offered a few pieces to us but ate the overwhelming majority all by himself.

Finally recharged and rehydrated, we started back up Route 219 with both a renewed level of energy and a new attitude. At Pennsylvania Route 53, very near the site of old Lake Conemaugh, we got off the four-lane and headed toward the town of Portage, where my water bottle cage had broken earlier in the day. It seemed in some ways that a week had passed. The long mileage and the long sustenance stop had pushed us well into the early evening.

Up to this point, I had been intimidated by Ken and John on these longer marathon rides. I could not imagine that I could keep up with them when the trip odometer went much over 100 miles. Ironically, it was just around the century mark that the hellacious climb occurred where I just didn't keep up, I blew everyone away. Though I had hoped that this moment would come, I was not certain it would. I tried to be modest when it finally did happen, but my inner self was jumping for joy. It was one of those watershed events some folks never experience in sports or life. For me, it was another in a series of momentous accomplishments with which I would be blessed. This one would not make any headlines in the paper, but was still one that I would be able to vividly recall for the rest of my life.

The same day we made the 145-mile adventure to Johnstown and Ligonier, Fred Long's son, Tom, another disciple of Ken Steel, set off on an adventure of his own. He hopped aboard an Amtrak train and set off for Portland, Oregon, with the intention of riding across the country. He chose Portland not just because it was a nice place to begin such a trip, but also because he loved Bill Walton and the Portland Trailblazers. But Tom's trip was important to me for another reason, as it was further proof that a cross-country trek was within the realm of possibility for me, too. I now knew and had ridden with four or five people that had accomplished this notable feat and was even more certain that it was something I could and should do.

I began a summer internship the first week of June, complicating my weekday riding more than ever before. Though much of the summer was pleasant, we experienced some very extreme weather, starting with record-breaking chill on June 8th. It actually fell into the twenties in Bradford, the traditional Pennsylvania icebox a couple hours north of us. The headline meteorological event, however, was the Johnstown Flood later in July. Despite the full-time internship and those extreme weather occurrences, I still managed to keep my mileage up by disciplining myself to ride every evening after supper. The overwhelming majority of evenings, I would ride to the Horseshoe Curve, up the steep climb to the village of Glenwhite, south to Gallitzin, and down Sugar Run past the boney piles of the strip mines near the Blair-Cambria County border. I would set off on a couple longer rides each weekend and any day-off that time and weather would permit.

July's most memorable ride was to Big Valley, the agricultural valley with the distinctive Mennonite flavor between Altoona and Lewistown. Ken Steel, John Bradley, Dave Berry, Gary Kephart, Tom Baldwin, and I enjoyed a perfect day of riding along a route that had a bit of everything one might ask for—demanding climbs, thrilling descents, beautiful woodland, peaceful farmland, and riverside scenery. And as so often would happen when Ken was leading a ride, we experienced an amusing side note as well. Rather than go down the busier main road, Ken took us on a parallel road closer to the eastern edge of Big Valley. As we rode together up the quiet road, Ken suddenly stopped, threw his bike into the grass and ran toward the field. Sure that Mother Nature was calling his name, we slowed and stopped to wait for him to answer the call. It was not the call that we thought he was answering, though, but the call of food. Ever vigilant of what was along the roadside, Ken had spotted an apricot tree along the road and decided that he could simply not let the tasty fruit go to waste. The apricot tree was also a bit of an oddity, for this was (before the days of serious global warming) the climatic border beyond which apricots often struggled to survive. This fact, as much as the lure of the tasty fruit, motivated Ken to take this unexpected detour.

Ken, as usual, was piling up the miles even when John, Gary, and I weren't along. He had been riding a bit sluggishly (by "Man of Steel" standards) the previous few weeks and we all thought he was just over-trained. We didn't realize it until he confessed it during a ride in August, but he been suffering through a chronic, month-long bout of diarrhea. Ken figured he had consumed some tainted water earlier in the summer when he was out West, and the doctor finally confirmed that he did, in fact, have a bacterial infection.

Though Ken's health made for a tough July for him, it was the flood on July 19-20th that was the most unpleasant memory of that summer for tens of thousands of people in and around Johnstown. Though the forecasts called for thunderstorms that fateful night of July 19th, nobody had any forewarning that yet another perfect storm would curse Johnstown on this dreaded night. Typically, Pennsylvania summer thunderstorms will travel in squall lines that can sometimes drape themselves in a narrow band (often oriented northeast to southwest) across much of the state. While they can be violent and bring much rain in a short spell, they usually pass quickly. When upper winds blow the same direction as the squall line, however, the showers can run along the squall line like a train, bringing much more persistent rain to the same place. This "training" can happen anywhere the squall line and upper winds line up the right way, bringing a soaking rain that can inconvenience those sitting underneath it. When it happens in a place like Johnstown, prone to flooding just because of topography, the results can be catastrophic. Despite the guarantee by Franklin Roosevelt when the flood walls were built after the 1936 flood, Johnstown was to experience yet another flood of biblical proportions.

The train of rain fell all night and brought double digit rainfall totals to a narrow strip of Cambria County. Witnesses to the east and west noted they saw lightning flashing and heard thunder crashing for hours on end while experiencing very modest amounts of rain themselves. Though the night and following day were rainy in Altoona, it was hard for us to comprehend the storm could do what it did in Johnstown and the surrounding communities. While the loss of life was not anything near what it was in 1889, the property damage was still overwhelming.

My supervisor at the planning commission office had family in Johnstown and his first-hand report on Monday morning was nothing short of staggering. He spent countless hours over the following weeks helping them dig out from sediment that measured in yards rather than inches. The luckier home owners had their basement filled to the rafters; less fortunate folks found the muck several feet deep on their first floor living spaces.

In Altoona, the recovery from the storm was much quicker than it was for the poor folks in Johnstown, just 40 miles away. Forty miles the other direction in State College, the storm wasn't much more than a passing shower. John Bradley and Ken had planned to ride in a locally organized road race there the next Sunday. Though I had been able to outride both of them on several rides through the first part of the summer, I had ridden nearly 100 miles the day before and opted to do a short ride on that Sunday. Just a few years later, by that point deeply infected with the racing bug, I would win a race over the very same course.

In the Summer Time

—Mungo Jerry
Written by Raymond Dorset
"In the Summertime"
From the album *Electronically Tested*
Dawn Records (1971)

WHILE I MIGHT NOT HAVE BEEN A FULL-FLEDGED RACER by that time, I had, nevertheless, become obsessed with the sport. When Mom and Dad talked about going to Ocean City, Maryland, during the first week of August, I was excited about the possibility of taking my bike along. We had made a similar trip the summer before. We couldn't fit the bike in the back of our smaller van and I was infuriated that I couldn't take it with me. So I went for a run each day since I had to leave the bike at home. The dawn run on the board walk before hardly anyone was up and about was peaceful, yet invigorating. The sun creeping up over the eastern horizon, the sound of the waves and sea gulls drowning out everything else in the world, the intoxicating smell of the salt air... Despite this idyllic scene, a crazed young cyclist yearned for something more.

My parents bought a new, larger van in 1977 and asked my mom's Uncle Fred, Aunt Margie, and Brian Weakland to join us on the trip to Ocean City since we had the extra room. That meant we could get both our bikes in the back of the van and still have plenty of room for luggage. Brian and I decided we would go for an overnight camping trip into Delaware while we were there. Late on the day we arrived, I squeezed in 40 miles before night fell. I saw the tidal marshes and farmland from a new perspective and came to recognize a different sort of quiet and tranquility on the flat backroads. Unfortunately, not all the miles were quiet ones, though, as the traffic around Ocean City itself was overwhelming.

When Brian and I set off for our overnight trip the next morning, we decided to follow the barrier island coastline northward toward Rehoboth Beach, Delaware. Almost all of the East and Gulf Coast beaches are not beaches in the true sense of the term but are actually beaches on narrow barrier islands. The islands are in essence overgrown sand bars. We were never more than a few hundred yards from the beach, since some parts of the islands that make up Ocean City, Bethany Beach, and Rehoboth Beach are only a few hundred yards wide in their entirety. Yet we seldom saw much of the actual shoreline because of the hotels and condos that lined the entire shore until reaching Fenwick Island State Park, just south of Bethany. I recalled that when we first started vacationing in Ocean City a dozen or so years before, not much was built in North Ocean City. The construction of a new bridge at the north end of town in 1971 changed all that, and very tall condominium buildings sprouted like bad weeds. Just a decade before, much of this area was covered with little more than sand, beach grass, and dunes.

North Ocean City was yet another textbook case of suburban sprawl precipitated by new highway construction. The character of the area had been changed profoundly now that access to it was easier. Traffic could be heavy at some times of the day as well, so Brian and I were delighted to turn west on Delaware Route 26 when we got to Bethany. Fenwick Island State Park was the only respite to this runaway development, a chunk of sanity and natural beauty sandwiched between the sprawl of Ocean City, Maryland, on the south and Bethany and Rehoboth Beaches on the north. The ride down Route 26, moving inland, was surprisingly different from the ride up the coast. Though the road was still surrounded by homes, stores and other businesses, it took on the small-town character that beach towns had possessed before the crazed condo construction boom of the seventies and eighties. Traffic was lighter and the town gradually faded into farmland.

Not all was ideal in Delaware though, for as we progressed further inland, the roadway deteriorated. The highways in the two states were shockingly different. Maryland's main roads were well marked and had generous paved berms. Beyond the US Routes, Delaware's had no paved shoulders at all. Worse yet, they were sand. When we had to bail out in heavy traffic, the sand swallowed our front wheels. More than a few times, we had to dive into the sand and get off our bikes when traffic forced us off the road. The roads were poorly marked, including the section that was named DuPont Boulevard after the family that built the state upon its chemical manufacturing business. Several times we feared we were on the wrong road because we went so long without seeing a sign.

When we finally crossed back into Maryland, we wanted to kiss the ground. At the border, the road widened and the narrow, sandy shoulder was transformed to pavement. A campground in the town of Denton, Maryland was a welcome site. As we ate our supper, we mapped out a return trip that would take us through Maryland rather than Delaware. The return trip through Mardella Springs and Salisbury was a dozen miles longer than the route the day before, but it seemed that many miles shorter. Leaving very early in the morning, we got back to Ocean City in early afternoon. It was a typically sultry August day, and Brian and I concluded that a relaxing afternoon in the ocean admiring scantily clad young ladies at the beach was in order.

Our two-day sojourn through the tidewater of the Delmarva Peninsula was enough for Brian, and he decided that an additional day on the beach was preferable to another day on the bike. Besides looking forward to one more ride on the flat roads of Eastern Maryland, I was also hoping to get one more tough ride in in preparation for the big Horseshoe Curve Classic road race the end of that week. I set off very early Wednesday morning, riding south toward the town of Stockton. It turned out to be a great ride, with the exception of the half gallon of rancid orange juice I choked down at the supermarket in Pocomoke City. Despite the stinging juice and accompanying heartburn that followed, I did the 85-mile solo ride in under five hours and found myself enjoying the sights at the beach before lunch.

Life's Been Good to Me

—Joe Walsh
"Life's Been Good to Me"
From the album *But Seriously Folks...*
Asylum Records (1978)

THE ONLY RACE IN MY HOMETOWN, THE HORSESHOE CURVE Classic, was the day after we returned from Ocean City. I felt as fit as I had ever been and was certain that I could again finish in the front group of riders. The previous year, I outsprinted Ken but did not have the kick to beat John Bradley. Now that I had been near the top of the mountain, though, I would have been disappointed if I couldn't get to the summit first this time. It would turn out to be a race very similar to the 1976 version, Ken, John and I pulling away from the rest of the field and rounding the final corner together, two blocks from the finish line. I had practiced this sprint a slew of times over the previous month, simulating the finish every time I rode this stretch of Beale Avenue on the edge of Altoona. I knew every crack in the road, what gear I could turn, when I could shift, and where it leveled out a block before the line.

I was a year fitter and smarter, I judged. I had better equipment, particularly real cycling shoes. I had out-climbed them both earlier in the season and was coming off a great week of training in Ocean City. Yet the shortness of the race worried me. Could I outsprint John, a powerful sprinter who would be nearly impossible to drop on the relatively short climb to the Curve? I just wasn't sure and for the first time, the pressure was on me. I was so nervous, my heart rate was at race level as we lined up for the start.

Just delighted to be able to stay at the front of the race the year before, I was resolute to ride so hard that I would make people hurt in the 1977 version. I went up the first climb out of town as hard as I could go and it looked like a rerun of the previous year. Only Ken and John Bradley could stay with me. With a big lead over the rest of the field, we had the luxury of doing some jockeying on the way back down, despite my pledge to make my competitors hurt. In a replay of the previous year, we rocketed down the last hill, all hoping to get around the corner in a good spot. Unlike bigger field sprints with unknown quantities, we knew what we were all capable of. I thought I would be hard to outsprint if I got around the corner first. The long, two-block sprint was painful and John stayed with me the entire length, but I hung on. I tried not to show it outwardly, but my ecstasy over the win was beyond anything I had felt before. Though I had outridden everyone at one time or another over the previous few months, this was the official confirmation that I could be the best. Given our area's near absence of any bicycle racing tradition, some might have thought the win to be the equivalent of being the leading hitter on the cellar dwelling 1962 Mets. At that moment of unbridled joy, I really didn't care.

As if I needed any more motivation to ride, my win in our little road race excited me even more about riding. Finished with my summer internship, I spent the last three weeks before school began either on my bike or working in my garden. I ate as much as I wanted, slept as long as I could, rode as many miles as possible, and enjoyed the fruits of my labor, both in the garden and on my bike. Life was good.

Not long after I returned to school in September, I found out the Penn State Cycling Club was meeting to talk with anyone interested in racing during the autumn racing season. My excitement for the sport rose to yet another level when I found out I could ride in intercollegiate races at the University of Delaware later in the month and at Rutgers in October. As a tune-up, the cycling club was having a hill climb time trial up Tussey Mountain the week before the Delaware race. My motivation to train was now at a fever pitch and I rode 430 miles the first two weeks of September, despite some rainy weather and demanding schoolwork.

I took off for a ride under threatening skies the afternoon of September 13th after my classes had ended, intending to do a brisk 30 to 40 miles. As I neared Pennsylvania Furnace, about a dozen miles south of State College, the skies opened up. I made it to the post office, an old wooden sided storefront, and ducked under the porch to keep dry. The building sat on the only notable street in the tiny crossroads named after the old iron furnace that had ceased operation nearly a century before. Lyons, Shorb and Company had made iron there for nearly 80 years, beginning in 1810. Though the operation had long since ceased, the nearby ironmaster's mansion would still stand in all its architectural splendor two full centuries after the ironworks were established.[7]

Before the rain began, it had been the warm and humid sort of day that I usually enjoyed, but the power of evaporative cooling brought a drop in temperature. I sat under the porch of the post office for a long time and had I been closer to home, I would have called for an automobile rescue, but my roomie was in the middle of the work day and Mom and Dad were 30 miles away. After more than an hour, I gave in and decided that riding through the rain was my only option. Never had I ridden so far in such a steady, drenching rain.

It was more than a dozen miles back to my apartment, and there was no place to hide from the downpour. Except for a cluster of houses at the crossroads in Fairbrook, the return route was lined by farm fields. There were few places to stop and catch your breath or seek shelter from heavier rain or lightning. Once I left the protection of the Pennsylvania Furnace post office, I was committed to making the whole trip. Once the initial shock passed, I was as wet as I could get. Though it had cooled down it was still relatively warm, and a combination of rain and sweat ran down my forehead and ultimately off the tip of my nose. I would stick my lower lip outward and blow the drops off when they became annoying. Yet I came to be surprised that the ride itself was not so bad. There was something peaceful and pleasant about riding through this still beautiful landscape in the unceasing rain. Only the sound of the falling rain and the water whipping off my tires interrupted the quiet that came with such a day.

The physical part of the ride did not bother me at all in the end.

I was horrified, though, that I would ruin my equipment. Water and moving bicycle parts simply do not mix. Back at my apartment, my bike and I dripped rain and road dirt through the entrance way and up the steps to the third floor. I leaned my bike against the railing at the top of the steps, not daring to take it into the apartment. Still dripping, I decided a generous dose of WD-40 was in order. I found a can with the tools in my bedroom and began squirting. I doused every moving part and anything that screwed into something else.

As I placed the WD-40 back on my closet shelf and got out of my soaking wet clothes, I was again struck by what an untraditional person I had become. College-age males often had girls or contraband in their bedrooms; I kept bike parts and tools in mine.

A New Racing Experience

"No one can possibly know what is about to happen: it is happening, each time, for the first time, for the only time."

—James A. Baldwin
American Author
1924-1987

THE RAIN PERSISTED FOR MOST OF THE NEXT TWO WEEKS but I managed six 40-mile rides between the rain showers. The hill climb time trial up Tussey Mountain was the day before the autumnal equinox. This was my first competition beyond my home town and, even though it was a minor club race, I was nervous. The weekly races were not always well attended, especially once school began. Just the same, a dozen or so riders usually showed up, and with a rich racing tradition, there were always a few very good racers. I didn't have the best bike in the race; in fact, I had one of the worst. So I was happy with a third place finish. I surprised some people, beating a half dozen more experienced racers the first time I tried. Yet despite this success, I realized that I needed to make the next big jump in equipment if I was to be competitive at this level.

The next improvement would be the wheels and tires. My Raleigh International had come equipped with traditional bike tires with inner tubes and they were slow. By Autumn 1977, they were also a source of embarrassment. Even though they were much skinnier than tires on cheaper bikes, they were still much wider and had higher rolling resistance than anything real racers were riding. I had come to be familiar with the higher end tires, sew-ups or tubular tires, because both Ken Steel and John Bradley rode them. Now that I was running around with the Penn State racing team, the narrower, lower rolling resistance of those tires became much more important.

I ordered a new pair of wheels from the bike shop and they were finished the day before we left for the intercollegiate race in Wilmington, Delaware. Everyone told me the brand new tires could be slick, so when I saw a chance of rain in the forecast, my pre-race anxiety turned to panic. The race went around a mile circuit in Rockford Park and the course featured an off-camber turn at the bottom of the only downhill. Though the rain had ended by race time, the wind and storm had knocked the first leaves off the trees, assuring that things would still be slick on the nasty turn. All that was missing was some ice.

When we arrived at Rockford Park, we were welcomed by a crowd of people and several hot air balloons. The bike race was part of a September festival at the park. A tall stone water tower overlooked the park near the shores of Brandywine Creek. The Brandywine was situated on the Fall Line on the edge of the Piedmont and, like other waterways along this sharp geologic boundary line, had many falls and rapids. Eastern Wilmington, near the Delaware River and the border with New Jersey, was as flat as a pancake, but the neighborhood where Rockford Park sat was a hilly and rocky landscape. If one wanted to understand the profound difference between the Atlantic Coastal Plain and the Piedmont, there was no better place to see it than Wilmington, Delaware.

Wilmington's historic roots went way back, the first European influence coming from Sweden and Denmark. Some street and place names still reflected that Scandinavian influence. Its nineteenth century industrial significance was closely connected to the need for gunpowder, ships and other instruments of war. In response to the demands for such things in wartime, it experienced significant growth during the Revolution and the Civil War particularly. It was no coincidence that Irénée du Pont found this to be a good place to start the gunpowder business that would ultimately become one of the world's biggest chemical companies. Even nearly two centuries later, the influence of the du Ponts, their political power, and economic stature was still conspicuous. Though Wilmington would come to be cursed by several dozen homicides a year and one of the highest HIV infection rates in the country, Rockford Park and the neighborhood that surrounded it was a pleasant area with vibrant residential neighborhoods and tree covered streets. The stone water tower, the only architecturally interesting water tower I had ever seen, was the focal point of the park.

The crowd at the park was not overwhelming, but was bigger than would usually end up at a modest bike race. While many came out for the balloon festival and good food, we soon came to suspect that many had stayed to watch not the bikes races but rather the bike wrecks. The leaves, wet road, funky turn and inexperienced riders made for some interesting fireworks. Word spread quickly among festival-goers that a short walk down Tower Road would provide a front row seat for the crashes that were sure to occur at the bottom of the hill. There was a whole series of races, several of which preceded ours. So we walked down to the infamous turn and watched the carnage. It was especially nerve-racking to watch the Junior race, the kids old enough to drive but not yet smart enough to ride a bike sensibly without crashing. Clearly, there was a recklessness that possessed the Juniors that far surpassed the other racers. It seemed there was a crash almost every lap of the race. After witnessing this, my panic turned to horror, for I came to learn that many of my racing comrades were less experienced, too.

Despite the new tires, my considerable anxiety and the inexperience of some of my race mates, I managed to stay upright for the entirety of the fifteen mile race. The nasty curve was followed by an uphill toward the finish line, so whatever I lost with my cautious approach to the corner was recovered on the hill. Nearly two dozen riders couldn't corner or climb as well as I could. Unfortunately, the race also included eleven people who could and I finished twelfth. I had hoped to crack the top ten, but I was happy to have been among the top third of finishers in my first collegiate race.

Though I had finished my first out-of-town race and was satisfied with the result, I also experienced my first moments of disillusionment over the sport I loved. Unlike the cooperation of a group ride with my cycling friends back home, racers snatched positions at the start line and in the field of racers during the race with reckless abandon and selfish self-preservation. Other cycling etiquette and basic good manners were similarly ignored. A few laps into the race I found myself in the middle of a group of riders, one of whom decided that he had to clear his nose. Placing his left index finger over his left nostril, he turned his head and blew out. The stream of snot flew toward me, a hint of the spray hitting my left leg.

The incidents might have seemed insignificant at the time but they were the first in a series of things that spoke to the profound differences in those I rode with at home and those that I would race against on the road. My riding partners at home were motivated by the same things I was. They enjoyed seeing the natural world go by from that unique lens mounted on the handlebars, they looked forward to the adventure that came with the experience, they enjoyed sharing it with their friends, and they saw it as part of a healthy lifestyle.

Whether it be to clear their nose or to get through the next corner first and at any cost, many racers focused on themselves, no matter what the impact on the person they spit on or cut off. They could be difficult, even abrasive. Wheel-sucking by racers averse to doing their fair share (rather than cooperative riding I had grown used to) was also all too common. My lack of such a cut-throat approach, especially in short-circuit criteriums, would ultimately be my downfall in some races, but it was difficult for me to adopt such riding habits. I felt that I could get by in a race without being an ass. Arrogance, too, was much more common than humility. I especially disdained people who were arrogant and hadn't accomplished anything to justify their attitude.

As I would get to know more and more riders, I also learned that many drank to excess, using their riding as justification for their excesses. Others would take caffeine pills to give them an extra shot of energy before a race. I saw such things as being wildly contradictory to the reasons I rode and raced. Beyond the health benefits, I was confident that clean living would pay dividends with race results, too. Despite the annoyance I came to have with some racers, there were also many that shared my philosophical approach to the sport, and I thoroughly enjoyed riding and spending time with them. My Penn State teammates were especially good guys and the laughs and frustrations we would experience together built lifelong memories.

Even though the days were getting shorter and the schoolwork longer, I hoped to stay sharp until the middle of October when the cycling team would travel to Rutgers. I was taking a heavier than usual class load that included heavy reading in an environmental law class, a major project in a soils class, and a bundle of math work in both a surveying class and statistical geography course.

My friend from Ehrenfield, Frank Galosi, and I decided we would benefit from a surveying class and scheduled Dr. Harmer Weeden's Civil Engineering surveying field class. It didn't take us long on the first day of class to realize we were in way over our heads. Frank and I were the only two non-engineering majors, and our missing pocket protectors were conspicuous in their absence. Frank and I decided before the class was even half over that we had to talk to the teacher and see if we could drop the class. Dr. Weeden was old school in every way, having graduated from Cornell in 1938, and was in his fortieth year of a distinguished career in academia. Yet he looked at Frank and me with patient understanding of our plight.

"Dr. Weeden, I'm a geography major..." I explained.

"...and I'm an Environmental Resource Management major," Frank continued.

"And we feel like we're in a little over our heads," I concluded.

"Yes, I could see why you feel that way. This is really for engineering majors," Dr. Weeden confirmed. He told us he taught a class for non-engineers and helped us make the change. Part of me thought the class would be good for a geographer that was interested in cartography and environmental issues. Another part of me was intimidated by Dr. Weeden's hard-core, old school, by-the-book engineering approach, but in the end, we took the class. It was an incredible amount of hard work, but I ended up using the skills a number of times in my career.

I had to work like a dog in my statistical geography class, too, and did not enjoy the instruction or classwork in the least. Another good friend from Penn State Altoona, Arnie Terry, took the class with me and we would often vent our frustrations when things were particularly difficult or the teacher was especially unclear. The craziness of the class reached its peak one day about half way through the fall term when the professor began erasing the left side of the blackboard with his left hand while still writing the end of the note on the right side of the board. The incident, Arnie and I concluded, was this crazy class in microcosm.

Arnie was one of my best friends in those days, and we both took our schoolwork seriously. Both of us were annoyed by our classmates' preoccupation with drinking and neither of us seemed to find much time for the fairer sex. We also ended up living very near each other when we moved to University Park, and we both rode our bikes to campus when the weather permitted.

We found ourselves sometimes forced to ride after dark when the days became shorter, and this put us in a few tough spots. Daylight savings time ended a few weeks before the end of fall term and that would not have meant much had my school day ended in mid-afternoon. It completely escaped me that my soils class did not conclude until 5:15 p.m., and I was shocked when I emerged from my windowless lecture hall to the darkness of an early autumn evening. I had no light and, to make matters worse, was at the far end of campus almost four miles from my apartment. Haunted by the voice of my mother ten years before telling me there was no bike riding after the street lights came on, I proceeded cautiously and as clandestinely as I could through the side streets, sidewalks and parking lots back to my apartment.

Arnie experienced a similar situation around that same time, but did not enjoy the same good fortune I had. One late fall evening, he had an obligation on campus and decided it was pleasant enough to ride his bike. As he was about to enter the first public street a few hundred yards from his apartment, he realized he had forgotten his light. Short on time, he decided he would follow my approach and navigate the side streets. He made it to within a quarter mile or so of his destination without incident. At the stop light on Beaver Avenue, a State College police car spotted him riding illegally without a light.

"Stop and get off your bike," the officer demanded.

"No," Arnie responded defiantly and to the point. Arnie sprinted down Burrowes Street and across College Avenue, confident it would take the cop a few moments to get turned around. In hot pursuit with lights flashing, the police car finally began to make ground on the rebellious cyclist as Arnie hit the hill at the edge of campus. He made the turn at the engineering building complex, knowing that it would be difficult for the police cruiser to overtake him on the single lane street. Though able to go faster than Arnie, the cop was unable to get by because Arnie stayed in the middle of the narrow street, reasoning the cop was unlikely to run him over for a light violation. At the end of the narrow street, a set of outside steps went under the complex back down to College Avenue. When he got there, he scooted down the steps and then down the sidewalk, leaving the defeated and frustrated police officer stranded in his car at the top of the steps. Otherwise a relatively straight-laced and law abiding individual, Arnie had successfully and proudly pulled off his first act of civil disobedience and lived to tell the tale without any repercussions. Given the statute of limitations on traffic violations and resisting arrest has long passed, we can tell the story now without fear of reprisal from State College's finest.

Despite all my schoolwork, I did manage to keep my fitness at a reasonable level until that last race at Rutgers on October 16th. It was a perfect autumn day and my uneasiness about pack riding made me happy to see the late date had reduced the size of the field of riders. Still uncomfortable with all the turns in the short circuit race around the Rutger's new fieldhouse, I finished tenth, respectable but not outstanding.

The race finished late Sunday morning and I had not made it to church, so I asked my teammates if they could drop me at the Rutgers chapel for the noon time mass. A beautiful chapel, the sun shone through the windows, making the setting almost angelic. But I was overcome with guilt that I was delaying my teammates from getting home at a more reasonable hour and became preoccupied with mass being finished as quickly as possible. As the lector began the first reading early in mass, a jet flew over the chapel, seemingly on que. The priest, feeling that we hadn't heard a word, asked the lector to read it again. And so began a series of longer, more drawn out episodes, prayers and hymns than I thought I had ever lived through in my 21 years of Catholicism. Finally, after nearly an hour, I felt I had fulfilled my minimal obligation and I hurried out of church, infuriated that the priest had drawn things out on the worst possible day. In reality, it was probably no longer than most Catholic Sunday masses. But because I had seven non-Catholic teammates waiting in the van, I was certain it had been the longest service in the history of the Church.

I ran to the van, hurried into my seat and began to spew a cacophony of expletives to express my frustration over what I thought to be an ungodly long service. After several sentences chalked-full of curse words and the Lord's name taken in vain, I gazed upon the Taylor brothers on the other side of the van and was immediately overcome with guilt and embarrassment. The Taylors were very religious and, as the old saying goes, wouldn't have said shit if they had stepped in it. Here I was, I thought to myself, giving a fine representation of the Catholic faith minutes after walking out of Sunday mass. I imagine they later discussed the contradiction of the occurrence at great length, wondering if all Catholic Church services were so dreadfully ineffective.

After recovering from the flood of profanity, we began the journey back home. Sunny, pleasant, and bordering on hot, we had been wearing shorts in the race. As we drove west on Interstate 80, we were met by a cold front that was exacerbated by our ascent into the Pocono Mountains. It actually began to snow as we climbed into the highest elevations. Near sea level on the east side of the cold front, it was nearly 80 degrees. Approaching 2,000 feet above sea level on the other side of the front, the temperature had dropped into the low forties. We had gone from late summer to early winter in a just a little more than an hour.

Even though the temperatures recovered after the early snow, the shorter days, combined with a very rainy November and December, managed to shoot the cycling season in the backside. Little did I know as November rolled into December, we were stumbling into another dreadful winter.

A Winter of Discontent

"Now is the winter of our discontent..."

—William Shakespeare
Richard the Third
Act 1, Scene 1

THE PREVIOUS WINTER HAD BEEN NASTY, BUT THE WINTER of 1977-78 would turn out to be even worse from a bicycling standpoint. When Saint Patrick's Day rolled around, I had only been on the road twice since the New Year had begun. I had spent 600 of the most boring miles known to man riding the rollers in the basement of my apartment, staring at the washer and dryer at the other end of the room.

I was back home in Altoona on spring break when the temperature finally hit the upper forties on March 11th. We had struggled through 43 consecutive days below 40 degrees and this was the first day above 45 degrees since December 2nd. Despite snow covering many shaded areas even in town, I exploded from the house bundled up and ready to ride. I tackled the challenging climb to Wopsy Lookout west of the Penn State Altoona Campus. In a replay of my first ride up the steep climb the February before, deep piles of snow were still lingering on the north facing slopes of the climb.

The winter had presented as bad a stretch of weather as could occur in Central Pennsylvania, and it had been very difficult to prepare for my first full season of racing. I came to realize how much so when we set off for the first race of the year two days after Saint Patrick's Day. It was a criterium on the campus of John Hopkins University and went around a very tight, turn-filled circuit on narrow campus streets. I was still riding in the shorter "B" race and that field was always filled with less experienced riders who were not yet particularly good bike handlers. Not having the greatest confidence in my own cornering abilities, I wondered if I should not have stayed at home and ridden in the Central Pennsylvania cold. After I rode around the course a few times to warm up, my doubts turned to terror.

The field of 42 riders seemed like 142 on the tight course. I was always trying to avoid the most congested parts of the peloton of riders in an effort to keep from running into someone else. Not surprisingly, I found myself trying to hang onto the back of the field just a handful of laps into the race. In the end, I had no idea where I finished because of the utter pandemonium that ensued as the race progressed (or should I say regressed). Riders were all over the place on the course before the race was three laps old. I know I was lapped by the leaders before it was over, and I could have easily been lapped more than once. But even the riders couldn't tell because few of us knew who the leaders were. The race organizers were completely befuddled and decided the only way to sort the mess out was to take the team leaders or managers, lock them in a room, and take their best stab at putting everyone in order.

Few schools had anything that even remotely resembled a real coach, so Mark Lyons, one of our racers, usually did this for Penn State. Before setting off for the meeting of the minds, he asked each of us where we thought we finished. He was able to piece together just enough to be totally confused. But it didn't matter because this race would be won or lost at the negotiation table rather than on the race circuit. Mark was good at it and reveled almost as much in that battle as the one on the race course.

We did not have the full contingent of our best racers on this opening weekend of the season, and when he went into the conference I feared the team had finished third or fourth. From my own standpoint, I hoped that he could talk them into a top 20 finish. I feared I might be as low as 25th. An hour later, he emerged from the fray, his red hair ruffled but a snicker on his face.

"Let's get the hell out of here before they change their minds. I don't know how I did it but we finished first." We tried not to laugh out loud. The rest of the team couldn't believe it. He shared the individual results with us, and when he told me I finished tenth I was just as surprised as I had been with the team result. Mark had convinced the race organizers that several of us had stayed in the same lap with the leaders in both races. We might have stolen one that day, but no one really knew for sure.

The dreadful winter had kept me off the road the entire months of January and February. When the weather suddenly turned spring-like the week after the Johns Hopkins race, my frustration was given a reprieve. I was actually able to ride in shorts when the temperature finally hit 60 the day after the Vernal Equinox. That single 60 degree day would be the only one between Thanksgiving and Easter. Like so many springs in Central Pennsylvania, a winter relapse occurred, this one on Easter Sunday as three inches of snow fell.

Penn State was traveling to Princeton and Rutgers for a two-day stage race the second weekend of April, and I knew I needed a pile of miles if I was to have any chance of doing well. I ventured out in all kinds of weather because I had to. The weekend before the New Jersey race was the only spell in a sixteen-day stretch leading up to the stage race that could be classified as pleasant. A rainy Wednesday ride to Stone Valley was my only ride on the road the week before the race.

We set off for Princeton late Friday afternoon, and I wondered how badly I would be embarrassed by my poor conditioning. Even though Eastern Pennsylvania and New Jersey lie at the same latitude as our part of Pennsylvania, the spring weather can be very different. The elevation difference of only a thousand or so feet could make the difference between the frigid lower forties and the tolerable upper forties so common in March. I could never seem to get warmed up at the low end of that range, but found myself quite comfortable at the upper end. The riders in those slightly warmer places found many opportunities to ride in the winter that we never realized in State College. Their lower snowfall amounts also meant when a warm day did come, they had much less snow melt to slop up the roads. Penn State seemed to be at a distinct disadvantage when compared to our more eastern and southern rivals.

As far as any of us knew, this was the first collegiate stage race that had been held anywhere on the east coast, and we thought it was a big deal. It was four stages over two days and started early Saturday morning with a team time trial. I was disappointed to be stuck on the second of Penn State's two time trial teams, even though I thought I was the best time trialist on our "B" team. Our first team ended up winning and my team finished fourth out of twelve squads. I finished 18th out of 63 entrants in the road race. Considering the training I had been able to do, I was not overly disappointed.

The next morning we started with a hill climb time trial. Being New Jersey, it had been difficult for the race organizers to find a notable hill, and the climb was tame by Pennsylvania standards. Still, it was a hill, and I found myself in friendly territory. My twelfth place buoyed my spirits as well as my stature on the squad. I had beaten several of the riders who had been assigned to the first time trial squad from the day before.

The weekend had gone as well as could have hoped given the sparse road mileage I had logged. I had not embarrassed myself as I feared I might, and my hill climb results made some folks take notice. The Eastern Intercollegiate Championships were at Penn State in three weeks, and I thought I just might have a chance to do well, especially if the weather would allow me to get in the miles I had hoped for.

April in the northeastern United States is best described as a yo-yo most years, and 1978 was a classic example. The week after the big stage race, the weather was incredible. That was followed by eight of the worst days April could bring. It poured rain the only two days it warmed beyond the low fifties. After the most miserable winter imaginable, the weather gods cursed me one more time. I suffered through three short rainy rides early in the week and finally decided I had to put in some serious miles no matter what the weather that weekend. I drug myself through two mountainous 50-plus mile rides on Earth Day weekend. Saturday's ride through Sinking Valley was one of the coldest long rides I had ever struggled through. The high reached only 43 degrees, and it was much colder than that through the shaded road that descended the back side of Brush Mountain.

Take It to the Limit

—Randy Meisner, Don Henley, Glenn Frey
"Take It to the Limit"
From the album *One of these Nights*
Asylum Records (1975)

THE WEATHER FINALLY BROKE THE MONDAY BEFORE THE Eastern Intercollegiate Championships and I managed to do 360 high quality training miles the eight days prior to the race. I was especially pleased when I pulled off a sub-two-hour State College to Altoona solo ride four days before the big race, completing the 40 miles in 1:53. The day before that, a group of us rode the race course, a hilly 3.5-mile circuit in the shadow of Beaver Stadium. I suppose it was appropriate that the most revered and well-funded athletic program at the university would literally overshadow the most obscure and poorly funded one, even on its most important day.

Despite having made great strides as a racer in general and during the month of April in particular, I still had a great deal to learn. What I had to learn included not only the finer points of racing but even the fine points of what to wear. Many years later, my mother still felt badly about my attire for the big race the final weekend of April 1978. I had spent as much as I felt I could afford on equipment and, consequently, did not spend much on clothing. In particular, I did not own a pair of cycling shorts, which even in those days could be pricey. Instead, I wore gym shorts or cutoffs.

When race day arrived, the final day of April, we were blessed with a glorious spring morning. It bordered on blustery at times but was warm enough to be comfortable in shorts, ugly as mine may have been.

My parents, brother, and sister P.J. all made the trip to Happy Valley, along with my Aunt Sally and Uncle Pete. I had my own little cheering section. My aunt and uncle's presence was particularly special because they had spent much of my childhood proudly boasting of their own children's athletic prowess. I had always been the little skinny kid on the end of the bench. Still very much the skinny kid, I was now in a collegiate championship athletic event competing with kids from every major university in the Northeast. If Pete and Sally's presence was not sufficient testimony to the magnitude of the event, a visit from Penn State's most well-known personality was. As riders warmed up for the 100 kilometer road race, Joe Paterno, the school's athletic director as well as football coach in those years, wandered down to the picnic pavilion where many fans and riders had gathered to shelter from the stiff April breeze. He talked with a few of us and wished us good luck. If Joe Pa, in the middle of his legendary career as college football's winningest coach, thought this was worth seeing, we knew beyond question we had reached the big time after all.

Though the university's support was sparse, we did get a modest supply of Penn State jerseys with the school's name emblazoned across the back. We wore them proudly and promised ourselves we would defend the home turf with the same vigor as the football team defended nearby Beaver Stadium. Our crowd was a good bit smaller but seemed every bit as enthused as we set off.

Our 50-kilometer event went off first, and the morning air was still chilly when the 62 riders left the start line. The intercollegiate events usually had a shorter race for the women, a slightly longer race for the less experienced male racers, and a long race for the national class racers. The "A" race was worth twice as many points as the "B" race. It meant we needed to score some significant points in the "B" race if we expected to contend for the championship, and some serious planning went into putting the right people in the right race. Given that we didn't have a truly national class rider like John Bare a few years before, we needed a true team effort. Though there were some real neophytes in our race, there were some very good riders, too. Several of the top finishers would go onto to have successful racing careers over the next few years.

Part of the course was open to auto traffic periodically. Additionally, racers from the next event were wandering around the circuit warming up and testing out their bikes as the "B" race progressed. So it really should not have been surprising when race officials actually lost track of the race leader. Cornell's Andy Ross launched a solo attack in the middle of the race, but hardly anyone in the race realized it. As we approached the line for the start of the last lap, almost everyone was under the impression the field was still together. Evidently the race would be won or lost on the last climb about a mile from the finish line.

The course began on a flat stretch across from the football stadium and turned left onto a brisk downhill near some of the university's agricultural and turf grass research facilities. It turned again at the bottom of the hill and wound through a wooded stretch and then up a sharp climb. We had dropped quite a few riders from the starting group, losing a handful more each of the first eight times we climbed the hill.

We also lost a few folks who had a hard time keeping between the ditches. One racer from West Point ended up entangled in the barbed-wire fence enclosing a pasture not far from the finish line a few laps from the end. We had poked fun at the cadets prior to that, but seeing that poor bloke snared by the fence induced another barrage of jokes about the dreadful bike handling skills of the West Point riders. If their riding abilities didn't give us enough fodder, their uniforms were a further source of amusement. The black stripes on their yellow jerseys made them look more like bumble bees than bike racers.

We reasoned there were a disproportionate number of crashes involving the bumble bees because some of the cadets were very new to the sport. This happened, we were led to believe, because cadets had to engage in some sort of athletic endeavor while at the academy. They were the best supported team on the circuit, and some riders got support they would have never gotten at other schools. Kids from other colleges were scrimping to buy equipment and clothing, paying their own way to races, and most had made a commitment beyond their college racing. Though Army developed some great racers, like eventual national team member Bill Watkins a few years before, many of their riders seemed to take up the sport as an afterthought. They took more chances than any other team, and their resulting aggressive riding could border on the insane. It seemed at times they wore their recklessness as a proud badge of honor, as if it were the only proper military way to ride a bike. The rest of us, a bit less self-destructive perhaps, preferred to stay upright and steer clear of barbed wire.

The wreckage and body were untangled from the barbed wire by the time we neared the finish line for the bell lap. The field had been whittled down, but there were still a good many riders remaining in the group who would contend for the top spots. The overwhelming majority still thought we were the front of the race as the race leader from Cornell dangled a short distance ahead of us. As we crossed the line to begin our last 3.5 mile circuit, the pace quickened. Most of the next two miles was downhill before the last climb about a mile and a half from the finish. The descent down Fox Hollow Road was a brisk one, and my pulse quickened even though we had not yet hit the gut-wrenching uphill that would decide the race. It struck me that this was, by far, the biggest athletic event of my life, and I was only a couple miles from completing an improbable metamorphism from twerp to exceptional athlete.

When we hit the base of the hill, I was unsure of how many riders were still hanging on, but I knew the number had been reduced to less than a third of what we started with. Just the same, 15 or 20 riders bunched at the finish line would be crazier than any of us cared for, so we all hoped the hill would sort out the best from the respectable. As the climb steepened, I stood up, pulled on the bars as hard as I could, and gave it everything I could muster. Perhaps halfway up the climb, I realized I was among a fairly small group of riders and we had already dropped a bunch. As the lactic acid accumulated in my legs, the burning was as intense as it had ever been. I saw my teammate, Paul Johnson, rocketing up the hill, seemingly propelling himself to victory, but also realized there were only seven or eight other riders that seemed capable of staying with this new front group.

My legs were on fire by this point, but I tried to surge one more time to top off the hill. Then anxiety struck yet again, when I recalled the top of the hill was still at least three quarters of a mile from the finish line and the persistent stragglers would do their best to close the gap we had opened on the ascent. A small group of us realized another group was in striking distance and it would behoove us to work together to stay in front of them. Just as we came together, things seemed to fall apart. The sight of the finish line only a few hundred yards away made it every man for himself. As we hit the finishing stretch, I could see Paul Johnson hitting the line, his arms outstretched in the traditional victory salute. I realized at about that time that I was going to finish among the leaders. As the line approached, I saw only three riders between Johnson and me. *My God*, I thought to myself as I crossed the line, *I just finished in the top five of the second biggest collegiate race in the Eastern United States.*

In our ecstasy over placing four riders in the top ten, we were oblivious to the escape of the rider from Cornell. As race officials tried to sort out the placings and scoring, the Cornell team protested wildly. Andy Ross had pulled off the ideal breakaway, one that hardly anyone realized had even taken place. It took a while and not everyone was convinced at the time, but it looked like Ross had won after all. Though we were disappointed we all finished a place lower, it didn't alter Penn State's dominance in the race.

The 100-kilometer race followed and we hoped that, despite not having that star racer like we had in past years, our depth would pay off in that race, too. Like many years, the best riders in the race were national class racers, and the three leaders, Penn's Ian Jones, Dickinson's Perry Fyke, and Lehigh's Murray Wilmerding, fit that bill again. They actually lapped the rest of the field near the end of the race, finishing 3.5 miles ahead. Jones particularly would go on to have a distinguished career, garnering national sponsorship from sports car maker Austro Daimler and racing for a time in Europe. Though Penn State missed the big break that would produce the race's winner, those leaders did not have the team support or depth that we enjoyed.

On the strength of our phenomenally deep B team and the determination of our no-name A team, we were in a position to win it all with a respectable showing by our more experienced riders. The longer distance would take a toll on the field as the race wore on and the temperature warmed through the afternoon. Yet we managed to hold things together despite the attrition of the field. Jerry Skurla ended up eighth, Steve Hammonds eleventh, and Phelan Fretz seventeenth.

Our quick math computations showed us in first place, but until the results were official, doubt and anxiety remained. Finally, the race announcer declared us the Eastern Intercollegiate Champion, and both the team and home crowd went crazy. The championship team was presented a rotating championship cup and my teammates promptly filled it with champagne. Phelan Fretz, his blood sugar tank bone dry after 100 gut-wrenching kilometers, gulped from the cup. It was the first case of instant intoxication I ever witnessed. I didn't have to drink a drop, though, to experience one of the most remarkable highs of my life.

The Eastern Intercollegiate Cycling Federation Champion Penn State Nittany Lions hoist the championship cup following their victory. Clearly, a few Nittany Lions partook from the champagne-filled cup. I'm the second from the left on the bottom row. Photo by P.J. Frederick.

The following day, prominent articles appeared in both the local paper and the Penn State's *Daily Collegian*. There in print was my name among the race's top finishers, leading the Nittany Lions to another championship. One of the worst performing athletes in Jay Perry's seventh grade gym class had just distinguished himself as one of the top 25 collegiate bike racers on the east coast. Perhaps the worst child athlete of a slew of athletic cousins in my clan, I had managed to be the only one to ever participate, let alone be part of a championship team, at the collegiate level. Some still might have considered it a lesser sport. I could have cared less what anyone else thought in that regard. I had done the training; I had spent the long, boring, sweaty hours on the rollers in the basement. I had felt the pain, the burning muscles when the lactic acid made it feel like someone had taken a blow torch to my legs. I had cramped so badly that I couldn't turn the pedals. I had been colder than I thought possible and ridden through the darkness of late winter afternoons. I had been on roads so obscure they weren't found on any normal map. So I really didn't care what anyone else thought. I had taken it to the limit, and knew that I put myself through much more than the overwhelming majority of football, basketball, or baseball players ever did. I knew it was a real sport.

Growing Your Own

"The glory of gardening: hands in the dirt, head in the sun, heart with nature. To nurture a garden is to feed not just on the body, but the soul."

—English Poet Alfred Austin
1835-1913

AS IS SO OFTEN TRUE OF LIFE IN GENERAL, I HAD LITTLE time to bask in the successes of the previous weekend. Five weeks separated the two biggest events of my cycling career to that point, while the rest of my life still kept on whizzing by. I was planning to set off on a cross-country trip the second week of June and I had bundles to do before I left. I needed straight A's in my last semester to graduate with honors, so the schoolwork alone kept me busy. Meanwhile, I was trying to stay fit for the big ride while getting my enormous vegetable garden prepared for my long absence.

Ah, the vegetable garden! Mom had purchased a 50-foot-wide vacant lot a block from our house, and the garden I plowed there had become my other passion. A fanatic member of the Organic Gardening Book Club, I read every organic farming and homesteading book I could get my hands on, including most of the titles available through the book club. In the idealism of one's college years and the bright sunshine of optimism that comes with young adulthood, I aspired to be an organic farmer and homesteader. Despite the cautionary advice from my mother and others, I trudged forward into the oblivion of *Total Loss Farm* and Helen and Scott Nearing's *The Good Life*.

The garden was an integral part of the back-to-the-earth lifestyle

I was pursuing that also included the bike. I was growing everything I could so I would have as much organically grown food as possible. I experimented with all sorts of things and tried growing just about anything that had a chance of surviving in Pennsylvania. When my classmates made such claims, "that they were trying everything," most frequently they were talking about alcohol, pot, and sex. My idea of new things included heirloom tomatoes, Jerusalem artichokes, lima beans, chickpeas, and Spanish peanuts.

My greatest challenge, and one that I reveled in, was trying to grow things that were supposed to struggle in cooler Pennsylvania summers. The first year I tried to garden, before I had any concept of growing season length or susceptibility to freezing, I simply opened up a seed catalog and picked out something I thought would be neat to grow. The first thing that caught my attention was a mammoth watermelon. I bought a packet of seeds, enthusiastically planted them and watched them sprout and grow through May and June. Small melons appeared in early summer and all seemed to going well until I started to do the calendar math. A week or so into August, it was clear that I would be cutting it close in our relatively short central Pennsylvania summer. When the first frost warning came in late September, the melons were only about two thirds the size of a mature watermelon. On top of badly misjudging the growing season length, the shallow and heavy clay soil in our yard was the exact opposite of the deep sandy soil that members of the melon family prefer. Doubtful that they were edible, I nevertheless stuck the biggest one in the fridge, hoping for the best. A day or two later, we cut it open to see an inside that was almost as green as the rind. I forced a few bites down, only because I hated to concede that all the hard work was for naught. I made all sorts of other dumb gardening mistakes, planting things too early, too close together, or in the wrong sunlight.

By 1978, I had figured out when the frosts should be expected as well as many of the other idiosyncrasies of growing fruits and vegetables in the Mid-Atlantic. I managed to grow all the traditional Pennsylvania crops and many of those that were not supposed to do so well in our cooler climate. I successfully grew watermelons (though much smaller ones than the variety I'd tried previously), Spanish peanuts, honeydews, and sweet potatoes.

Despite my own passion for gardening, like many post-war families, the propensity to grow their own food had faded for my parents. All four of my grandparents, by contrast, had closer connections to farms or farmers and were ardent gardeners even though they lived in the city. While my father had been forced to work in his father's massive garden many times in his youth, he hated the work and offered little insight into how to grow anything. Similarly, my mother had little to offer, though her father always had a big garden during her younger days. Pappy Weakland was more than happy to share his experiences growing fruits and vegetables over the previous half century. As far as I knew, I was the only one of his grandchildren that ever showed notable interest in vegetable gardening, and he was always eager to talk about it with me. His stories about his days on the farm with his friend Mayberry Claar didn't just convey helpful farming tips, but were often funny too.

Mayberry, or "Burry" as Pap called him, lived near the town of Queen, about 25 miles south of Altoona. Queen, not surprisingly right next to the village of King, was a beautiful area just south of the Blair County line, and I came to enjoy riding there. When I rode through Queen, I would always think of Pap and Burry and imagined what it would have looked like and what life would have been like during those days. Though the roads were paved and the farms were much less diverse in what they grew, it seemed likely the area had changed little otherwise.

As Pap told the tale, Burry would regularly come to town in his huckster wagon, a rather fancy compartmentalized wagon that had specific spots for all kinds of produce and dairy products. One compartment held ice and below it was the cooler for milk and meat. Other doors opened to display fresh produce. Even well into the twenties, the wagons were horse-drawn. Sometimes there was a need for Burry or other farmers from the Cove or the Claysburg area in southern Blair County to stay overnight in Altoona. A place was set aside for them in Downtown Altoona at Seventeenth Street and Eleventh Avenue that came to be known as Huckster Row. Long before supermarkets or even many corner grocery stores, these folks were the source of farm-fresh food.

Pap had many amusing stories about his years working with Burry, but the two that made me laugh the most were both connected to the huckster wagon and the horses that pulled them. One summer evening, Pap was returning home with Burry in the wagon when the exhausted farmer decided he needed to catch a few winks. He told Pap he should take over the reins, but not having much experience with horses, Pap voiced concern over the assignment. Burry reassured him the horses knew the way and lay down in the back of the wagon. Not long afterward, Pap spotted a narrow covered bridge ahead and began to worry that it was more than he could handle. As the bridge loomed closer, Pap sized up the width of the opening and became certain that he was about to wreck the wagon. Not wanting to bother his now snoozing friend, he held on tightly to the reins and prayed as he entered the bridge. As they passed through the one lane span, the wagon cleared the wooden walls by a few inches on each side. Mayberry's reassurance that the horses knew what they were doing proved true.

As further testimony to the resourcefulness of Burry's horses, Pap also relayed a story about another trip from Altoona to the farm in Queen. On his way home from the big city, Claar decided to stop in the village of Claysburg for a haircut. He left the horse and wagon untied in front of the barber shop and went inside. After a short wait, his haircut and the traditional "barbershop bullshitting," as Pap called it, Mayberry stepped back outside. The team and wagon were nowhere to be seen, having decided on their own that it was time to go home. He concluded as much and began the five-mile walk home from Claysburg to Queen. His suspicions were confirmed when he saw the horses peacefully grazing in his front yard, the wagon still trailing behind.

Beyond the funny stories that came from his time with Mayberry Claar, Pap still marveled about the farm, all the things he grew, and all the animals he raised. It was the quintessential early twentieth century family farm and testified to the profound difference in the way we produced, transported, and delivered our food to consumers in those days. Just like the large urban garden Pap tended over the next few decades, it spoke of times when we were much closer to our food and those who grew it. The enthusiasm to garden might have skipped a generation, but the stories and experiences lived on. Pap's connection to that earlier time and his ability to convey the tales was one of the reasons I had the urge to grow my own food.

This particular summer also taught me a new lesson: that it was difficult for any serious farmer or gardener to leave his crops in the middle of the growing season. Setting off on a month long cycling trip, I needed to have everything planted and mulched before leaving. I also needed someone's help in my absence. My family helped a great deal but it was my Great Uncle Fred, an experienced gardener himself, who did the yeoman's share.

While frantically trying to prepare the garden for my long absence on the weekends, I was also working hard during the week to make the Dean's List and graduate with honors. I had the luxury of taking a light class load and classes that were of great interest to me. The highlight was Peirce Lewis's geomorphology class. My geography studies in general had complemented my cycling interests, but this particular class was especially fascinating to a cycling geographer. I came to know cyclists that rode only for the physical test that came from the ride. While I came to enjoy that part of the sport, it was the interesting landscapes and the adventures that came from riding through them that kept me coming back for more. No single class had made those connections any better. It was the perfect class at the perfect time, not just because it brought all the other academic work together, but because it was the perfect study of the nation's geography. If a cross-country bike trip was given for credit, a geomorphology class should have been a prerequisite.

Despite all the hard work at school and in the garden, I still managed to rack up some big miles, great rides, and fast times during the last few weeks before setting off on my adventure. I was climbing like a mountain goat and did a wind-aided solo ride down the Nittany Valley at over 25 miles per hour the week before graduation. A rerun of the infamous 150-mile ride to Johnstown and Ligonier from a year before was the final test the weekend before we set off for Oregon. The next week, we would be on the West Coast, poised to start the adventure of a lifetime.

A Grand Adventure Begins

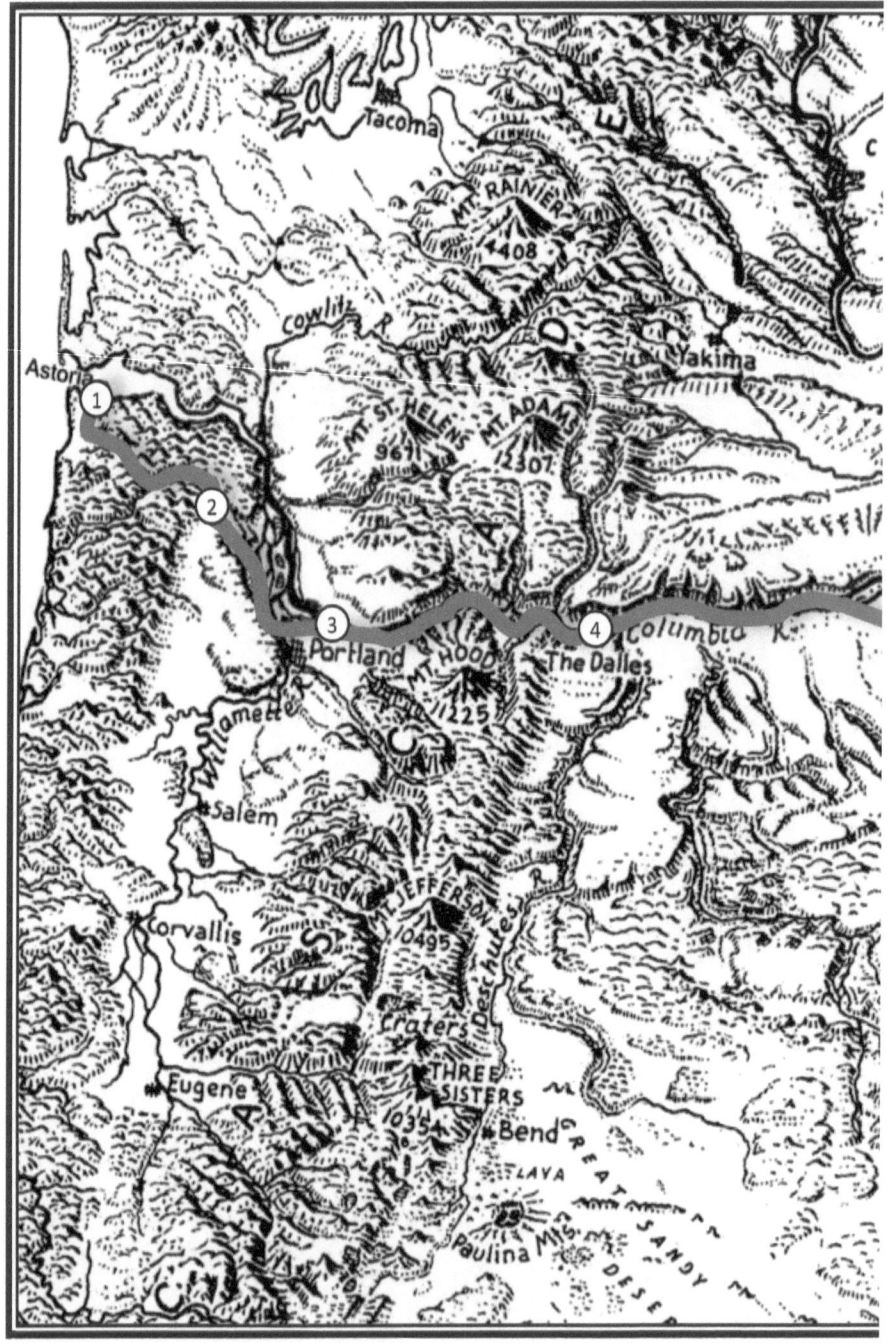

Ramblin' Man

—Richard Betts
"Ramblin' Man"
From the Allman Brothers album *Brothers and Sisters* (1973)

IF YOU EVER SO SLIGHTLY ALTERED THAT LINE OF THE Allman Brothers tune to "stuck in the cramped seat of a Greyhound bus," you would have accurately captured the three and a half days I endured on one in June of 1978. I had decided to take the bus to the west coast because it was cheap, forgetting again that wise old axiom that you get what you pay for. Greyhound was offering a deal; transportation to any city in the United States for $79. The train seemed like a much more pleasant way to go but who could pass up a deal like the one Greyhound had offered? Meanwhile, my traveling partners took the rail and air options.

I was told that Greyhound would treat my bike like any other piece of luggage. I discovered if I removed my wheels, took off the pedals, shoved the seat post down into the frame, and pulled the handlebars out of the head tube, I could fit the bike into a modest sized box. Mine ended up being not much bigger than two suitcases. I shoved my sleeping bag in the triangle between the top and down tubes and packed the rest of the things I would need for the bus and bike trip into my bike panniers.

Around mid-day on Thursday, June 8, 1978, Mom and I packed up the box in our Plymouth station wagon and drove to the bus station. Our bus station was not the nicest of public spaces and I would soon learn this was true of far too many bus stations throughout the country. But hope springs eternal and, like the bus trip itself, my vision of the places I would pass through was still one of charm and scenic adventure.

It took only a few hours for reality to set in. I had to switch busses in Pittsburgh, a station that was only marginally nicer than the one in Altoona. When it came time to load my bike on the westward-bound bus, the crotchety old freight master refused to put it in the baggage compartment, complaining that it was too big and would not fit. At first, I cordially and patiently asked that he find some room because the bike was my only way home from the west coast. As he became more belligerent, I grew increasingly impatient until the two of us were yelling at each other.

"Can't you please find a spot for it?" I pleaded.

"No, it don't fit," the baggage man shot back, in less than perfect grammar. "This is just for passengers' baggage."

"This is my only baggage and I was told it would be treated like any other baggage," I explained. As I peered under the bus, I saw dozens of boxes of flowers. (Greyhound did a great deal of express shipping in those days.) Now this really perturbed me, and I tried hard to think of a snappy comeback.

"Oh," I retorted in the most sarcastic tone I could muster, "do you have a contingent of hard-core flower fanatics headed to a garden show?"

Unable to think of a similarly clever response, he hesitated, then blurted out, "The damn bike's staying right here," as he pointed to the sidewalk next to the bus. I might have won the war of words, but he had won the conflict and I boarded the bus. Though the bike would eventually be packed on a subsequent bus, at that moment, I worried I would never see it again.

The bus was not the most comfortable way to travel, but it proved to be interesting none the less. In Cleveland, a gentleman from Live Oak, California, just north of Sacramento, sat down next to me. A fit man in his early sixties, he would be my traveling partner for the next day and a half and 1,700 miles. He had a small farm about an hour north of Sacramento where he grew almonds and walnuts. He was orphaned as a child and had been a drifter during the Great Depression, hopping trains and living in hobo cities. He had just remarried after losing his first wife to suicide the previous summer. She had shot herself for no apparent reason while heavily sedated in July 1977. I decided as I listened to him this surely had to be true, because this was the sort of stuff he just couldn't make up.

We got our first taste of Great Plains wind when we took a break in North Platte, Nebraska. It was a very warm June night and rather than the breeze being a source of comfort, the warm wind just moved the hot air around. My farmer friend and I were just getting to the front seats of the bus as a slightly-built older lady was making her way down the steps. As she cleared the door, a particularly strong gust came along and blew her down the sidewalk, making her stumble as if she had been drinking. The bus driver caught her by the arm before she hit the pavement, but it was a comical scene that made us laugh.

Our bus drivers were usually cordial and accommodating, but we managed to get a few that must have missed out on the "Be pleasant to passengers" part of the Greyhound training course. Whenever we got to a stop around mealtime, we'd have a few extra minutes to grab a bite. Most of these places were the prototypical greasy spoons, and many were overwhelmed when a whole busload would come in to dine. On one occasion in the Midwest, a grouchy driver would conspire with some slow service to actually abandon a passenger. The driver grumbled as we got off the bus that we should be certain to be back by the scheduled departure time, explaining he wasn't going to get behind schedule and would not wait for tardy diners. Just as he promised, the appointed time arrived, he closed the door, and put the bus in gear. To the shock of all of us, he began pulling away as the soon-to-be-stranded passenger came running out of the station with sandwich in hand, screaming to the driver to wait. As passengers in the bus implored the driver to stop, he shot back, "I told you all to be on time. Besides, there'll be another bus along." The passenger ran after the bus for a block or more before finally giving up, much like a dog chasing after a passing bicyclist. We could almost hear him whimper as he realized his fate.

After the California farmer got off in Ogden, Utah, a cute young lady ended up sitting next to me. She was heading back to Portland, where she attended Reed College, majoring in Psychology. I wrote in a letter home that, "She was a refreshingly deep-thinking person in a predominately shallow-minded world." Like my previous seatmate, we talked about things reserved for old friends. Her dad and mom had divorced, and her step-mother died at a very young age from a heart attack that April. Her dad was still shaken and she worried about him. We ended up talking about our philosophies on life and I found her to be on much the same wavelength as I was. She encouraged me to read *Zen and the Art of Motorcycle Maintenance*, since it, too, chronicled a cross-country trip, albeit on motorized two-wheelers. Even though I was never able to muster the enthusiasm for the book that she had, I enjoyed the discussions and was sorry that we lived 3,000 miles away from each other. In my classic ineptitude with the opposite sex, I never got an address and can only recall vaguely that her last name might have been Weber.

Like the farmer and the Reed College coed, folks on the bus were generally civil and pleasant. But two less pleasant incidents still stick in my mind. The first reinforced a principle I had identified while still a child. In almost every group, there's one (and sometimes two) really annoying people that can't shut up. In school, these were the ones well marked by the brown spots on their noses.

One such obnoxious young lady got on the bus somewhere in the Midwest at the same time a quiet middle-aged black man boarded. I had been close enough to both of them at the stop or on the bus to be able to pass some judgment on their personalities and demeanors. I found the man to be a pleasant gent and despised the insufferable woman after being around her for just a few minutes. Just as we were ready to pull out of the station a few stops later, the woman came running to the bus driver, screaming that she had been propositioned or that the man made some inappropriate remark. Though I didn't think anyone would have wanted to proposition her, I could have understood how someone would have wanted to tell her to shut up. So any remark along those lines would have been one she likely deserved, but not one that would have called for ejection from the bus. The poor guy pleaded his innocence, it appeared in great sincerity, but it was to no avail. The driver eventually called for the police and the shocked and still pleading man was escorted from the bus.

There were a few stretches when the bus had a great many empty seats, and we would all get a double seat to ourselves. Through one stretch of desolate country in Idaho, a rather disheveled soul ended up a seat or two behind me. Though I was hesitant to criticize anyone for hygiene deficiencies after going three days without a shower myself, this guy went another level up the grunge scale. His aroma both preceded and followed him, and it appeared he and shampoo had long ago parted company. But it got worse. I awoke at one point to a conversation back in his section of the bus, but he was still sitting by himself.

After three nights on the bus, I finally arrived in Portland at 7:00 a.m. on Sunday. I was to meet my riding partners at Fort Stevens about an hour northwest of Portland later that day. Even though Portland is a well-known port, it is not a coastal city. To get to Fort Stevens, I had to once again board a bus to Astoria and yet another local run to the crossroads of Warrenton, near Fort Stevens.

I decided to wait for an afternoon bus with the hope my bike might be on the next westbound bus from Salt Lake City. Meanwhile, I went to church and sat down on a bench in Downtown Portland to write a letter home. I was struck by the beauty and vibrancy of downtown Portland in the day and age of fading downtowns and the malling of America. Many streets in Portland were pedestrian malls (making you wonder how the word mall could mean two such drastically different things), and many others were bus and bicycle-only streets. Contrary to the national pattern, it was clean, pretty and a place people would feel safe rather than threatened.

As I walked to church and around the downtown, I stumbled upon the Paramount Theatre and was surprised to see one of my favorite bands, Little Feat, was playing there that same night. I so much wanted to stay for the concert and certainly had an excuse to do so given that my bike was still in transit. With only $300 in travelers' checks, I thought it unwise to spend five percent or more of all the money I had for a concert ticket. Much as I wanted to go, I decided against it.

I had often regretted the decision and felt even worse after doing some research for the book. I had not realized it, but band leader Lowell George died a year after the 1978 tour. It also happened that the last stop on their nationwide tour was in Los Angeles the next weekend, and it was still getting rave reviews 30 years later. From all of this, however, came a curious happy ending; recordings of both the Portland and Los Angeles concerts were made and downloadable from the internet. Three decades after I walked away from the concert, I had the chance to hear it after all. It wasn't quite like being there, but it took the edge off.

With Little Feat preparing for the concert I wouldn't hear for more than 30 years, I set off for Astoria on the afternoon bus. The icing on the cake (or more appropriately the mold on the bread) of my cross-country bus adventure came on the final leg to Warrenton, Oregon. After more than three days without a shower, the trip to the coast was more like a sauna than a bus, as the air conditioning had broken down. As the bus approached that final stop in Warrenton, I breathed a grand sigh of relief the bus ordeal was about to end. While an adventure unto itself and a source of its own volume of crazy stories, the trip was long and uncomfortable. I was sure a hundred-mile bike ride could never be as painful as the same period of time in the confines of a Greyhound bus.

The tepid bus ride ended in the parking lot of the Warrenton Dairy Queen. As I stepped off the bus, I was surprised to see Anita Petrusky, John Mencke and Tom Baldwin enjoying the cuisine. In a remarkable bit of timing, it turned out that my riding partners had decided to come to town for a Brazier Burger and a DQ sundae. As they explained how far up the road the campground was, I realized my unpleasant journey to the west coast was not quite over.

Everyone felt bad about my bicycle predicament. Even this early in the trip, we had come to realize that an endeavor of this magnitude would not be without considerable inconvenience. We ate and exchanged other stories about our westward journeys, and their less painful trips by rail and air reminded me I would never again travel cross-country by bus.

As we were finishing our food, an interesting character wandered into the Dairy Queen in a decade-old station wagon, obviously on the road as well. He recognized our Charles Kuralt fraternal bond and struck up a conversation with us. It turned out he was headed up the same road we were, and he offered to get me a bit closer to our campground after learning of my circumstances.

The rest of the Pennsylvania crew headed up the road on their bikes, and I walked over to my new-found friend's car. My first impression was not a good one. It seemed that every square inch of seat and floor space beyond the driver's seat was covered with the detritus of a lone traveler. I wondered if George Carlin's routine on "Stuff" might have been inspired by this guy's car. There were clothes, camping equipment, pots, pans, all kinds of cooking utensils and boxes and bags of all shapes and sizes. I could only imagine what sorts of contraband he might have had underneath the mess.

He apologized and tried to shovel the debris off the front seat to have enough room to get my backside in the car. It wasn't until I was in the seat that I realized he was coughing and sneezing. Oh, God, I thought, if I don't get arrested for possession of a controlled substance, I was likely to be infected with tuberculosis. Or worse yet, he would kidnap me, torture me to a painful death, and bury me under some old fishing shed. It was just the sort of end my mother warned me of when she told me to never, ever hitchhike.

My driver turned out not to be any of the things I feared. Instead, he was actually a Jesus Freak (in the vernacular of the time) and was on his way to church. Just what kind of church this was, though, was unclear to me. I knew better once we arrived. About halfway up Pacific Drive, we arrived at the "church," which was not any congregation I had ever heard of. One of the crew at the church asked me if I wouldn't stay for a bite to eat but I politely declined. They also offered me a sleeping bag (since mine was somewhere in the Midwest with my bike). Though I might have normally balked at using a stranger's sleeping bag, after four days in a Greyhound bus, I eagerly accepted the offer.

The skies became more threatening as I walked the two final miles to the campground, and not long after I got there, it began to rain. I don't recall it stopping most of the next few days. I had hoped all along my trip would help me better understand the physical and cultural geography of the nation by experiencing it firsthand. But it is human nature to romanticize a trip like this one, anticipating the pleasant parts and selectively dismissing the possibility of the unpleasant prospects—like a three-day torrential downpour.

I had lived through many a rainy spell in Central Pennsylvania but it became clear (in all the fog and clouds) that coastal Oregon was a different animal. This part of the Oregon and Washington coast gets about 70 inches of rain per year, 30 inches more than the Pennsylvania average. Like the rest of the west coast of the United States, much of their rain falls in the winter, a relatively uncommon climatic characteristic. The way the rain fell this particular week in June of 1978 made me wonder what it was like in November. By the end of the first night, it seemed like everything we owned was soaked. If we had been there in the true rainy season, we were certain that boats, rather than bicycles, would have been our only way out.

The first night, I discovered Tom Baldwin came prepared for everything. He was the only one to have brought a tent and he graciously let me share it on that first very rainy night. As the rain had persisted, we wondered what the future held. Tom whipped out a transistor radio. As the rainy hours drug on during incarceration in the tent, Tom suggested a game of checkers, which he also happened to have stowed away in his bag. I, by contrast, had brought only the bare essentials and was struck by all the things Tom had. I wondered if I was traveling too lightly.

When I had occasion to pick up Tom's bike for the first time and later when we climbed our first serious mountain, I was reassured that I had taken the right path. Though Tom could get the weather report and would stay a tad drier than the rest of us, he would pay for his conveniences every time we went uphill.

Despite plenty of rain during the day, it seemed to diminish a bit the few evenings we were there, and we made several warming campfires. We came across some beans somehow or another and tried cooking them up over the fire. The bland flavor of the baked beans straight from the can made me appreciate my mother's bean casseroles. It was the first of a long string of campground meals that were interrupted only by a few restaurant treats over the next four weeks.

Though it rains a great deal in the Pacific Northwest, the coast is not uniformly damp. It might seem a bit odd to some that rainfall amounts are dramatically different from San Diego to Seattle. Many places in coastal Southern California get under 20 inches of rain annually and not many miles inland it is technically a desert. Port Orford, Oregon gets 140 inches. Why would there be such a dramatic difference in this stretch of only 600 miles?

While it might look like the same ocean when we look at it on a map, the ocean currents drag warm water into the more northerly coast and relatively cooler water into the Southern California coast. The relatively warm water produces more evaporation and subsequent rainfall to the north.[8] The mountains help bring more rain, too, providing lifting that cools air and condenses the water vapor into clouds and precipitation. The mountains also provide a physical barrier that brings abrupt decreases in rainfall east of the mountains. A few days later, we would appreciate that firsthand.

All this rain near the coast made for very lush vegetation, and it became easy to understand why the Pacific Northwest was such a great place for harvesting timber. Trees grow very fast when presented with 70 or 80 inches of rain each year. We found other things grew well in such a damp climate, most notably the slugs. Slugs could be a nuisance in Pennsylvania, chomping on lettuce in gardens, especially on the heels of a wet spring. But these Oregon slugs were the Godzillas of gastropods. A large slug in Pennsylvania might get to be the diameter of your little finger, while the west coast cousin could easily grow to two or three times that size. If not so inherently grotesque, west coast slugs might even be considered pretty, coming in a variety of colors and patterns unseen back east. They were prolific on top of being gargantuan. Every plant and bush was covered, and they would seemingly fall from the sky. We were constantly flicking them off each other as they dropped from the trees and crawled onto us from surrounding vegetation.

Even though I did not have my bike, we decided we all had to touch the Pacific Ocean to make our trip a truly cross-country trek. So the next morning we slogged over to the beach in the rain. Though I was prepared to see a different kind of beach from what I had grown used to in Delmarva and New Jersey, I was still surprised by the west coast. Besides the narrow beach and rocky cliffs, I was further struck by the desolation. So much of the east coast has become choked by seaside resorts and buildings almost to the shoreline. Even protected shorelines of state and national seashores are very busy places in the summertime. Except for a few signs and the remnants of an old shipwreck, this shore looked similar to what Lewis and Clark would have seen in 1805.

The expedition had built Fort Clatsop just south of current day Warrenton, very near where we were staying. Much of our first week on the bike followed the Lewis and Clark Trail eastward, and though much had changed since their trip, much had also stayed the same. The Columbia River gorge was nothing short of spectacular, the western portion one waterfall after another tumbling over the bluff carved by the Columbia. The Columbia River gorge and the Missouri River on the eastern leg of Lewis and Clark's trip provided for a relatively easy passage for them. The part over the Northern Rockies was quite another matter, just as it would be for a group of cyclists 170 years later.

It turned out that Fort Stevens had nothing to do with the Lewis and Clark era; it had been built as a precaution in case Canada joined the Civil War as a Confederate supporter. Later it was part of a series of west coast forts designed to deter any Japanese attacks in World War II. It holds the distinction as the only place in the contiguous 48 states to have been fired upon during the war. A Japanese sub fired shells in the vicinity of the fort on June 21, 1942, but the US commander never even returned fire. It was deactivated in 1947, never having fired its guns in anger, and became a state park just three years before we began our cross-country trip.[9]

Have You Ever Seen the Rain?

—John Fogerty
"Have You Ever Seen the Rain?"
From the Creedence Clearwater Revival album *Pendulum*
(1970)

LATE THE NEXT DAY, JUNE 12TH, AFTER TWO DAYS OF NEAR-ly non-stop rain, the station master at the Greyhound bus station in Astoria told me my bike had finally caught up with me. We awoke to a torrential downpour on Tuesday morning. I cannot recall how I got from the campground to the crossroads at Warrenton, but I do remember I was soaked from head to toe as I stuck out my thumb to hitchhike into Astoria. As I looked at the bridge crossing over the bay, arching high over the waterway, I feared no one would pick me up on such a dreadful day. It turned out that quite the opposite held true. A man on his way to work from one of the nearby coastal communities slowed and stopped to pick me up. He noted he never picked up hitchhikers but could not possibly leave me standing in the driving rain. Fascinated by my story, he wished me good luck as he dropped me off in downtown Astoria.

    I picked up my bike at the bus station and found that a bike shop was not far away. The shop manager welcomed me to use his repair stand to put things back together. I was still not a mechanical whiz by any stretch of the imagination. But I realized that Ken and Roddy, the two people most responsible for me standing there next to my bicycle, 3,000 miles from home, had taught me enough to get by. I patted myself on the back for remembering the left pedal was threaded left-handed so it didn't unscrew as you rode.

The rain let up a bit by the time I had pieced the bike back together, and John, Tom and Anita met me in mid-morning. Covered in our rain jackets, we set off for Portland, or so we had hoped. Portland and the Pacific Coast seem much closer together in easterners' minds than they actually are and we often forget the Coast Ranges are situated between the coast and the Cascades. While much smaller (and older), the Coast Ranges are mountains nonetheless and these two misperceptions conspired with the weather to make our first day in the saddle an arduous one.

The result of cooled lava flows pushed upward by two colliding crustal plates, the Coast Range's ocean-made rock ended up several thousand feet above sea level. [10]

Though built by a much different process than the folded Appalachians, the roads between Astoria and Portland could be mistaken for Pennsylvania's back roads at first glance. They could be narrow, curvy and steep but, also like Pennsylvania, they were marked by their beautiful, tree-covered slopes. Beyond the first glance, there were many differences. In Pennsylvania, conifers are the exception rather than the rule and this part of Oregon is quite the opposite. Though Coast Redwoods or Giant Sequoias don't grow this far north, the Sitka Spruce and Douglas Firs can still grow to extraordinary sizes in these parts. Western Red Cedars and Western Hemlocks are common, too.[11]

Like coal country in Pennsylvania, these rural roads were also cursed by large tri-axle trucks, but here these big trucks hauled logs, not coal. To Pennsylvania bicyclists, coal trucks are the most feared of road hazards, and these log trucks seemed to present similar dangers. A few thousand miles can make a difference in attitude, however, and we found the drivers of these behemoths as polite as could be. While most coal truck drivers seemed to revel in buzzing a cyclist at 60 miles per hour, the loggers would slow and courteously pass, giving a wide birth and waving as they went by. Dozens passed us without incident over that 100 miles through the Coast Range.

We stopped at a tavern to refill our water bottles in the town of Jewell on Route 202. From the exterior, it could have passed for a mountain town bar in Pennsylvania, but it was apparent from their dress and conversation these were lumbermen. Just like their genteel driving habits, they showed a friendly disposition in conversation as well. When they discovered what we were up to, they wanted to hear more about the trip and how we liked Oregon so far.

I thought back to my trip through rural Virginia two years before when I was often treated like an unwelcome foreigner. I could still picture my cousin being struck by a car in the frantic congestion of Trenton, New Jersey. I recalled a number of scary experiences with coal trucks in Central Pennsylvania. Though only the first day on the road, a clear pattern had begun to emerge. Westerners were clearly friendlier, more personable, and more polite than most Easterners.

Logging was and remains big business in these parts, and more than a third of the land is held by the big lumber companies. In addition to the logging trucks, the clear-cuts were conspicuous indicators of the magnitude of the lumber industry in the region. The scope of these clear-cuts makes one realize how the term clear-cut came to be, for every tree was taken down, often as far as the eye could see. To witness one first-hand and up close hammers home why concerns over erosion, sedimentation, and habitat destruction are so great. Tire ruts on steep hillsides through soil nearly scraped clean of any vegetation results in an indescribable quagmire of eroded topsoil. On top of being an environmental debacle, it was an aesthetic abomination as well. It was just damned unpleasant to look at.

Hummingbirds and the Old Man

"A flash of harmless lightning,
A mist of rainbow dyes,
The burnished sunbeams brightening
From flower to flower he flies."

—John Banister Tabb
Humming-Bird

ALREADY A DAY LATER THAN WE PLANNED BECAUSE OF MY bike taking the long way around, our first day on the bikes fell short as well. Several rain delays and sloppy roads in between made it impossible to get to Portland as we had planned. It was the first of many miscalculations we would make, as we also underestimated how many miles and how long it would take to get to our destination. So when we came upon Big Eddy Park Campground in Pittsburg, Oregon, we decided it seemed as good a place as any to camp. Two cyclists from Corvallis, Oregon, also ended up at Big Eddy that evening, our two parties making up the vast majority of the evening's guests.

When we arrived (and admittedly for years afterward), I thought it was Big Eddy himself who welcomed us to the campground. I didn't find him particularly big in stature and wondered about the unusual spelling of Eddy, but nicknames often come about in peculiar ways, so I discounted the inconsistency. It turned out the park was named after the big eddy in the Nehalem River, not the one in the office. The park proprietor (who we thought was Eddy) was housed in a modest structure, an aged trailer sitting near the entrance of the campground that doubled as an office. Like his abode, the campground was a humble establishment as well. The only other structure of any note was a concrete block building among some trees that housed the bathrooms.

It had stopped raining by the time we got there, but it remained damp, and I was sure the mosquitoes would be along directly. Sometime the previous spring, I had been offered a cigar on the occasion of the birth of a baby. Though I did not smoke, I took the cigar with the intention of using it as an insect repellent at some point during our trip. As we settled in for the evening, I pulled the stogy from my pannier and dug into my waterproof medical kit for a match. I lit it up and waited to see the mosquitoes scurry away from our campsite. Being among a group of nonsmokers, none of us really understood one had to keep drawing in air to keep the thing lit. Not wishing to inhale the foul smoke that emanated from the cigar, my refusal to inhale meant it repeatedly went out. Not surprisingly, the mosquitoes descended upon us like the plague.

The traffic through Big Eddy was clearly not sufficient to justify a pay phone, so we sauntered back up to the big house and asked "Eddy" if I could use his phone to call home. He led me into the trailer and showed me the phone. As I spoke to the family back in Altoona, I peered out the kitchen window to the covered patio and noticed several bird feeders, including one for hummingbirds. After finishing my call, we conversed with "Eddy" for a few minutes and the conversation eventually wandered to the topic of the birds.

"Have you ever seen trained hummingbirds?" he asked.

"Why no, I don't believe I have," one of us replied, sure this was a setup for a joke.

"Well, you've come to the right place," the old gent explained. "I'm the only hummingbird trainer in the country near as I can tell, and I can get them to do all kinds of tricks."

Hummingbirds doing tricks? This was something I had to see. So we egged him on.

"It might take a few minutes," he continued, confirming that he didn't keep them in a cage under the trailer. He poured some nectar onto a small spoon, stuck the handle of the spoon into his mouth and waited patiently. After a few minutes, a hummingbird flew under the patio roof and swooped around the bespectacled campground proprietor. After several approaches and retreats, the bird flew toward him and began to take the nectar from the spoon. A second bird soon followed. We had not paid particular attention to it at the time, but before he began, "Eddy" had picked up a couple rings, each about a foot or so in diameter. As the birds retreated, he held one of the rings eight or ten inches in front of his face. The birds flew through the ring on queue. He held up the second ring at arms-length and the birds flew back through both the rings like a well-trained dog would have jumped through rings in a competition. He moved the rings around and the birds went back and forth, dashing off into the nearby brush and then back again. Maybe he wasn't the only hummingbird trainer in the United States, but that did not diminish "Big Eddy's" stature in my mind. I was duly impressed and Eddy was justly proud.

Big Eddy's American flag was wet and limp as we awoke to Flag Day 1978 on June 14th. The rain delayed our departure and prompted us to splurge for a cooked breakfast at Roach's Coffee Break in Veronia, a few miles south on Route 47. I ate three of the biggest buckwheat pancakes ever thrown on a griddle, and it helped me forget, at least for a few minutes, how miserable the riding had been. Despite enjoying some of the most incredible scenery and pleasant people, the rain had made our first day in the saddle difficult. Day two seemed to have little prospect of being any better meteorologically. Everything seemed wet and dirty, from the bike right down to my underwear.

Though the people of Oregon had shown us nothing but kindness and hospitality, we would not have quite the same good fortune with their dogs. We met one ill-tempered canine on a nasty uphill in the wooded landscape of Columbia County. One of our group had riled the barking beast, and when I came upon him, he had worked up a good head of steam. After thirteen happy years with our family mutt Kelly, my subsequent experiences with dogs had not been pleasant ones. I had been chased by at least a dozen different breeds in my few years of long-distance riding and had riding companions take nasty falls after colliding with dogs on training rides. Even my cousin's Chihuahua had taken a nip at my ankle a few years before.

Most of the time when chased by a dog, a good hard sprint will leave the critter in the dust. But when the dog sees the rider or gets ahead of him, it takes some fancy footwork to avoid collision or getting bit on the leg. So when this one got a warning we were on the way, I was at a distinct disadvantage. A rather steep hill was the *coup de grâce*. Particularly since it was a larger than average dog, I decided I needed to do something to prevent getting bit or knocked over. Rather than dismounting on the uphill, I grabbed my pump, hoping a swing in the dog's general direction would discourage him. I was surprised when the first swing plunked the beast on the head. The dumb animal that lost this battle, however, was me rather than the dog. As I swung, the base of the pump flew off, leaving me holding the handle. Using my rear wheel as a shield, I walked back down the hill to recover the rest of my pump. If dogs could chuckle, this one was having a good one at my expense.

Ken had taken the train to Portland and intended to meet us there since his time off work was limited. The weather and the pump incident were among several other things that delayed us, and our lunchtime rendezvous with Ken Steel happened about 3:00 p.m. In early afternoon, when it became clear we would be very late, I told my riding partners I would ride ahead to let Ken know the rest of them were on the way. But a few miles outside of Portland, I was again foiled by the rain and the rest of the group caught up before I could meet Ken. Things did not get much better once we got to Portland. I was confronted by a very narrow tunnel on US Route 26 and walked back up a long hill to find a way to ride around the dangerous stretch of road. The rest of the group braved the tunnel reluctantly, figuring they'd rather take a chance of getting run over than walk back up the hill.

Eventually, we found our way to I-80 with the anticipation we were finally on our way. We looked forward to riding the interstates in Oregon, one of only a handful of states that allowed cyclists on the limited access highways. This part of I-80 was not such a hospitable route though. It was urban rush hour traffic, speeding by at 60 miles per hour, as close to bumper-to-bumper as it could be at that speed. Still, we struggled along, being especially careful at the interchanges so as not to be creamed by a commuter exiting the freeway. With good reason, it so happened we were not allowed on this portion of the interstate after all, and a trooper would soon inform us of this.

The five of us were pulled over and told, in no uncertain terms, we would have to exit the highway.

"We understand, Officer, but we honestly thought we were allowed on the road."

"No, you're not allowed on this road. Unless, of course, you'd like to get run over," the officer shot back.

"We'll get off at the next exit," one of us responded.

"No, you'll get off right here."

"Where?" I sincerely inquired.

"Right there," the officer directed, pointing to a parking lot on the other side of a four-foot-high fence.

The scene that followed could have won a prize on *America's Funniest Videos* had the show existed at the time. We struggled to heave the bikes and ourselves over the barrier. It was not until that moment that we really appreciated how heavy fully loaded touring bikes could be. Lifting Tom's over our head, with the tent, radio, checker game, and God knows what else, was the biggest back-breaker of all.

But that was not the end of the story. As we gathered ourselves and tried to figure out how we would proceed east, we were confronted by two highly perturbed security guards. Our police friends had ordered us to trespass into the parking lot of a fenced manufacturing facility, and the security staff did not take kindly to our intrusion. In the matter of three minutes, we were nearly arrested twice.

The Leader of the Pack

—Ellie Greenwich, Jeff Barry, George "Shadow" Morton
"The Leader of the Pack"
The Shangri-Las
Red Bird Records (1964)

THE SKIES WERE STILL THREATENING WHEN WE ROLLED into the eastern Portland suburb of Gresham. It had been another problem-filled, rainy day and we had barely clocked 70 miles. Ken rode a block north of US 26 to a motel and came back to report the place was a bit pricey. One of the locals suggested we make the climb to nearby Mount Tabor Park, where we would find a spacious pavilion and bathroom facilities. Mount Tabor was a small volcanic cone, long gone dormant. It was a steep climb from downtown Gresham but worth the effort to find a quiet (or so we thought) and covered place to camp on the rainy night.

Our stumbling upon Mount Tabor was further evidence that amazing geology was all around us. The cinder cone's peak sets about 400 feet above the valley and is one of many cinder cones and shield volcanoes in the Boring Lava Field. (It's named for the town of Boring rather than for its lackluster reputation.) The two million year-old volcanoes rise above the surrounding landscape like bubbles. They extend from just southeast of Portland into southwestern Washington, interrupted topographically for a brief time by the Columbia River.[12] Unlike similar volcanoes in Arizona, the smaller cones of coastal Oregon and Washington can be more difficult to spot, having undergone a few million years of erosion and more likely to be tree covered in this humid climate.

We hiked up the last hundred or so vertical feet to the top of the volcano, confident that this one would not blow in the traditional tectonic fashion after at least 1.5 million years of dormancy. The closest thing to an eruption was the flatulent-like sound created by Ken's air mattress as he blew it up for the first time on the trip. After a hearty laugh about the mattress, we grabbed a bite and started to get ready for what we hoped would be a relaxing (and dry) night's sleep. The park had a spacious new pavilion with enough picnic tables that all of us could enjoy a night's sleep away from the creepy crawlies and dew.

One at a time, we wandered down the grassy hill to the bathroom to wash up, answer nature's call, and brush our teeth. Tom had ventured down first and John went down a few minutes later. Upon entering, John spotted the tell-tale feet below the door of the stall and asked Tom, "How's it going in there?" Much to his embarrassment, it was not Tom at all but some total stranger.

Anita and I ran into Tom as he was walking back to the pavilion and he commented on how nice the facilities were for a public park. As I walked into the men's room, I wondered if Tom's long couple of days in the rain had dulled his senses, for I found the place to be a typically dirty, malodorous public bathroom. John was just finishing up and he told me of his embarrassing interlude with the mystery man in the stall he had mistaken for Tom. I washed up quickly in the cold water at the sink and walked back up the hill with John.

When we returned to the pavilion, Tom was still marveling at the cleanliness of the bathroom and how much he enjoyed his sponge bath. Anita agreed the ladies room was remarkably clean as well. It hit John and me at the same moment as we pieced the facts together in our minds and we broke into hysterical laughter. Laughing too hard to speak coherently, we tried to explain to Tom, still oblivious to his mistake, that he had relieved himself and stripped down to his skivvies in the ladies' room.

After many more laughs and jabbing about Tom's intrusion into the wrong bathroom, we finally settled down to sleep. We were all physically tired and mentally weary from four days in the rain and welcomed the roof over our heads (even if there were no sides). Our sleep was abruptly interrupted sometime after 10:00 p.m. by the roar of motorcycles. It was clear this was a group of riders, and it was also clear they were headed our way. We were all uneasy with the prospect of a confrontation with a motorcycle gang and quickly discussed how we would handle the situation. Many gangs would evolve into more fraternal and philanthropic groups a quarter century later, but in 1978, most were gangs in all the most negative and intimidating ways possible. We quickly strategized how we might defuse a potentially difficult situation and concluded that some sort of friendly greeting might mute any violent tendencies they would harbor.

As they approached, we all lay still in our sleeping bags. This was a rather ridiculous attempt to feign nonchalance, considering that the sound of their engines was enough to vibrate items off the picnic tables. Our hope that our apparently sleeping bodies would prompt them to simply ride off into the moonlight was soon dashed. The leader of the pack stopped his bike and walked toward us. I was now far past "uneasy" and was approaching horrified on the panic meter.

Lined up across the picnic tables like bodies on the autopsy tables, John was the first person they came upon. In an attempt to shock the gang with kindness, he sat straight up in his sleeping bag. He cordially asked the motorcyclist, "How's it going?" with much the same tone he used inquiring of the other stranger's well-being in the bathroom stall two hours earlier. The biker stepped back, clearly surprised as much by John's unintimidated demeanor as by his casual salutation.

"Ah, okay, man, how about you guys?" he replied.

"We're doing all right. Had a rough day on the bikes with the rain and all," John explained to the now diffused leader of the pack.

"Yeah, it's been messy riding for us, too. Where ya headed?"

"Riding across the country. This is day two," John continued conversationally.

"Cool, man!" The biker was duly impressed and we were greatly relieved. The rest of our group and several of his riding mates joined in the conversation, evidently bonding in the fact that we were all two-wheeled warriors.

A cool front had helped produce the rainy weather and it prompted clearing, cooler temperatures and drier air after it had passed. This was magnified by the fact we were also passing through the rain shadow of the Cascades and into a vastly different climatic zone. Average June rainfall in The Dalles, where we would stay that night, was one tenth of the June average in coastal Astoria, where we began two days earlier. Even in the rainy winter months, the rainfall disparity is four to one. It is one of the most abrupt variations in rainfall amounts in the world. In just 150 miles, three hours in a car, one goes from a temperate rainforest to a semi-desert. Soaking wet on Tuesday, we were sunburnt on Thursday.

Just east of Gresham, the Historic Columbia River Highway begins along the Sandy River, a tributary of the Columbia. The Sandy River marked the eastern border of Metro-Portland's urban growth zone and the suburbs ended emphatically when we crossed the tributary. The scenic highway skirted the bluff of the Columbia River a short distance south of (latitudinally) and above (topographically) I-80N. Similar to the way the Colorado River carved the canyons of Arizona's Colorado Plateau into sedimentary rock, the Columbia and its tributaries came to be incised into the igneous rock of the Columbia Plateau.

The rocks near the surface of the Columbia Plateau are primarily basalt, a rock made from lava that hardens at or near the surface. When you look closely at the topography of the region, it's easy to see the many volcanic cones that might have produced all this lava. They range in size from the smaller cinder cones like Mount Tabor to the gigantic composite cones (or stratovolcanoes) like Mount Hood south of Portland.

On a clear day (which are hard to come by much of the year) Mount Hood is a dominant feature in the skyline, and can be seen for many miles on either side of Portland. About three dozen of these distinctive cone shaped peaks, stretching from southern British Columbia to northern California, exceed 8,000 feet, and fifteen are higher than 9,000 feet. It's easy to understand why they would be called composite cones. To make a cone that big, it surely must be the result of a long series of eruptions over many years.

Volcanism in these parts began 37 million years ago, but ten of these larger peaks have been active in the last 200 years, the most notable of these being Mount Saint Helens, only 50 miles north of where we rode in 1978. Just two years after our trip through the Pacific Northwest, the top of the peak blew off and dumped four million cubic yards of debris into the Columbia River and its tributaries.[13] More than a half billion tons of pyroclastic debris blew across the western United States, and cities as far away as Spokane, Washington, were clouded in darkness during the late afternoon and early evening of May 18, 1980.[14]

Ken, in his typically adventurous spirit, set off on a bike trip through the area later that summer so he might experience the devastation firsthand. He was particularly struck by the moon-like appearance of the areas most impacted by the massive ash deposits. Many roads and bridges were still impassable when he made the trip in July, and he was overwhelmed by the scope of the destruction. Large trees had been tossed about and carried downriver, many miles in some cases.

Thirty million years of volcanic activity piles up a great deal of lava, and the Columbia Plateau is testimony to the scope of these deposits. The eastern half of Washington, the eastern two thirds of Oregon, and most of southern Idaho are plateaus and canyons through this basalt and other similar volcanic rock. To a passing tourist or bicyclist, the most amazing of the resulting features along the Columbia River are the waterfalls that spill off the bluff carved by the river. Overcome by the beauty of that landscape, we spent most of the morning of June 15th taking pictures and hiking around the waterfalls. The waterfalls are especially interesting because of the columnar jointing of the rock on the cliffs. When the lava cooled, it shrunk in volume several percent, forming joints that made five or six sided column-like shapes and a very unique cliff that made a similarly unusual waterfall. The lichen and moss from the damp climate added an additional patina that made the Columbia River Gorge National Scenic Area one of the most beautiful scenic highways in the country.

After the scenic highway ended, we found ourselves on I-80N (later I-84) along the Columbia. The wind was from the west and pushed us along to The Dalles. Despite the long but welcome distraction of the scenic highway, we managed to get in 90 miles. Not having had the luxury of a hot shower since we departed from Fort Stevens, we decided against another night of camping and stumbled upon the

Shamrock Motel a short distance from the highway. Beyond the shower, it was a nondescript evening except for one amusing image that persisted in my memory even decades later.

The speck on the right side of the bridge is riding partner John Mencke. We spent hours hiking and taking pictures of the many waterfalls tumbling down the side of the ancient lava flows of basalt rock eroded by the Columbia River. Photo by John Frederick.

I knew Ken liked to eat and would do so deliberately and for as long as it took to get his fill. But this night, it took on a new dimension. Beyond what we had left over from our trip to the Safeway supermarket in Portland, we stocked up on fresh bread, cheese, and peanut butter. Ken spread the whole mess out on the desk in the motel room. He prepared and devoured one sandwich after another, after another. We called it the Ken Steel Smorgasbord.

I left his room to return to my own and came back 20 minutes later to see him still parked at the desk next to the television, eating yet another sandwich. He had consumed all but a few slices of a loaf of whole wheat bread, a good portion of the jar of peanut butter, and all of the extras from our trip to Safeway. He washed it down with massive quantities of whatever fruit juice he had on hand. Ken recognized we were using up large amounts of fluids and calories every day, and he clearly intended to enjoy himself while replenishing them.

Though we didn't see the sun too often, the view of the Columbia River Plain was spectacular when the scenic highway hugged the top of the bluff. Interstate 80N (now I-84) can be seen on the bottom left. Photo by John Frederick.

The Wind at My Back

"May the road rise up to meet you.
May the wind always be at your back.
May the sun shine warm upon your face,
and rains fall soft upon your fields.
And until we meet again,
May God hold you in the palm of His hand."

—An Irish Blessing

A STRONG WIND BLEW IN FROM THE WEST ON I-80 AS WE pulled out of The Dalles along the Columbia River. We put up the sails and enjoyed some fast riding, cruising along at 30 miles per hour for long stretches, despite carrying a full load of gear. Particularly after the rain that we struggled through the first few days, this was mighty fine riding.

The last 20 miles brought us back to earth quickly as we left the Columbia Gorge and began to climb. We ascended 1,000 feet from the time we left the valley until we got to Pendleton. I wrote in my journal I had already grown tired of riding up long climbs through boring terrain in the burning sun. Little did I know, I had only seen a small sample of those discomforts. John and I got split up from the others and had to backtrack in an effort to find everyone. We finally spotted them at the bottom of the long hill, struggling to fix the second flat tire of the day. After making the necessary repairs, we rode into town and found a military base turned campground, RV Park, and its pleasant proprietor. The campground and its immaculate bathroom facilities were a much-needed tonic for our weary band, but we lamented it also came with our most expensive campsite of the trip—the fee of $7 plus tax split five ways cost us each $1.45.

The next morning, we were met by a nasty headwind and more cloudless skies. John Mencke was the prototypical fair-skinned, red-haired Caucasian that could get sunburnt by just thinking about sunlight. Just a few days before the summer solstice and the highest sun of the year, two full days in the blazing sun was taking its toll on all of us, but especially John. By Saturday afternoon, his skin was close to the color of his red hair, despite every effort to shield himself from the strong ultraviolet rays. John didn't care how silly he looked; he donned his ball cap, strapped his handkerchief around his neck, and pulled on his long sleeve denim shirt despite temperatures in the mid-eighties. The nearly treeless landscape provided little relief from the sunlight, and the first consideration for any rest stop was shade.

Had I brought my Raisz Landform Map from my geomorphology class, I would have seen the base of the Blue Mountains before us as we started out that morning. I would have, at least, been prepared for the pain soon to be inflicted upon us. But on the Oregon state road map, it just looked like more dry, boring, relatively flat eastern Oregon landscape. The Blue Mountain region was significant for another reason; the area was home to the oldest geologic formation anywhere in Oregon.[15] A seemingly endless climb, the full magnitude did not hit home until we saw a sign noting an elevation of over 4,000 feet.

Though we had enjoyed a much safer trip and cooperative group of drivers than we were used to in many parts of Pennsylvania, the climb out of the river valley brought my first scary roadside incident. The wide berm of the interstate highway was a great place to ride under normal circumstances. Being the days of the nationwide 55 mile per hour speed limit, the cars went by at a reasonable speed and were always in their own traveling lane. So long as the vehicle was of normal dimensions, there was seldom anything to worry about. Part way up the climb, however, something of unusual proportions was bearing down on me. Fortunately, cyclists come to recognize when something is amiss even if they can't see it. The sound and the shadow struck me before the truck could. I thought I should gander over my shoulder when I sensed the big rig was too close for comfort. The cab of the truck marked "Oversize Load" passed me as I turned to see the mobile home just inches (or so it seemed) from my left elbow. I bailed out toward the guardrail, unleashing a cacophony of selective curse words at the careless driver. Must have been an Eastern transplant, I thought to myself, most likely from New Jersey.

Someplace north of La Grande, we caught up to Tom and Fred Long, hoping to ride with the father-son duo for a day or two before climbing into the mountains. The Altoona contingent of the group knew the Longs from the bike club back home, and though of vastly different ages and abilities, we all got along and enjoyed riding together. Fred came to love bicycling, even though it might take him a little longer to ride from one place to another than the rest of us. The climb through the Blue Mountains was grueling for everyone, but especially for Fred. Yet when we got to the end of the day, he was still smiling, and it was clear he had enjoyed the day as much as any of us. Just like the cross-state ride he had organized two years earlier during the national Bicentennial, Fred enjoyed the history along the way as much as he did the bicycling. He was a pleasant, selfless, and jovial man that enjoyed life in general, and sharing his knowledge and enthusiasm of history in particular.

With Fred especially feeling the effects of the tough ride and the rest of us enduring the 135-mile day on Friday, La Grande seemed like a good place to stop for the day. The Longs, Tom, Anita, and John decided a motel sounded like a good idea and found one in town. Ken suggested a camping alternative at a roadside rest area down the interstate. Though La Grande sits in the Grand Ronde River valley, its elevation is still nearly 3,500 feet above sea level. Yet it was still a dry place that could support trees only near rivers or where extensive irrigation was done. Though we should have fully realized this as we approached the beautifully landscaped roadside rest, it did not occur to us at first that the oasis owed its existence to the unnatural assistance of irrigation.

Though the Ken Steel Smorgasbords had to get by with slightly more spartan provisions out here in the semi-wild Oregon countryside, he and I managed to throw out quite a spread of food after we got settled. As we sat at the picnic table eating and talking, we heard an unusual click, followed by the sound of spraying water. In a comedic scene, the two of us hastily grabbed the food and then our bikes and sleeping paraphernalia as we tried to avoid being drenched by the park's sprinkler system.

After days of nearly nonstop rain near the coast, the sun became unrelenting in central Oregon. When we found this shaded overpass, we simply couldn't pass it up. From left to right are Anita Petrusky, Fred and son Tom Long (partially obscured), me, Tom Baldwin, and John Mencke. Photo by Ken Steel.

As night fell, we cleaned up and threw our sleeping bags out on the spacious picnic tables in anticipation of a peaceful night's sleep. At midnight, precisely six hours after our first surprise shower, we were awakened by the same distinctive clicking sound that had interrupted our evening meal. Absent the flying slices of bread, our scurrying about to get out of our second man-made rainstorm was every bit as silly looking as our dinner time sprint to dry ground. We ran back to the same tables we were at for dinner and hoped that the rest of the night would go by without incident. As the sun, creeping over the horizon of the eastern sky, shone in my eyes, I rolled over in the hope of going back to sleep. Still half asleep and content to lay on my table for as long as I could, I thought I heard the now infamous clicking sound of the sprinkler system again. Chuckling to myself in my dazed state, I discounted the sound as something else, certain that this involuntary baptism surely could not drench us for the third time in twelve hours. My optimism was short-lived as the cold water came raining down upon us yet again.

It's strange how stupid things can be entertaining in circumstances like these. Ken and I laughed until we cried and our traveling partners found even more hilarity in the incident. "I slept very well," Anita joked with a broad smile of satisfaction that she had the foresight to stay this night in a dry and comfortable bed.

Though still technically in the Columbia Plateaus, the ride south of the La Grande took us between two block faulted mountain ranges, the Elkhorn Ridge and the Wallowa Mountains. The mountains are about 150 million years old and, with peaks over 9,000 feet, are the highest mountains in Oregon outside the Cascades. Their highest point, just shy of 10,000 feet, is Sacajawea Peak, named after the legendary Shoshoni Indian guide on the Lewis and Clark expedition.

After enjoying that incredible tailwind along the Columbia River, a headwind blew incessantly from the south for the next three days. The scenery on the day's ride was diverse and beautiful, though I noted in my journal that the near-desert landscape was not one in which I would want to live. Even if the rainfall was more abundant, deep and fertile soil could be hard to come by. Those early travelers on the Oregon Trail actually avoided parts of the Burnt River Canyon. The rocky landscape was brutal on their wagons (and very likely their backsides as well). Closer to Express (now Durkee) the soil improved and the Durkee Valley became a desirable area for sheep ranching, just as it had been valuable hunting ground for Native Americans.[16]

As the day wore on, it cooled down, we got a few sprinkles, and the temperatures dipped into the forties as the night approached. We built a campfire to cozy up to and I made a futile attempt to bake a potato I had bought at the market. As I gazed disappointingly at the inedible spud on this crisp Oregon evening, I promised to never again take my mother's potato preparation skills for granted. Yet despite the chilly evening and the lackluster supper, it was difficult to complain about where we had ended up. Farewell Bend State Park was situated on the shores of the Snake River's Brownlee Reservoir and the landscape was like few others I had ever seen. The view from our campsite was dominated by the southern end of the Slaughterhouse Range, a treeless ridge that jutted more than 1,500 feet above the Snake River Plain. As the sun sunk in the west, the mountainside was surreally inflamed by the late day sun, and we caught the sight of two hikers walking along the spine of the mountain. My challenging potato baking endeavor aside, the relaxing late afternoon and early evening in this beautiful place brought a peaceful end to a difficult day.

Given the trials and tribulations of the Oregon Trail travelers, I really had my nerve complaining about the day's difficulties. For eastbound trail trekkers, this was where things got especially difficult, for this was where the trail left the Snake River Valley to begin the difficult journey over the mountains. For those going westward, this was the easier leg of their trip (but only relatively speaking). Navigating the Columbia and Snake in the days of those early pioneers, and before them in the days of the Plateau Indians, was challenging for many reasons. Strangely, those traveling on the river now would find it challenging for another reason. Brownlee Dam, built in 1952, was one of fifteen dams on the Snake, making life difficult for salmon as well as people trying to go up or down the river. At the time of our trip in the late seventies, the many dams on the Columbia and Snake were awash in controversy as well as water. The dams had seriously impeded the ability of Pacific Salmon to make their annual pilgrimage to the headwaters of the river system where they spawn. Eventually, all the lower dams were modified to allow the fish to migrate back up the river system, but the three in Hells Canyon were never rebuilt.[17]

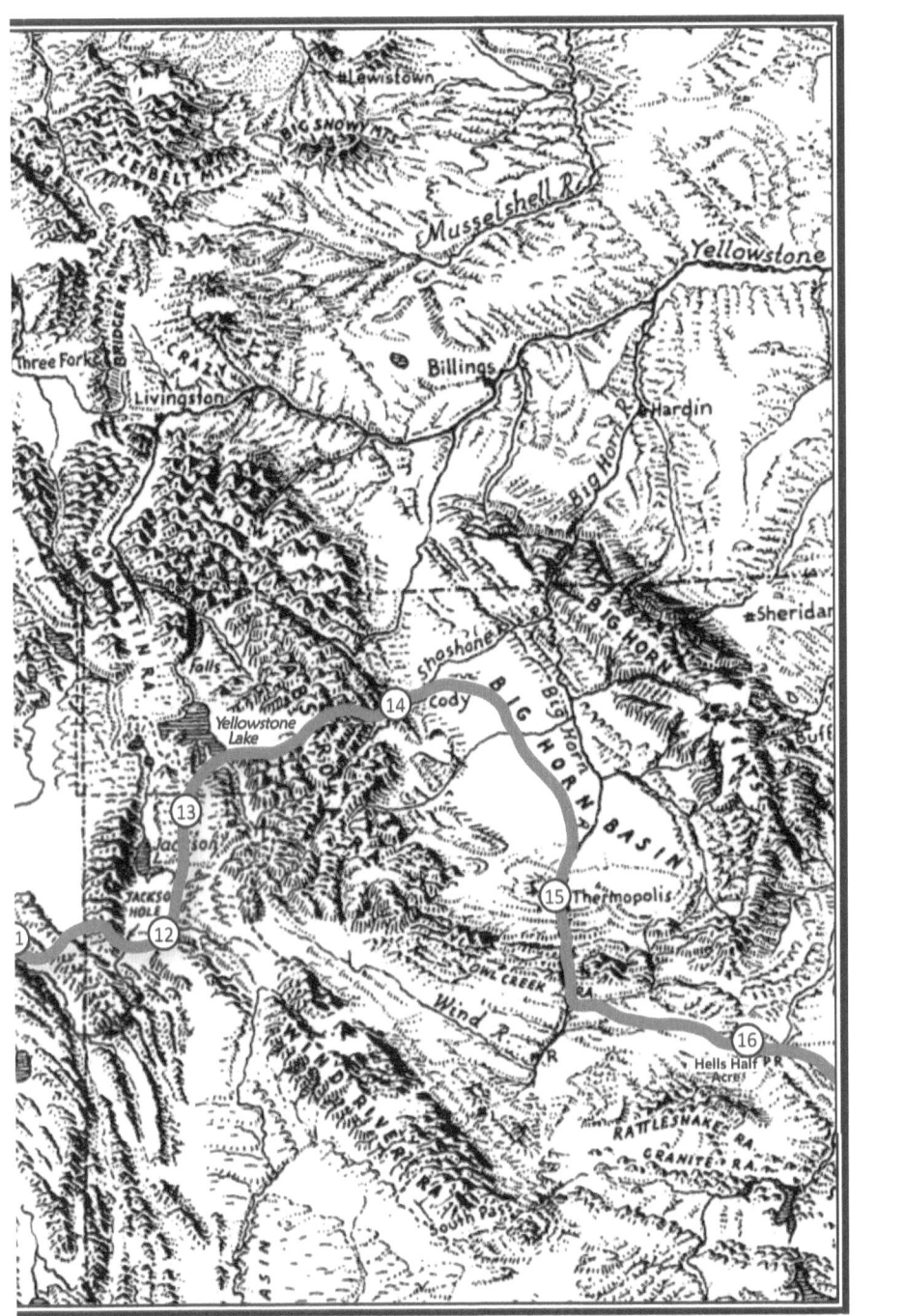

Take the Long Way

"Take the Long Way Home"
Roger Hodgson
Supertramp from the album *Breakfast in America*
A & M Records (1979)

JUST OUTSIDE OF ONTARIO, OREGON, THE ARID LANDSCAPE suddenly turned into lush farmland supported not by a sudden increase in rainfall, but rather an extensive irrigation system. The entire valley was irrigated from just west of the Idaho border to beyond Boise and turned a place cursed by sparse rainfall into an agricultural oasis.

We left the interstate and took US Routes 20 and 26 into Boise, and although a pretty ride through the aforementioned farmland, it ended up being out of the way. It was the long way from both a mileage and time standpoint, as both John and I got flat tires. Adding insult to injury, my tire still would not hold air after I patched it. The staple that had punctured it ripped several holes in the tube, and I had to go through the whole exercise the second time. Adding further insult, I discovered my pump head was broken, a casualty of my altercation with the dog in the Coast Range a few days earlier.

I found a bike shop, but it was several miles outside of downtown Boise and took us another half hour out of our way. When we finally got back on track, we rode back to City Hall, where we all had planned to meet. Ken ran into several delays himself and we ended up waiting two hours for everyone to get back together. When the disjointed day finally began to wind down, we stumbled upon the Americana Campground, eager and ready for some food and a comfy picnic table on which to sleep.

The first major climb in the Rocky Mountains was the ascent to Mores Creek Summit north of Boise. I caught this photo of Ken on one of the four nasty switchbacks that took us up 800 feet in the final 2.5 miles before the summit. Photo by John Frederick.

The next morning, we set off up Idaho Route 21 for our first day in the Rockies. Much like my hometown of Altoona, Pennsylvania, Boise sits in a valley surrounded by mountains (though these are much larger than the Appalachians). Also like Altoona, this means the city's growth is constrained by its physical geography. Soon after leaving the city limits, we found ourselves in tree-covered foothills. The mountainous geography discouraged development much beyond the valley, providing land use constraints to suburban sprawl that local government has often been hesitant to enact.

The last of the man-made features before the serious climbing kicked in was Lucky Peak Dam at about 3,000 feet elevation. Although the dam was originally constructed in 1949 and operational in 1955, the electric generating station was not built until 1984. As we rode by, a massive geyser of water exploded from the base of the dam. We all agreed we had never seen water shooting so far into the air and watched in disbelief until the release ended. Clearly, it didn't take much to entertain us.

After Ken caught up to me on the first summit we conquered in the Rockies, he said we needed to memorialize the auspicios event. So I turned around and rode the last hundred meters or so over again so as to get me and the summit sign on film. Photo by Ken Steel.

The rest of the day was equally entertaining, albeit in a different way. We were treated to some of the most magnificent scenery we had yet experienced as we climbed Idaho Route 21 out of Boise. At the top of one of the early climbs, I wandered into the woods to answer nature's call. Having a young lady along, I was apprehensive to do so too close to the road, as I might if the party was all male. With Ken watching the bikes, I stepped a few dozen yards back into the woods and was surprised to see our first snow. Though it was a north facing slope and the elevation was over 8,000 feet, the sight of snow on a warm June afternoon was still a bizarre sight.

Even though it was late June, we found snow on a north facing, tree-covered slope above 6,000 feet. Anita is ducking because that white spot half way between us is a snowball aimed at her. Photo by Ken Steel.

Anita was a ways behind, and it gave us time to plot a snowball attack. Ken had his camera ready when she crested the hill and John and I left the snow fly, resulting in one of the trip's funniest photos. Ken's snapshot caught both the snowballs in mid-flight and Anita's shocked expression. Tom was still struggling up the climb and gave us time to repeat the prank on him. The greatest insult to Tom, however, was the dismay that overwhelmed him just a few moments later. It was evident he was whipped when he got to the top of the climb and was looking forward to the opportunity to catch his breath. As he started to dismount, Ken matter-of-factly declared that we better get moving if we wanted to get in the miles we had hoped to. Tom looked forlornly at his old friend. "Ken," he responded in disbelief, "I just got here." Ken reconsidered and generously gave Tom a few minutes, but just a few.

The only settlement of any kind we came across during the latter part of our day was the town of Lowman. We saw several places on the map along the route after Lowman that appeared to have camping provisions, the most inviting of which seemed to be Warm Springs. Had we known then what we would know a few hours later, we would have stocked up at Lowman. It was a beautiful ride along the South Fork of the Payette River. The Payette River was named after French-Canadian fur trapper François Payette, who traveled from Astoria, Oregon, to this region in 1818. He evidently followed much the same path we would traverse 160 years later and would head the Fort Boise trading post for the British Hudson's Bay Company from 1835-44. Payette was a friendly guy, well known for the assistance he gave to travelers coming through the fort. We could have used his help this day, as it was a demanding leg of the trip. After much climbing, we were getting anxious to settle in for the night. A turn off what looked like it might be Warm Springs turned out to be the gravel road to nowhere, and the ride back over the rough surface seemed twice as long.

Back to the highway, we finally found the turnoff for Warm Springs, a National Forest Service Campground. The road into the campground made the gravel one we had been on a half hour earlier look like the Autobahn. This road was a road only in the loosest sense of the term. A very fine light brown dust provided the base for fist-sized rounded rocks that seemed particularly well-suited to cracking rims, rather than providing a surface for them to ride over. I tried riding over the mess for a short distance and finally succumbed and pushed the bike much of the distance to the actual camp site. It would be the only stretch of road on the entire cross-country trip that I did not ride.

The campground brought more disappointment. Our map interpretation skills, clearly lacking on this day, led us to the assumption this was a place with food, water and bathroom provisions. We were wrong on all three counts. The facility was terribly run down and the one-hole privy was full to the brim. The water pump, not that awful far from the outhouse, generated a sediment-filled liquid that we suspected could have (at least at one point in its existence) been water. Though I was parched, I refused to drink the foul looking liquid. Ken boiled some over a campfire but, despite his assurances, I still could not bring myself to touch the stuff.

Especially following the trip up the dusty campground road, we were tired and dirty on top of being hungry and thirsty. Several of us had been talking about the prospect of a relaxing soak in the warm spring but could not find hide nor hair of that either. We asked a few of the other occupants what they knew about it and finally found a couple that had actually been to the spring. They directed us down the path and cautioned us that it was a long walk and the water was, indeed, very hot. Having looked forward to this with great anticipation all afternoon, John and I declared, by God, we were going to enjoy the spring or die trying. We threw our towels over our shoulders, grabbed our soap and headed down the path.

It was a longer walk than we would have suspected, just as our campground mates had conveyed. The path skirted the bottom of a steep mountainside following a tributary of the South Fork of the Payette River. While we agreed the canyon was breathtaking, we also knew what we wanted. "I'll be royally pissed if we can't swim in this," I declared as we walked along the stream of snow melt water. Finally, we caught a whiff of the tell-tale sulfur smell that accompanies geysers and hot springs. This was the first time either one of us had seen, or been around, a hot spring. We were struck by both the pungent smell and the extreme temperature. Soon after, we came across several wooden signs warning ambitious explorers of the dangerous 180 degree water.

John expressed a few choice words. "We walked all this way, rode up that miserable road, and then we can't even get in the water." I grumbled in agreement. But not ones to give up easily (especially after all we had gone through) we continued on. We opened the door to a crude wooden hut the hot water was flowing through, but it too was emitting water much too hot for bathing. Down the hill, where the hot spring water met the stream, we spied a man-made pool built from the rounded rocks and small boulders smoothed by erosion of the rushing creek. We stuck our foot in the pool of water and, to our uncontrollable delight, found perfect 110 degree water. The pool had been perfectly positioned to allow the near-freezing creek water to mix in just the right proportion with the 180 degree hot spring water.

John stripped and got in the water. I could not bring myself to strip to the buff and climbed into the pool in my underwear. John told me to be a rebel but I just couldn't cast aside the inhibition, even in this very remote location. After ruminating in the warm water for a spell, a rush of frigid creek water spilled into the pool. The drastic drop in the temperature prompted us to jump out of the water. Though we never saw anyone, we thought we heard a rustling in the brush and feared that some campground voyeur had been watching us in our scantily clad and naked states. But we would not be undone, not even with the threat of open lewdness charges by the Idaho State Police, and climbed back in again. I cannot recall precisely how long we soaked, but I do remember we stayed in the pool long enough to thoroughly wrinkle the skin on our fingertips.

We dried and worked our way back to the campground, able to temporarily forget the long and difficult ending to our day. The lack of potable water and the overloaded outhouse quickly brought us back to earth. Keeping with the pattern of misery that had been broken only by our soak in the hot spring pool, even our picnic table beds were shaky and on the smallish side. After another rough night's sleep, we awoke to a sunny sky that seemed to spark initial enthusiasm for the prospect of a better day.

But for me, several things were brewing that would turn that enthusiasm into despair. My water bottle and stomach were both empty. As we made our first major climb, my legs turned to mush. I could not remember ever feeling this bad on a bike, not even when I bonked on my first century ride three years before. It was so bad, Tom and Anita easily out-climbed me. At one point, I almost fell off the bike because I was turning the cranks so slowly. I was not only bonked from the low blood sugar but was also suffering from dehydration (or something darn close).

Stanley, the next town likely to have any provisions, was at least 25 miles away, and I did not know if I could make it. The climb was a long, grueling, and very slow one and the resulting downhill was the only thing that saved me from collapse. Stanley seemed like the proverbial one-horse town, but they did have a new general store and that was all I really cared about. I got a loaf of whole wheat bread, some orange juice and bananas, but I could not find any cheese. I asked the young man behind the counter if they sold cheese. After some initial confusion, he managed to find a block of American cheese in the meat cooler. Clearly this cheese cutting business was new to him and he fumbled with the package and the slicer for what seemed like ten minutes. He finally handed me a package of cheese wrapped up in white paper. We went to the wooden benches in front of the store and dug in to our most welcome lunch treats. I was so ungodly famished, I had jokingly said I could eat almost anything as I struggled up that first climb. I had not realized just how much I would be tested on that front, for when I opened the cheese, I was perplexed to find something extra attached to each slice. My confused cheese slicer did not understand that the plastic wrap around the cheese was supposed to be removed before the cheese was sliced. I needed food and a good laugh and Stanley, Idaho, was able to provide both.

A Mysterious Disappearance

"Lord! It's a miracle! Man up and vanished like a fart in the wind!"

—Warden Samuel Norton
The Shawshank Redemption
Castle Rock Pictures
(1994)

ANOTHER IN THE SEEMINGLY ENDLESS SERIES OF DIFFICULT mornings had taken a turn for the better after getting something to eat and drink in Stanley. Despite the threat of a shower, I appreciated the surrounding Sawtooth Mountains so much more after I got something in my stomach. Stanley, population 100 in a good year, sits in a basin where Idaho Routes 21 and 75 meet in the shadow of Thompson Peak, the highest point in the range.

Though sunny, the altitude helped keep the temperature cool and the differential heating of the mountain landscape provided a fertile environment for development of sometimes potent afternoon thunderstorms. The resulting instability brought highly variable cloudiness that finally generated a few showers as the day wore on. Riding south on Idaho 75 after our lunch stop, one such shower prompted our group to gather under a small outbuilding a few feet off the highway. Most days, Ken and I would lead the front of the group, John and Anita would dangle in the middle somewhere, and Tom would bring up the rear. We always tried to keep Anita in the middle so we could be sure she was doing okay. But at this stop, Anita never showed. Being certain she had been between the beginning and end of our stretched-out cycle train, we became worried when she seemed to disappear into thin air. I always thought the best in such a situation, and I had convinced myself there was a logical explanation. Anytime now we would find her stuck somewhere with a mechanical problem or sauntering up the road following a food or water break in the shade.

But as the minutes turned into an hour, even my eternal optimism turned to serious worry. Now my visions were of her unconscious in a ditch or kidnapped, tied up in the remote cabin of some looney mountain man. So we called the sheriff's office. After what seemed like hours more, Custer County Deputy Sheriff Carl Ellis met up with us and began the search for Anita. We backtracked down the road looking in every possible place she might have been and Sargent Ellis called the surrounding sheriff offices to see if anyone had any news.

As the afternoon approached early evening, we decided one or more of us should ride ahead to Sun Valley to see if Anita might have somehow or other ridden ahead. It was getting late, though, and our rough calculations told us it would be tough to get to the resort town before nightfall. The challenge was magnified by the fact that the highest highway summit in the Northwest sat between us and our destination.

It was already past 6:00 p.m., we guessed we were nearly 40 miles from Ketchum, and the 8,701-foot Galena Summit had to be conquered. Even though I felt good, I wondered if it was possible to make it. We were encouraged by two facts. We were nearing the edge of the time zone where Mountain Time stretched further west than any other spot in this part of North America, pushing sunset uncommonly late into the evening. And in a strange coincidence, it was also the summer solstice, the longest day of the year. I would need both of these advantages and the good fortune not to have any mechanical or physical problems.

In those youthful days, there were several times a year (a few times a month in my best years) I felt like I could ride up the toughest Tour de France climbs with Eddy Merckx. I never saw those days or rides coming; they just seemed to be bestowed upon me. On this otherwise disconcerting evening, all those physical, mental, mechanical, and environmental factors that figure into how well one rides converged to put me in the Zone. As the Sawtooth Basin yielded to the mountain, I began the climb of Galena Summit. I ascended it with ease, further pushed along by the truly breathtaking view at its peak as the sun faded lower into the evening sky. Somewhere between 7,000 and 8,000 feet, I found myself above the tree line as the road swept to the east. The incredible vistas were unobstructed. I climbed along the west flank of the mountainside, and to the east was the broad valley of the meandering Salmon River. The river snaked along in textbook fashion, one meander running into the next, forming small oxbow lakes and scarring the plain with abandoned river beds. After turning east and crossing the Salmon, the river faded toward the south and finally disappeared from view as I descended the other side of the mountain. Beyond the geomorphology lesson my landform professor Peirce Lewis would have thoroughly enjoyed, the river was almost surreal, glistening in the late day sunshine. The silence was broken only by the wind blowing by my ears and an occasional bird calling out as it rode the thermals along the mountainside.

I had already been blessed to see some incredible things in my 21 years and would see many more later in life, but that ride climbing up to Galena Summit was perhaps the most overwhelming and moving scenes I had witnessed. But amidst my feeling of ecstasy, both of my physical conquest and of the natural beauty before me, I felt cheated. My battle with the fading daylight meant that I did not have the time to stop and relish it all. Confident that Anita was safe up ahead somewhere, my worry faded for a moment and I cursed her for stealing this opportunity. Yet, I realized later that had we made this climb in mid or late afternoon, we would have seen the valley in the washed-out light of the high sun. In a strange twist of fate, her disappearance provided me with the opportunity to see the valley below the summit in the most extraordinary lights.

Someplace in Blaine County on my descent into Sun Valley, someone from one of the sheriff offices caught up to me to let me know they had found Anita. She was already snug and secure at the Sun Inn in downtown Ketchum. I was greatly relieved she was all right, but it did not take long for my relief to turn into annoyance. She had turned our day upside down, worried us beyond any anxiety we had ever experienced, and had three sheriff departments wandering all over central Idaho looking for her.

Despite my frustration, I pledged I was not going to let that ruin the remainder of my ride. I was, after all, in the midst of the most incredible descents of my life, following a climb of epic proportions, through some of the most awesome landscapes on the planet. I put my head down and pushed my biggest gear through the still warm and remarkably pristine early evening air. It was truly a sliver of heaven on Earth. Too frequently, those special moments in life are not fully appreciated until they are over. This was one that was clearly majestic as I experienced it. Whatever your perception of God may be, it was clear that He was riding with me that evening thoroughly enjoying his handiwork.

I rolled into Ketchum about 9:35 p.m. and there was still a bit of daylight despite the late hour. The Sun Inn was on the main street in Ketchum and it didn't take long for me to track down our wayward sister. When I told her the story of our day, she was understandably upset and apologized profusely. It turned out she had hitched a ride with a guy in a pickup, certain that she would be hard pressed to get to Ketchum on her own. Earlier in the day, Ken had stressed we had to make it to the resort town by day's end, if for no other reason, because there were not many other options. As my ride from Obsidian to Ketchum had proven, there was nothing but wilderness on that stretch of road in 1978.

Not long after I had started to Ketchum, Ken decided to give it a go, too. He hoped he might catch up to me, but my incredible ride made that impossible. When he got to town, fifteen minutes or so behind me and in complete darkness, he couldn't find either of us. Anita and I, unaware he was in town, walked over to a pizza shop for a late supper. The pizza place was a converted church, and it was packed from vestibule to sanctuary when we walked in. Anita and I, both famished, patiently waited in the pews near the front door. Once at our table, we proceeded to do what long distance bicyclists do well—eat like hogs. We ordered a large pizza and easily downed the entire pie in short order. We laughed that the opportunity to eat as much as you wanted anytime you cared was one of the great and often overlooked perks of endurance athletic endeavors.

Anita had gotten a room with space for the whole group, but it ended up being just the two of us. Under some circumstances, such an arrangement would have seemed scandalous, but the two of us were probably two of the straightest, clean-living twenty-somethings you could find. Beyond that, Anita and I had the classic platonic relationship. We were just two good friends that happened to be in the same motel room after a long day on the road (though much of her day on the road was seen from the comfort of a pickup truck). Having ridden 102 miles over some nasty climbs, I was dead tired and slept soundly in the quiet and comfort of a real bed. Even if I had been so inclined, I was far too exhausted to do anything but sleep. We slept in, knowing that John and Tom would be awhile catching up with us. We thought Ken would be with them, too, not knowing he had made the trip to Ketchum the night before. When Ken couldn't track us down, he found a motel not far from us that advertised hot spring showers.

With some spare time, I stopped at the bike shop in Ketchum, bought another water bottle, and replaced the pump that I had ruined swinging at the dog in the Oregon Coast Range. Though the bill was only $8.80, I was still miffed I had ruined a perfectly good pump on the bothersome mongrel that had chased after me.

Somehow, we all eventually found each other. We felt bad we had missed Ken, forcing him to spend money on a room when we had enough space for John Boy and the rest of the Walton family in ours. Anita's hitchhiking had managed to turn another day upside down but, like so many days, we would soon be laughing about yet another unexpected event. It was Ken that managed to take the edge off this time as he recounted his experience in the hot spring heated shower. His excitement over taking an earth-friendly geothermal shower collided with the reality that hot springs reek of sulfur. Whether it persisted that long or not, Ken would swear the aroma was still with him two days later.

Idaho 75 would take us south, out of the mountains and back toward the Snake River Valley. Our foray into this portion of the Northern Rockies was technically coming to an end. The magma that built the Idaho Batholith uplifted this section of the Rocky Mountains, much as the Sierra Nevadas were built in California. The granite that formed within the mountains is a durable, valuable building material likely to survive not just everyday wear and tear but probably thermonuclear war, too.

Coincidentally, we were wandering into the part of Idaho that had been part of the early development of thermonuclear weapons and energy. The next day we would ride just north of Atomic City (nearly a ghost town by 1978) and pass through Arco, home of the first nuclear breeder reactor that generated electricity in 1951. The legacy of mining in the area became an even bigger concern by the seventies. A lucrative silver, zinc and lead mine in the town of Triumph, just south of Ketchum, would become a toxic Superfund site in the nineties. Two massive piles of tailings and a deep mine sat near the East Fork of the Wood River, and lead and arsenic were detected in wetlands and groundwater in the area. Though the mine closed in 1957 after 75 years of mining activity, elevated levels of arsenic were found in the blood of nearby residents many years after the closure.[18]

Other than precious metals, this area is more obviously marked by its volcanic topography and geology. The Snake River Plain is a crescent shaped flatland south of the Idaho portion of the Rocky Mountains and is covered with lava rock. It also makes a trail that traces the eastward migration of the volcanic hot spot that now resides in and around Yellowstone National Park. It's why Old Faithful is so faithful. Though we were moving considerably faster than the 4.5 millimeters per year that the plate was sliding along, we would be following much the same route as the hot spot.

The first obvious sign of the volcanic activity were the lava fields spread along US 20. This was a vastly different landscape from the previous two days, both geologically and biologically. The alpine woodland had faded into a semi-desert. Such places, just like eastern Oregon, are often called deserts but do not actually meet the standards according to most climactic classification systems. Deserts are very dry places and this region does not meet that standard, averaging more than 15 inches of total precipitation and 50 inches of snow.

Yet, especially in midsummer, it's easy to see why people would call this a desert. From a biological standpoint, it is as devoid of vegetation as any true climatological desert. The relatively young volcanic soil (which really isn't even soil at all in many places) supports very little flora. Despite its lack of plant life, we would find out later it played host to more fauna than we might have otherwise suspected. In fact, it only took a few minutes at the campsite to realize how full of animal life this apparently barren landscape could be. The roads and campsites in the national park wandered through the rough and jagged lava rock (called aa) wherever a gap or lower spot could be found. The campsites themselves were stuck in a gravely, cinder-like soil among the nooks and crannies of the rocks. The rock was so porous that small animals could live in the voids, though they were initially invisible to the unsuspecting human guests.

Before settling down to eat, I decided to ride some of the trails and take a few pictures of the lava fields. Craters Loop Road roamed through the park, but the Park Service had also constructed asphalt trails well-suited for road bikes. It was not long, however, before I became unnerved by the unpleasant prospect of crashing into the jagged rocks. For the trails were narrow and the leg-lacerating rocks were sometimes actually jutting into the pathway. It occurred to me that the term "aa" may very well have originated from some poor South Pacific islander who had fallen onto the jagged-edged rocks, crying "ah, ah" as his skin was torn from his limbs.

We eventually settled in for the evening, partaking of our traditional mega-calorie repass at our campsite. Many small mammals and a few lizards scurried through the cavities of the lava rock, and it proved to be a source of amusement to us, at least for that moment. Once we bedded down for the night, the bewilderment turned to annoyance. An endless parade of critters scurried from one place to another, and it was unnerving for those sleeping on the ground especially. John bounded from his sleeping bag at one point, frantically brushing his clothes and hair and exclaiming, "It feels like there's a highway going by my head!"

I claimed one of the picnic tables (as I did on most nights) to sleep on and thought at first I would not be bothered by the furious flurry of fauna beneath me. It so happened, though, that someone had carelessly left a plastic peanut butter container lid on the ground below my head, and one of the moles latched onto it and started chewing after we were all snuggled in our bags. This proved to be the most amusing of all the animal frivolity surrounding us, and everyone was soon shining their flashlights on the little rodent enjoying his own private nocturnal picnic treat.

Enjoying their fill of the entertaining scene, the group returned to their sleeping bags and the critter ran off into the rocks, taking his tasty possession with him. I did not realize initially that this would have repercussions that would drag well into the night. The mole took the lid into the aa just beyond my head and proceeded to chew and gnaw on the plastic for what seemed like hours. Tired as I was, the constant chomping kept me awake for a long time. After an atypically wonderful night's sleep the evening before at the motel in Ketchum, sleep did not come easily this night. Not even through our second state, sleep deprivation seemed to have become the standard for the trip.

Next Gas 43 Miles

"We ride unnoticed down this empty highway through this strange country I've never seen before, and now a heavy feeling of isolation and loneliness becomes dominant and my spirits wane with the sun."

—Robert M. Pirsig
Zen and the Art of Motorcycle Maintenance
HarperTorch Books (1974)

IT WAS IMPOSSIBLE TO GET MAD AT TOM BALDWIN. HE HAD been struggling to keep track of some of his belongings, and each time he lost something else, his role as the tragic hero was further confirmed. His proclivity to lose things was perhaps a function of the fact he had brought so much with him. He lost his riding gloves on the ride into Craters of the Moon, adding to his general frustration the trip was more tedium than adventure.

I had not lost things like Tom, but like everyone else on the trip, I had my share of difficulties. Though this had not been a trying day when compared to the rest of the first week, I was nevertheless frustrated when the cleats fell off my cycling shoes. This might seem like a small detail to some, but it was so much more efficient and comfortable when the shoe was secure in the old style pedals and toe clips.

Each day brought some sort of anxiety with it, even if things were otherwise going well. This day's concerns centered on a barren stretch of road east of Craters of the Moon National Park. Ken was prone to understating the severity of just about everything, so when he told us it was a particularly long and deserted stretch, we took notice. Our anxiety turned to near panic when we came to the sign that read,

"Next Gas 43 Miles." The scope of this desolation could not be fully appreciated until it was experienced first-hand, for there was nothing in those 43 miles except a bunch of sagebrush and a run-down roadside rest near the halfway point. The State of Idaho was kind enough to provide non-potable water at the meager way-station in case of an overheated automobile engine. While my engine was pretty darn hot by the time we got to the rest area, all I could drink was the tepid water in my own bottle.

Having grown up in the northeast United States, such desolation seemed incomprehensible. While this was the most extreme case, we would later realize many of the towns in Wyoming and Nebraska were small islands of human activity separated by a sea of sagebrush or grassland devoid of any man-made features beyond the berm of the highway. This particular stretch of desolation, however, had an interesting story that went beyond the sagebrush. We didn't think too much about it as we passed to the south, but this wasteland was part of the nuclear legacy left by the federal government in the forties and fifties. The death and destruction associated with the bombs dropped on Hiroshima and Nagasaki were still fresh in the minds of many Americans and the push to find "peaceful" uses for the atom was in full swing. This sort of isolated, out-of-the-way place was ideal for the experimental work many still feared could bring a rain of nuclear fallout upon them. The National Reactor Testing Station, about 20 miles from the town of Arco, was built in 1949 and its reactor was installed two years later. Just before Christmas 1951, the facility became the first to generate electricity made by a nuclear reactor.[19]

Two years later, President Dwight Eisenhower gave his "Atoms for Peace" speech, kicking off our stumbling venture down the nuclear power trail. Two years later, the Idaho facility experienced a partial meltdown of its core, the first in a series of "almost" catastrophes that beset the nuclear power industry. Like the Three Mile Island accident a quarter century later, the 1955 accident was attributed to "operator error." The "operator error" rationalization always seemed to somehow excuse the inherent danger of the material the industry used and produced. It wasn't the radioactive and deadly plutonium we should fear, after all, it was those silly operators who were unable to deal with it.

What's more, they had no idea what to do with the radioactive waste in 1951, and remain similarly perplexed more than a half century later. It seemed clear to me the industry was always ahead of itself, never quite sure how to handle the extraordinarily high temperatures of the reactions or the overwhelmingly toxic and radioactive nature of their waste. Yet we blindly plowed ahead, starting right there in Eastern Idaho in 1951.

The desolation and related boredom of the landscape was finally interrupted by two interesting geologic features that would become, quite literally, the butt of a class joke in my Earth Science classes for years to come. As we passed the dirt road turnoff to the near-ghost town of Atomic City, the Twin Buttes could be seen on the horizon. These two cinder cone volcanoes were about the same size, each rising about 1,000 feet above the plain over which we were riding. From the right angle, the two peaks, now rounded by erosion, took the shape of two buttocks. Coupled with the fact that many of my ninth-grade students in Pennsylvania had never heard the word butte (with a long U), and it's easy to see why these later became "Twin Butts" in Mr. Frederick's Earth Science classes. In reality, these two cones were the next features left behind by the migrating hot spot that built the volcanic cones and lava fields we had been riding through for the previous five days.

Though uneventful (which was nice for a change), June 23, 1978 may have been the most desolate and scenically unpleasant days of my cycling and hiking life. Such isolation in the mountains usually translated into breathtaking scenery, but in eastern Idaho (and we would later find out in eastern Wyoming), it meant only sagebrush and wind-blown sand.

If the Phone Doesn't Ring, It's Me

—Jimmy Buffett
"If the Phone Doesn't Ring, It's Me"
From the *Last Mango in Paris*
MCA Records (1985)

WE WERE OVERJOYED WHEN WE SAW SIGNS OF IDAHO FALLS in the distance. A tailwind had turned into a strong crosswind in the final miles, but we had made good time nonetheless. The KOA campground was just a few blocks from the square where the falls fell. The falls themselves could have been aesthetically pleasant, but a manmade dam and a gaudy sign spoiled the site. The campsite was not the most scenic or luxurious either, and our campground neighbors added an unpleasant ambience to our end of the campground. Before the neighboring crew unpacked a single thing from their car, we were overwhelmed by the smell of dirty, wet dogs. Coupled with the fact that some of our group had not had a cooked meal since we were in Boise four days before, we decided against eating on the shaky table next to the soggy and aromatic dogs. Freshly showered (unlike our neighbors), we decided we really deserved a night out and went to a nice restaurant we had seen across from the falls.

We parked the bikes out front and strolled into the restaurant to find a distinctly sixties motif. Red vinyl covered chairs surrounded round tables, each with a single red phone in the middle. A waitress brought menus and ice water and quickly retreated to the kitchen. We all made our selection from the menu and waited patiently for the waitress to return. And we waited. And we waited some more.

After what seemed like an eternity, the waitress motioned to us from the kitchen door.

"What's she trying to tell us?" I asked.

"I think she wants us to call her," Anita speculated.

"Call her? Call her what?" someone joked.

"Call her on the hotline to the Kremlin," somebody else concluded.

Tom Baldwin, he of quick, dry wit, raised his eyebrows in disbelief and simply said, "Oh my."

We had found the red phone (with no dial) peculiar when we first arrived and joked that it looked like the infamous red phone that connected the White House to the Kremlin. After the visual hint from the waitress, we urged Tom, who was nearest the phone, to pick it up. We could faintly hear it ring in the kitchen and the waitress promptly answered it.

"Can I take your order?"

"This is how we order?" Tom asked.

"Yes, that's why each table has a phone."

"Yea, we were wondering about that. You'll have to forgive us. You see, we're from Pennsylvania." By this time, we were laughing so hard the tears were rolling down our cheeks.

Tom placed his order and passed the phone on. When the phone came to me, I eagerly ordered the eggplant parmigiana. Hungry as a horse and looking forward to a real meal, I savored each bite. I nostalgically recalled a similar evening meal (but without the phone) three years before in Boyertown, Pennsylvania, as Brian Weakland had finished his cross-country trip. I had come many miles, and in many ways, between those two tasty eggplant meals.

As we exited the restaurant across from the falls, we were again struck by how different this part of the Snake River was when compared to the scenic canyons on the other side of the state. The Snake River's most famous and scenic portions cut deep gorges through the plateaus of ancient lava flows. But in Idaho Falls, the shallow river mostly cuts into sedimentary rock from alpine glaciers and river deposits. Ironically, the Snake now washes away the same sediments it laid down.

Idaho Falls is one of the last communities along the Snake River

Plain that owes its existence to the river or one of its nearby tributaries. The influence of a river on settlement and growth is seen along the Snake as profoundly as we can see it anywhere in the United States. More than half the state's population is in or around the river cities of Boise, Pocatello, and Idaho Falls, and nine of the ten biggest cities owe their existence to the Snake.

Idaho had experienced a population growth of more than 30 percent in the seventies, and the cities and their suburbs experienced growing pains. Despite this growth, Idaho and neighboring Wyoming remained as white and conservative as they always had been. Even their early growth was predominated by those same demographics, post-Civil War growth being dominated by conservative southern and Midwestern Democrats. As the Republican Party became more conservative, the political allegiances in both states swung accordingly to reflect the deeply conservative politics. Only once between 1960 and 2016 did a Democratic presidential candidate win either state, Lyndon Johnson taking Idaho and Wyoming in 1964 by the slimmest of margins.

These politically conservative leanings would often be in direct opposition to environmental conservation of the region. Preservation of what would become Grand Teton National Park was met with considerable local opposition and would be embroiled in controversy until the park was expanded in 1950 to include much of the valley floor. Philanthropist John D. Rockefeller had established a land holding company in the late twenties to quietly acquire land to be handed over to the Park Service, and it was that 35,000 acres that became the basis of the 1950 expansion.

Our path to Jackson Hole and onto Grand Tetons went through Targhee National Forest, established by Teddy Roosevelt in 1908, and it would go over the southern end of the Tetons, a massive block faulted mountain range. The crescent shaped lava fields and endless miles of sagebrush and sand of the Snake River Plain came to an abrupt end as we approached Wyoming and the Tetons. Short of adding at least a half day of additional riding, there was no easy way to go east. Two separate mountains, separated by one brief respite, covered almost 30 miles. The second was a particularly steep twelve-mile ascent over

Teton Pass. When even Ken, the King of Understatement, described a climb as very long and difficult, there was reason to be wary.

Like much of the Rocky Mountain system, what we saw and climbed in 1978 was a remnant of much bigger mountains. This particular range had been block faulted, the initial elevation change perhaps as much as 30,000 feet from the top of the block to the bottom of the resulting valley to the east. This impressive uplift, a relatively recent occurrence 13 million years ago, unearthed 2.5-billion-year-old metamorphic rocks on the east side of the Tetons. These same rocks are buried deep beneath Jackson Hole. This burial is even deeper than what would have been caused by the faulting alone since the valley was being filled by the erosion of the still-rising mountains.

As I climbed the worst of the ascent, I was especially grateful we had not come along a few tens of millions of years earlier in this process. The initial parts of the climb were tough (even with at least 30 million years' worth of erosion), but the end was longer and steeper than anything I had ever ascended. The last twelve miles from the town of Victor to the top climbed 2,217 feet, and it would take me an hour and fifteen minutes. The last eight miles pitched up most dramatically, ascending more than 250 feet per mile to the top of the pass at 8,431 feet above sea level. I was used to steep Pennsylvania climbs, but the very steepest portions of those were rarely more than two miles. This one was four times that length. Carrying close to 20 pounds of additional gear, it was an overwhelming climb. I stood up when the worst part began, and my backend never hit the saddle the rest of the way—at least five miles. I did not think I could keep the pedals turning if I sat down. I also suspected that if I stopped, I would not be able to get started again.

Long before this climb, I had resolved I would not walk one step of the actual cross-country ride. So it was incumbent upon me to keep stomping on the pedals and not stop until I reached the summit. Any climbing is tough on the lower back, but this extraordinary effort was excruciatingly painful. I had trained hard for the racing season, but this ride put me in more sustained pain than I had ever experienced in any athletic endeavor. When I would come to the final sweeping curve on lesser ascents back home, the end was near. But the magnitude of this climb, coupled with being above the tree line, meant there were nearly two miles to go when I came around the last bend. And the whole thing was laid out there right in front of me.

When I finally got to the top, I couldn't get off the bike fast enough. With my heartrate still through the roof, I looked back down the road to see how far back everybody was. I couldn't see a soul (and I could see a long way). Finally, after a few minutes, I saw Ken, a tiny speck on the road, coming around the far-off final bend. He would finish the climb nearly fifteen minutes after me but more than 20 minutes ahead of John and Tom and a full half hour ahead of Anita.

My average speed over those last twelve miles was just under ten miles per hour and Ken's was just a bit over eight, but we still knew we had done an incredible ride. Anita had decided she was not so proud and would walk part of the climb if it became too overwhelming. While still showing signs of fatigue, she was unquestionably the least taxed of the group when she got to the top. John and Tom were quite the opposite. They were riding nearly side by side when they came into our view. Tom had been saved by his extremely low gearing, which made the steep climb a bit less daunting. As the slope steepened one last time in that last half mile, John decided he had enough and surged in an attempt to win their derby to the top. As he moved ahead, he tried to grab his water bottle and dropped it onto the pavement. The quiet of the desolate mountain pass was broken by John's scream of frustration.

"I've got you now," Ken and I could hear Tom chuckle from our ringside seat atop the mountain.

John would not go down without a fight. It was difficult to get restarted on the steep slope, but he finally managed to get himself upright and the race was on again. Though contrary to Tom's riding style to accelerate with resolve, he gave it his best shot and opened a gap over the frustrated young man a dozen years his junior. Ken and I were treated to what was perhaps the most exciting bike race ever waged at seven miles per hour. John caught and passed Tom a few dozen yards before the summit and we collectively had another hearty laugh, John and Tom still gasping for air as they did so.

From the summit of Teton Pass above Jackson Hole, Wyoming, I photographed John Mencke and Tom Baldwin struggling up the pentultimate switchback of the very long climb that actually began in Idaho.

The sign at the top of Teton Pass read "Howdy stranger, Yonder is Jackson Hole, Last of the Old West." We would come to realize when we actually arrived that nothing could be further from the truth. Before we came to witness the inaccuracy of the sign, we had an incredible descent into the valley. The mountain had been uplifted so as to make the western climb similar to a partially-raised drawbridge.[20] So the dramatic drop down the other side guaranteed this would be a brisk ride. Ken further cautioned us that our heavy bikes would make the descent even faster. He reminded us to use our brakes with discretion, as rims could overheat and tires burst if we kept them on continuously. It was, indeed, a remarkable, high-speed descent through hairpin turns and stunning alpine scenery.

Before arriving in Jackson, we passed through the town of Wilson and again crossed the Snake River, not many miles from the source of the 1,040-mile-long river. Here the Snake is a braided river, much different in form than it is through the basaltic plateaus of Hells Canyon or the monotonous desolation of eastern Idaho. A broad plain (like the Jackson Hole basin) sitting below large mountains provide ideal conditions for massive amounts of sediment to be deposited, but not necessarily washed away. River bars form, and the waterway becomes an intertwined, ever-changing mess of braided streams.

While we would be somewhat disappointed by the commercialization of the city of Jackson, the scenery we saw on the mountain and then through the edge of the valley was as figuratively breathtaking as the actual descent was literally breathtaking. Though the sign at the top of the pass claimed this was the "Old West," the town itself looked like the prototypical tourist trap. It even included the simulated gun fight six nights a week, just in case you had any doubts. Three US routes shared the main street through town, and the traffic reflected both the number of routes and the level of tourism that plagued the city. We spotted Kampark in the heart of town and decided that some nasty weather on the horizon made the otherwise touristy place a bit more attractive.

Like so often happens in many parts of the Rockies, thermal convection from the heating of day produced some impressive thunderheads, and one was moving toward us. From the front porch of the store we could see the dark and ominous clouds descending as if someone was pulling a gray blanket over the entire valley. When it finally arrived, it brought more wind than rain. It would be the most violent windstorm I had ever experienced, and its descent upon us was surreal as it came over the steep eastern face of the Teton Range and showered us with dirt and dust.

If it looks cold on this shot, it's because it was. It snowed on these peaks in the Tetons the day we went through the park and the temperture was in the low forties even where we were riding in the valley. Photo by John Frederick.

After the storm passed, I found a Catholic Church for Saturday evening mass. It wasn't until I returned to the campground that I fully realized this was one of those dreadful urban campgrounds similar to the one I had tolerated in Las Vegas five years before. The sites were on top of each other without tree cover and very little grass. To make matters worse, we found ourselves with difficult camping neighbors for the second night in a row. Before the night progressed very far, we came to long for the stinky couple and their dogs in Idaho Falls.

Drinking to excess, our Jackson neighbors were loud, rude, and still going strong at 2:00 a.m. Sunrise awoke me after less than four hours of sleep. Our drunken neighbors were sleeping soundly.

Unbeknownst to us, the windstorm the previous night had been brought courtesy of a cold front and upper level low pressure system that was now settling right over eastern Idaho and western Wyoming. The weather got worse as we progressed northward. A look at the historic weather maps of the day showed the weather was coming from the Gulf of Alaska, and coupled with higher altitude, spelled a meteorological nightmare for a group of bicyclists ill-prepared for winter weather in June.

It never got out of the forties and I was chilled to the bone despite wearing every article of clothing I could pull on. When one of my riding partners took my picture at the continental divide (usually a pleasant and momentous occasion) I had a look of disgust that testified to my frustration. Shortly after noon, John Mencke and I stopped at Moose Village Visitor Center, deciding we would wait there until the temperature hit 50. Instead, we watched the visitor center's thermometer drop from 46 to 42 while we waited. Under other circumstances, the day's ride would have been among the most beautiful of the trip. With snow falling on the mountains to the west and a stiff north wind in our face, it was breathtaking for all the wrong reasons.

Late in the afternoon, we arrived in Flagg Ranch, just two miles south of Yellowstone's southern gate. Flagg Ranch had its beginnings as the Snake River Military Station and served that purpose until about 1905. The camp could be spotted by the flags flying over it, so its first owner decided to call it Flagg Ranch. Why the second "g" was added is a mystery.

Ken went into the office to talk with some of the staff to ascertain how things were up the road. Though we wondered about the distance to our next camping options, we were more concerned about the weather. They confirmed the bad news that it was indeed snowing ahead and advised us to get a cabin there at the resort. After a particularly trying day, one that fell far short of our lofty expectations, we were consoled to find the cabin to be charming, comfortable, and, perhaps most importantly, warm.

The three beds were well-suited for our group, Ken and Tom sharing one, John and I another, and a third single bed for Anita. As we started preparing for a good night's sleep, Tom unrolled his sleeping bag and threw it on the floor.

"What are you doing, Tom?" Ken asked.

"Getting ready for bed," he answered.

"We got two doubles so we would all have a bed," Ken explained.

"Oh my, no, Ken. I could never sleep with anyone," Tom told his old friend.

"I can't let you do that, Tom. I'll sleep on the floor. You need a good night's rest," Ken continued, surely realizing the slowest rider of our group could use every edge he could muster.

"No, no. I'm fine. I often sleep on the floor," Tom replied with a straight face, in the sort of typical Tom Baldwin reply that got us all laughing again.

Rocky Mountain Way

—Joe Walsh
"Rocky Mountain Way"
From the album *The Smoker You Drink the Player You Get*
ABC Records (1973)

THE AIR AT 8,000 OR 9,000 FEET DOESN'T LOOK ANY DIFferent than air at sea level. Any athlete that has been taken to elevations above a mile will attest to the profound difficulty of performing and breathing at that altitude. Over 7,000 feet or so, folks that are not so well-conditioned will find it difficult to do much of anything that requires much exertion. Believing that I was the best conditioned of the group, I had little anxiety about riding in the mountains. With the exception of the infamous morning after the Warm Springs fiasco when I had not eaten or drunk anything, I was otherwise the first one to the top of every climb we had tackled. So I thought I had proven I was immune to the maladies of the mile and a half high mountains.

But after brushing my teeth before bedtime, my nose started to bleed profusely. Not having had the experience before, I made no connection between the altitude and the sudden cascade of blood. Headaches and nosebleeds, it turned out, are two of the most common things that happen to people when they are affected by the thin air. The very dry air and lower air pressure (resulting in your blood pressure being relatively higher) conspire to make these nosebleeds much more common at altitude. After I got the bleeding stopped, I hoped to settle down for a long winter's nap. I was to be foiled, though, as we started to talk and laugh about the trip in general and the day's craziness in particular. Like a bunch of silly adolescents, we laughed again until we cried. At one point, Tom peered up at us from his nest on the cabin floor.

"Oh, my," he gasped between snorts of laughter, "I can't tell you how much fun these crazy conversations are at the end of each day. It's just the other 23 hours of stuff in between that I can't take." This made us laugh all the harder.

Unfortunately, Tom was completely serious about the frustrations of those other 23 hours, and it was this day he decided he finally had enough. Even though he chuckled about how refreshing his sponge baths were, the days on end without a shower alone could drive one crazy. Add that inconvenience to the demands of the terrain, the lousy weather, and the short nights of sleep, and it could be torturous.

Anita felt much the same. "I just can't stand the day after dayness of it all," she lamented as she rationalized her decision to head home the next day. I was saddened by the development but not particularly surprised. John and I persisted in part because of our stubbornness, not because we were having the time of our life. That said, it prompted me to take stock of where we were, what we had experienced and whether or not it had been worth the trouble. Despite the "day after dayness" Anita had so accurately described, it had been a most amazing journey and I would not miss the rest of it, no matter how miserable the weather, how rough the road, or how sore my backside became.

Ken had to be back at work in a few days, so he had already planned to catch the train back to Pennsylvania. Tom and Anita were riding to Billings or Livingston to catch the train east. When morning arrived, John and I decided to wait for a while in hopes things would warm up. Morning also brought me a special gift to add to my already considerable frustration. Whether altitude sickness or bad water from somewhere on the road, I had developed gastrointestinal distress of the most unpleasant proportions.

After a 9:15 a.m. departure, seven miles out, we stopped for another hour, fed up with my upset stomach, the cold, the poor road, and intolerable traffic. I had read about the concerns over the degradation of the National Park experience in the most popular parks because of the overwhelming traffic congestion. But it could not be fully appreciated until I was forced to experience it in person.

About 20,000 visitors came through Yellowstone every day at that time of year, and 5,000 of them came through the same South Entrance John and I would enter. An inordinate portion of them seemed to be in motor homes. An alarming number (or so our anecdotal experience would indicate) were ill prepared to drive them down a straight road, let alone on the harrowing serpentine highways along the steep cliffs that climbed onto the Yellowstone Plateau. Keeping in mind the vast majority of those drivers drove sedans most of the time, it was a miracle more of them did not plummet over the cliffs or send several bicyclists to their deaths.

The snow flies later and stays longer on the Tetons and other nearby Rocky Mountain ranges. We lifelong Pennsylvanians never grew accustomed to summer snow, but still enjoyed the scenic landscapes they presented. Photo by John Frederick.

Beyond being challenged by their overall size and weight, the drivers of these behemoths also forgot how long they were. Most left little margin for error when they passed us and then moved back into their lane much too quickly. To make matters worse, many left their side steps extended, evidently thinking they could break the cyclist's left ankle if they missed with the body of the motor home.

I suppose in an effort to make the landscape appear as natural as possible, the National Park Service avoided guardrails on some stretches of park highways. Many roads in National Parks, Skyline Drive in Virginia being a good example, utilized rock walls using native stone to provide a degree of roadside security. But many western parks simply sat boulders along some of the steep cliff sides. These rocks would have conceivably been able to slightly slow a wayward auto or motor home. They were usually so far apart, however, odds favored that a cyclist would either miss them all together or run into them headfirst, being thrown forward off the bike into the great abyss.

So rather than this being the awesome natural experience it could and should have been, the 22-mile ride through the southern portion of Yellowstone was at times a nightmare. Three fourths of the park visitors entered via entrances relatively close to Old Faithful with the intent of seeing the world's most famous geyser. As we figured this out, we wondered if we should avoid that part of the park all together. As each mile passed on our journey northward, we became more convinced the visit to Old Faithful simply would not be worth the trouble.

This made me melancholy even many years later. It infuriated me in 1978. It was bad enough that one of the most amazing places on earth was overrun with cars and recreational vehicles. That those hoping to experience the area in a more environmentally sensitive manner would be driven away seemed to be the height of injustice. My utopian park would be one with thousands of bikes and dozens of motor vehicles (instead of just the opposite). The elimination of recreational vehicles the size of small houses would be a big step in the right direction. After all, if you intend to enjoy nature, a modest sacrifice to assure you don't undermine that experience for everyone else seems to be a reasonable concession. Beyond the struggles with the traffic, I remained sick in the stomach the entire day. Despite devouring Pepto Bismol tablets like they were candy, I couldn't get off the bike fast enough each time we came to a bathroom.

We turned eastward when we came to the crossroads at West Thumb, the western inlet of Yellowstone Lake. Our hope had become reality and the majority of the overwhelming traffic had indeed turned west to visit Old Faithful. It remained cold and I was still under the weather, but the decrease in traffic and incredible view along the north shore of Yellowstone Lake gave us a new outlook. Despite that, we could not forget how miserable the first 25 miles had been and decided we would get out of the park as quickly as was practical.

A Close Encounter

"Every creature is better alive than dead, men and moose and pine trees, and he who understands it aright will rather preserve its life than destroy it."

—Henry David Thoreau
The Maine Woods
Published by Ticknor and Fields (1864)

THE RIDE ALONG YELLOWSTONE LAKE WAS BEAUTIFUL AND a long stop at Fishing Bridge was every bit as amazing as everyone told us it would be. Everywhere I looked from the bridge was wildlife. It looked like a spread in *National Geographic* or *Sierra* magazine. Bison. Elk. Moose. There were too many to count. So relaxed (or perhaps exhausted) as we sat on a bench watching, I fell asleep in the warming mid-day sun.

At 7,735 feet, Lake Yellowstone is the largest alpine lake in the United States. Even though it freezes over each winter, subsurface geothermal activity produces hot spots of over 200 degrees Fahrenheit. The lake is the result of the last of three calderas (or volcanic craters) to be created in the Yellowstone basin over the last few million years. This last one formed the basin for the lake just over 600,000 years ago. It was partially filled in by subsequent lava flows but is still nearly 400 feet deep.[21]

A long climb out of the lake basin took us to just a few hundred feet shy of 9,000 feet. The long descent followed Middle Creek until it met the North Fork of the Shoshone River, and it was every bit as beautiful as the ride along the lakeshore. The invigorating downhill and amazing landscape helped me forget, at least for a while, that I was sick as a dog.

Just short of 9,000 feet, my bike leans against the Sylvan Pass sign marking one of the highest elevations on the trip. The pass is just east of Fishing Bridge and Yellowstone Lake near the east entrance to the national park. Photo by John Frederick.

The road went along the North Fork through the Wapiti Valley, named after the town of the same name between Yellowstone and Cody. A testimony to how profoundly environments can vary over time, fossil findings along the river and its tributaries show that this was a turtle paradise and that crocodile-like creatures also called it home about 50 million years before we rode through.[22] The river had carved a deep valley that laid among a number of massive mountain peaks in the Absaroka Range, Fortress Mountain (12,085 feet) to our south and Sleeping Giant Mountain (11,193 feet) to our north being the two most notable. The Absaroka divided the Yellowstone highlands from the Big Horn Basin to the east. The range's name comes from an Indian term meaning "children of the large-beaked bird." In a slightly botched translation, it gave rise to the English name of the Indian tribe: the Crow.

Though still a beautiful landscape, the Absarokas do not enjoy the scenic notoriety of other parts of the Rocky or Cascade Mountain systems. Their volcanic rocks are easily eroded compared to the resistant granites seen in so many other parts of the Mountain West. Though the range was glaciated, the poorly consolidated rocks show little of the evidence one might observe in places like Glacier or Yosemite National Parks, with their dramatic U-shaped valleys or proliferate glacial lakes. While perhaps not as spectacular as the more famous ranges, the high peaks on either side of the valley and the river rushing along the road still made for a splendid ride.

We ended up in the Three Miles United States Forest Service campground at a place called Pahaska Tepee just a few miles (I presume three) beyond the eastern entrance to Yellowstone. The campground was a stark contrast to the busy and crowded facilities in Yellowstone. We were the lone human beings (for as far as we could see at least) in the remote campground. Though that isolation was a relief after the hectic beginning to our day, it was also a bit unnerving since we were still in grizzly bear territory. We made a small fire and I cooked some rice in my Sierra Cup, hoping the bland food would settle my upset stomach.

The Sierra Cup was itself an interesting story. An eight-ounce cup with a slotted handle that could be slipped through a belt while backpacking, it had been around since the early part of the twentieth century. Countless outdoor adventurers had used the cup over the previous three quarters of a century. One can be seen on the belt of renowned nature photographer Ansel Adams in pictures from early in his career. The authentic model had the words "Sierra Club" stamped on the bottom of the stainless steel cup. In my hopes of carrying as little as possible on my cross-country adventure, I had opted for the Sierra Cup instead of a full mess kit. And trust me, it was not easy to cook rice in such a small "pan." I meticulously cleaned out the cup and wiped off the concrete picnic table (three times) after eating supper. I did not want to see a bear staring me in the face looking for leftovers in the middle of the night. Years later, the Forest Service would forbid tent camping, allowing only hard-sided campers, at Three Miles Campground because the problems with grizzlies had become so serious. I'm not sure if I'm happy or disappointed I didn't know that at the time.

As we finished cleaning up our supper, we did spot an animal that looked like a horse coming up from the creek across the clearing, just a silhouette in the fading daylight.

"There must be a ranch of some sort nearby," I speculated.

"That's odd," John added. "We're in a National Forest. Do you think there are some wild horses running around these parts?"

"That would be neat if there were."

"Oh, look, there's a colt with the mother," John noticed.

"Holy shit!" I gasped as quietly as one could exclaim such surprise. "It's not a horse; it's a moose."

Neither of us had ever seen a moose up close in the wild and we were shocked by the animal's size. Hoping not to spook it, we grabbed our cameras, naively optimistic we'd have enough light to get a picture of the creatures, now just a couple dozen feet from us. We felt certain everyone would think this just another "Big Fish" story unless we had photographic proof of the beast. In retrospect, we probably got closer than we really should have. Like all animals, defense of their young is a high priority for moose, and this mother moose could have kicked or butted the daylights out of us. But the two animals were about as nonchalant as they could be, gazing our way only once or twice for a few moments and then moseying off into the dusky light of the early evening.

By this time, light was fading quickly in the shadows of the trees and we realized we needed to settle down for the night. Keeping the bears in mind, we placed everything that contained food as high up in the trees as we could conveniently climb and reach. In my paranoia, I also opted to look for another place to sleep rather than the picnic table on which we had eaten. I dug my net hammock out of my bag and found two trees to connect it to. Naively thinking I would string it up and doze off into a blissful night's sleep, I threw my sleeping bag onto the swinging contraption and climbed in. The bag sagged despite my best efforts to string it up as tightly as I could. Like hammocks everywhere, it swayed to and fro, no matter how hard I tried to lie still. Like far too many nights on the trip, I found myself lying awake in the middle of the night, wondering how I would ride another hundred miles the next day in my sleep-deprived state. When I finally gave up on sleeping as the sun tried to shine through the forest canopy, a chilly dew covered everything. Though it was the end of June, we were still 7,000 feet above sea level, and the mornings here in the summer were much cooler than the same latitude in the lower elevations of the Central Plains. We would find out how much warmer it could get just a couple thousand feet lower in eastern Wyoming a few days later.

Though the campground at Pahaska Tepee was not near as famous as Old Faithful or some of the other well-known spots in Yellowstone, we were glad our journey had taken us there. The canopy of trees, the pungent smell of the pines, and the quiet of this isolated place almost erased the images of the parade of recreational vehicles we tolerated the day before.

Not far from the campground was Buffalo Bill Cody's Lodge, the more famous part of Pahaska Tepee. Built in 1904, Cody saw it as an opportunity to capitalize on the growing fascination with the West in general and the recently dedicated Yellowstone National Park in particular. I'm not sure we even knew the lodge was there, but it likely would not have mattered; we had splurged for a lodge two nights before and would have thought that two nights in a row was beyond our means.

When we started out on Tuesday morning, we did not fully appreciate how the landscape, topography, vegetation, and our related demeanor would change so dramatically by the day's end. Happening so gradually that it was easy to miss the subtle changes, the trees became fewer and fewer as we descended from nearly 7,000 feet and left Shoshone National Forest. The North Fork of the Shoshone River was the feature that tied the changing landscape together and provided for a scenic ride even as the rest of the roadside was turning to sagebrush and rocky hillsides. By the time we got to Cody, the mountains were fading into the western horizon. By contrast, to the east, we were overcome by gaudy billboards and a proliferation of tourist traps of every size, shape and description, almost all of them with a reference to old Buffalo Bill Cody himself.

Cody was certainly Buffalo Bill's town; even the reservoir formed at the juncture of the north and south forks of the Shoshone River bore his name. The Shoshone had been called the Stinking Water River only 70 years before, thanks to the hot springs and fumaroles found in the region. One of the few notable features that was not named after Buffalo Bill was the center of that geothermal activity, Colter's Hell. When mountain man John Colter passed through the "stinky water" in the winter of 1807-1808, he made note of the extensive geothermal hell-raising that was going on. The reservoir submerged many of the hot springs and geysers, and several of the remaining larger features had become inactive, only their cones remaining to confirm Colter's observations.

Once we left the river valley outside of Cody, the landscape was transformed from a tourist trap theme to a stark one out of an old black and white cowboy movie. The cross-wind west of Cody became a brisk headwind as we turned south toward Meeteetse on Idaho Route 120. The stretch between Cody and Meeteetse was another one of those stretches of desolation that were so common in the more arid parts of the West. This one was 30 miles. About halfway between the two towns, the skies started to darken. Perhaps five or six miles from the town of Meeteetse, it became painfully evident the dark clouds were bringing a nasty thunderstorm that we couldn't avoid. In the middle of no-man's land, I decided to make a run for it. Meeteetse was in sight, but I had learned that in this landscape, being "in sight" didn't mean much.

The skies opened up in a way that I had experienced only a few times in my life, and never while out in the open on a bike. Still probably three miles from the nearest shelter in town, the storm pelted me with hail and gusting winds that threatened to toss me into the roadside ditch. Though I was extremely concerned over my own plight, I was even more worried about John, who was sure to be at least two miles further back by this point. Beyond there being no man-made shelter, this austere landscape seldom offered any other protection from the worst of such a storm. I pushed myself as hard as I could, fearing the lightning even more than violent winds. The hail was hitting me so hard I could have cried. I put my head down and closed my eyes to all but just a tiny slit. I was barely able to see where I was going. The last mile or so was downhill as Route 120 dropped from the bluff toward the Greybull River valley. I don't know how fast I was going at that stage, but I can't fathom there was another bicyclist on the entire planet that had gone as fast under such adverse conditions on that particular day in June 1978. Of course, it was likely there weren't any other cyclists stupid enough to be riding in such a blinding hailstorm in the first place.

As I turned onto the street at the edge of town and ducked under the overhang of an abandoned storefront, I said a prayer of thanks that God delivered me there without being electrocuted. The building was a wood-sided place that hadn't been painted in many years, and I couldn't see a soul anywhere. From this spot, Meeteetse looked like a ghost town and could have served as the set of a post-apocalyptic episode of the *Twilight Zone*. After the storm finally subsided, I found a store and grabbed some grub. After a long wait, I finally saw John laboring into town, looking more like a drowned rat than a recent Penn State grad. Resigned to the fact he would never even come close to getting into town before the storm hit, he found a low spot off the road a piece, covered up with his tarp, and hunkered down. The ordeal had frightened me as much as anything in my life, and John had experienced a similar scare, despite having run for cover. We were not ashamed to admit as much to each other.

We had already covered 85 miles by the time we got to Meeteetse and had a difficult decision before us. Like the stretch we had just completed, there was little between Meeteetse and Thermopolis. It was more than 50 miles and the thunderstorm and strong wind had put us way behind schedule. Yet it seemed too early to stop for the day; we decided to shoot for Thermopolis. It would later be one of those decisions that would cause us to wonder, *What the hell were we thinking?*

The brisk southerly wind continued thanks to a high-pressure system over Nebraska so as to blow southerly and southeasterly winds the entire day. We stopped at a crossroads around mile 115, exhausted and frustrated. With another 20 miles still to go, we were getting low on food and drink. I found a bag of dried prunes in my bag and inhaled them, ignoring the possibility that their mighty laxative powers might disable me. Instead, thankfully, they gave me the glycogen boost I needed to make it to Thermopolis.

It was dark by the time we hit the outskirts of town around 9:00 p.m. Much to our chagrin, the KOA Campground we were looking for was on the other side of town, and it was 9:15 p.m. before we finally arrived. Thermopolis owed its existence to two somewhat unrelated water features: the Big Horn River and the Thermopolis hot springs. The hot springs also gave the city its name, literally meaning "City of Heat."

We were so tired we thought we could have slept through just about anything—anything, that is, except the loudest bird in the Western United States. At 4:00 a.m. this bird began its loud song in the tree directly above us. John and I crawled out of our sleeping bags into the cold morning air. When throwing stones did little to deter the bird, John eventually resorted to throwing his shoes. He hoped the larger object would scare the pest away, but instead, John got his shoe stuck in the tree. Somehow or other, we finally got the shoe down, and John's persistence also got the bird to fly to the other end of the campground. Though we could still hear it, it was not near as bothersome, and we both were able to return to sleep. Someone on the other side of the campground was not nearly as delighted by the bird's change of venue.

Our clothes were as nasty smelling as they had been the entire trip, and we were delighted to have the luxury of a washer and drier at the campground. It delayed our departure, but we looked and smelled much better than we had when we'd arrived. With our later start and the fact that we would have had to backtrack several miles to see the hot springs park, we decided we couldn't afford the detour. Casper was 125 miles away and the wind and weather remained a great uncertainty.

Ken had told us the Wind River Canyon was spectacular, and it certainly didn't disappoint us. The first handful of miles south of

Thermopolis had been the same drab landscape as we had tolerated the end of the previous day. When the Owl Creek Range jutted up in front of us, we were again reminded that a notable change in topography can also bring a change in spirit. So steep-sided was the canyon, some places it was incised 3,000 feet into the mountains. Even in the high sun the week after the summer solstice, we would sometimes find the early morning sun creeping behind the mountain. Had we realized this was the last majestic mountain scenery we would experience until we hit Pennsylvania, we might have savored it a bit more.

The Wind and Bighorn rivers are actually the same river, but were given two different names when the early explorers mistakenly thought they were two different waterways. Having explored the Bighorn closer to its mouth at the Yellowstone, the inaccessibility of the canyon at the Owl Creek Mountain end of the river left many uncertain as to where the river really came from. The canyon road today is the only easy southern escape from the Bighorn Basin, but the gorge was practically impassable in stagecoach days.

The mountains themselves owe their existence to a thrust fault thrown on top of very old rocks that formed the large dip making the Bighorn Basin. It was further testimony to the complexity of the Rocky Mountains, where faults are covered by lava flows, or intruded by magma over many different geologic time periods. This makes for confusing surface geography and almost incomprehensible geology. In the Appalachians, the cards are merely wrinkled and slightly askew; in the Rockies, they have been crumpled, shuffled, and thrown across the table.

Headwinds and Flatlands

Headwinds and Flatlands

Douglas, Wyoming to Sioux City, Iowa

June 28, 1978 - July 6, 1978

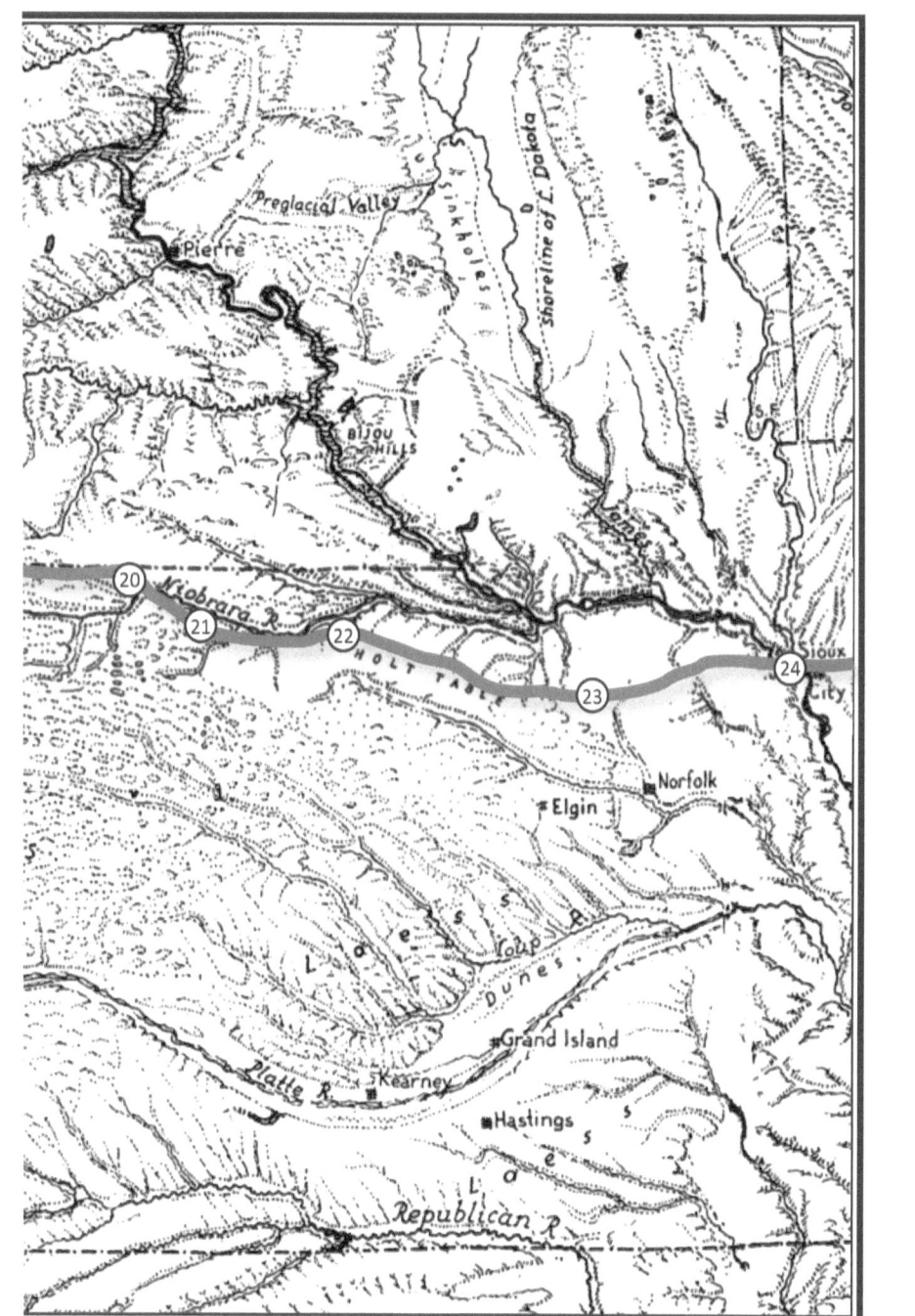

Hells Half Acre

"If you're going through hell, keep going."

—Sir Winston Churchill (1874—1965)
British Prime Minister
Nobel Prize for Literature (1953)

WITH THE EXCEPTION OF OUR TRIP THROUGH THE TETONS and Yellowstone, we had been following US Route 20 since we left the Sawtooth Mountains in south central Idaho. While not enjoying the notoriety of US 66, US 1, or even US 30 through Pennsylvania, US 20 was still a fascinating cross section of America. More by accident than design, we would follow it for 1,500 miles into Chicago.

After leaving the Wind River Canyon, the Boysen Reservoir was to our west as we went south on US Route 20. As we turned east in Shoshoni, the wind was in our face. Historic weather maps would show we were stuck smack dab between two high pressure systems and cursed by an unusual easterly wind for the second straight day. We again found ourselves in the desolate old western movie landscape, tumbleweeds included. To make matters worse, the wind had slowed us to a crawl. To our north was the Badwater Creek, and somewhere just to our south was the Powder River. It was a safe bet they got their names for obvious reasons. When the water did flow, it was a turbid mess that could sometimes seem to be more sediment than actual water. Though the maps said we were between two waterways, all we could see was more sandy soil and sagebrush. We passed through the crossroads of Waltman and looked at the map again. We realized if we tried for Casper, we might be worse off than we were the previous night. It was more than 30 miles and the wind was still making us feel like we were going backward.

Waltman wasn't much of a town, with the old oil well parts and junked cars exceeding the number of people. So we figured that Hells Half Acre, just a few miles down the road, might be a good place to stop for the night. When I called home and told them we were in Hells Half Acre, my mother thought I was making a joke. Rest assured, it was no joke. The sign at the entrance said it was a "unique setting of natural beauty." John and I joked that the public relations con artist that drew such a conclusion surely must have been smoking something illegal. The "Half Acre" was actually more than 300 acres and was some of the most depressing landscape known to man. These were badlands, full of deeply eroded, flat-laying sedimentary rocks of various colors and consistencies.

A party of men led by French fur trapper and explorer Benjamin Louis Eulalie de Bonneville came through here in 1833, said the sign. Washington Irving would later write an account of the Frenchman's adventures. It should come as no surprise that Bonneville passed up the Half Acre and built his fort in Green River, in the more scenic and more fur-rich western part of the state.[24] Someone eventually did build something here, albeit not much more attractive than the landscape surrounding it. The "visitor center" was a greasy spoon, just a few dozen feet from the Hells Half Acre Motel. With one look, John and I feared we would catch something should we take the motel option. It was almost incomprehensible to me that the motel lasted several years into the 21st century before finally succumbing to the wrecking ball. It appeared it was about to collapse in 1978.

We were even more certain upon entering the front office of the motel that we would not be well served by staying there. We were greeted by an ill-groomed woman who looked like she might be in her forties. Already missing a good portion of her teeth, her greasy hair indicated that she had misplaced her bottle of shampoo along with her toothbrush. She told us a motel room would be almost $15 but a campsite was only four. Given the likelihood of bed bugs or other unthinkable maladies in the motel rooms, we eagerly opted for the campground.

As we walked out the door, she warned us that a tornado a few weeks before had done a bit of damage to the facilities but everything still worked. But when we got there, we found the bathroom door had been ripped off the hinges and the electricity was out. Looking forward to a shower with great anticipation, we decided it would be wise to stand guard for each other just in case the innkeeper from hell or another guest happened upon us. We finished our showers in the nick of time, as a family in a trailer joined us a bit before dusk. Just in case we needed anything additional to set the mood, a chilly, dry, and dusty wind persisted through the night. I could not imagine anywhere on earth had been given a more appropriate name. This was indeed Hells Half Acre.

As further testimony to the desolate landscape in this part of Wyoming, one need only peer at a map and note some of the names. Devils Gate, Deadman Butte, Hole-in-the-Wall, and Lost Cabin certainly did not paint a picture of the Garden of Eden.

We were anxious to move on that next morning, having had our fill of our hell on Earth. John and I were delighted when the day began with a robust tailwind and we flew into Casper. The barren landscape continued, but the favorable wind renewed our spirits. Our arrival in Casper, however, would bring a series of unpleasant and unexpected changes. The scenery, the wind, the traffic and then our speed and mood went from the best to the worst in the matter of a half hour. Casper was one oil well after another after another. Just a few miles outside of town, I could not have imagined that the landscape could become any more unpleasant. The pumping oil wells spread across the skyline abruptly showed me it was possible.

In what seemed a mystery at the time, the wind had changed directions thanks to a high pressure system passing over eastern Wyoming. An upper air high over the southeast United States would continue to pump gulf moisture into the Plains. Coupled with the incredible power of summer thermal convection, this upper air pattern would provide the moisture that was needed to give us nine consecutive days of afternoon thunderstorms. These kinds of thunderstorms were foreign to a couple of easterners. While thermal convection could contribute to summer thunderstorms back east, the storms in the

Plains look and act much differently. A clear morning turns into a thunderstorm-riddled afternoon, the storms seeming to appear out of thin air. This is a result of the land heating up quickly on a brutally hot summer afternoon, causing the air to rise quickly. As it rises, it cools and available moisture condenses to make clouds. When this lifting happens slowly and gradually during the passage of a cold front, the rain clouds spread out over a large geographic area, bringing steady, longer duration rainfall. The convection-induced storms, however, build upward, rather than horizontally, making them not just shorter in duration but also more violent.

When extra moisture fuels the convection, the storms are more frequent and formidable. This particular summer, upper winds would drive weather systems supplying plenty of moisture from the Gulf of Mexico. A conversation that afternoon with a transplanted New Jersey native confirmed just how wet a year it had been in the High Plains. He noted some places in the region had already received a year's worth of precipitation even though we were a few days short of mid-year. The pattern would continue into July and rainy weather would persist throughout the Plains.

While we rode in the sun nearly all day, we were in the shadow of a black eastern sky. Already frustrated by the headwind, we eventually wandered into the showers as well. It took us an hour and a half longer to cover the 30 miles into Douglas than we had planned. Even though eight miles short of our hundred, we decided to call it a day. There was a KOA Campground in Douglas and based on the size of print on the map, we feared towns east of there did not amount to much. The next day, we would find out how true that was.

We hoped we would receive a brief reprieve from the refineries, oil wells, the urban blight of Casper, and the sagebrush of its hinterlands when we began riding along the North Platte River. But it was not much of a river this far west and couldn't even support the Cottonwood trees more common east of the 100th meridian. Despite being next to the river, the landscape changed little. The easterly wind had continued persistently into the evening, bringing us to the end of another frustrating day. This had been the second day in a row filled with negative experiences and ugly landscapes and it was driving both of us crazy. For the first time, John spoke of giving up and going home. I wrote in my journal that I feared I would not be far behind if he decided he just couldn't take it anymore.

The Van Tassell Hassle

"The last town there was called Van Tassell,
And the whole state was one big hassle.
We had some snow up in Yellowstone,
And now John and I are all alone.
Tom and Anita have gone and hopped a train
Because the whole stinking trip was such a strain.
We have chosen to see the nation by bike,
But there is only some that I really like."

—John Frederick
Fledgling Poet & Frustrated Cyclist
Van Tassell, Wyoming (June 1978)

THE MILES FROM DOUGLAS TO THE WYOMING BORDER WERE more of the same. The same landscape, the same sandy soil, the same scrubby vegetation, the same miserable headwind, the same late day thunderstorm, the same sore bottom. Only the names of the towns were different; Mometa, Hiland, and Natrona had been replaced by Orin, Keeline, and Lusk.

The most memorable, though, was the last town in Wyoming — Van Tassell. It wasn't any less drab and desolate than anyplace else nearby, but its name became a source of amusement. Now nearly a ghost town, it was actually named after the original owner of a nearby ranch, Dutchman Van Rensselaer Schuyler Van Tassell (R.S. for short). Mr. Van Tassell became most infamous for marrying women (five to be exact) so he could add to his vast land holdings. When a Union Pacific spur line came through in 1886, Van Tassell seemed like an appropriate name since the scrupulous Dutchman owned land as far as the eye could see. Van Tassell had taken Theodore Roosevelt on a demanding 50-mile horseback ride through the region two decades later,[25] and our ride through southeastern Wyoming 70 years later was similarly trying. We were struck by the fact that the town's name rhymed with hassle and I told John I thought a limerick was in order. That evening I composed the "Van Tassell Hassle," a bit of bad poetry, but a very accurate description of Eastern Wyoming.

We had decided to skip the Black Hills of South Dakota and Mount Rushmore because we feared the traffic there would rival that of Yellowstone. Our next consideration, then, was to look for the most pleasant way across the Central Plains. We concluded, partially on Ken's advice, that we should avoid the very hilly southern portion of Iowa. So US Route 20 through northern Iowa looked like it made the most sense. Ken failed to tell us, however, that western Nebraska's Sand Hill region might have been hillier than southern Iowa.

The topography remained fairly flat as we crossed the Wyoming-Nebraska border. But as the sun faded in the northwestern sky, the landscape began to undulate. Those undulations soon turned into a series of annoyingly steep hills, the beginning of the Sand Hills. And they were indeed hills and again reinforced the notion that the Plains really were not plains at all much of the time. (I guess the Great Hills just didn't roll off the tongue like the Great Plains.) Despite the wind, the fatigue, and the renewed difficulties of the topography, the western part of the Sand Hills was one of the most unique landscapes we had seen. The late day sun cast a peculiar light over them. Where cattle grazed, windmills turned and the shadows of the turning arms created a unique flicker on the hillsides. These remote grasslands were often far from the electric lines, and the windmills were the only way to provide water for the cows.

Had the region been a bit drier, this vast expanse of land, a quarter of the state of Nebraska, would be the classic desert sand dune landscape. But it's just high enough and wet enough to support tall prairie grass, stabilizing the dunes and creating this unique landscape. The sand was blown out of the Rockies, the remnants of glacial till of the last period of significant glaciation. It's well-suited for range land but far too dry, sandy, and prone to erosion for extensive cultivation. The eastern edge gets a bit more than 20 inches of rain per year, the western edge a bit less.

The Sand Hills of Nebraska were a unique landscape in many ways. The sand is generally very deep, presenting engineering challenges like seen on this bridge over this usually slow-moving braided stream. Photo by John Frederick.

That doesn't mean it doesn't rain much west of the 100th meridian! While this was certainly the case during the Dust Bowl years in the late twenties and early thirties, it was not the case in 1978. Like the previous few hundred miles, the Sand Hills were enjoying (or suffering through, depending on your perspective) one of the wettest years in memory. Few creeks and rivers flowed through the Sand Hills, the depressions between the dunes capturing the water. The resulting ponds and lakes supplied water for the cattle and added another interesting feature to this unique landscape.

The now daily thunderstorm rolled in just before we left Wyoming, and the easterly wind seemed even stronger and more persistent as the evening wore on. More by our own stubborn determination than good fortune or favorable winds, we covered 114 miles and ended up in Fort Robinson State Park. One hundred-one summers before, and just one year after Custer's Last Stand at Little Big Horn, the legendary Crazy Horse led 1,100 of his people to a peaceful surrender at the then Camp Robinson. Following four months of what amounted to house arrest, Crazy Horse had shown signs of restlessness, and whites feared he was planning an exodus north. This prompted officials, including tribal police, to formally arrest him, but he resisted as they tried to incarcerate him in the guard house at Camp Robinson. He was stabbed and killed in the resulting melee. His death closed a most unpleasant chapter for both the Sioux and the United States government.

As we wandered along US 20 a century later, we were never more than a few dozen miles south of several expansive Indian reservations in South Dakota. We would be frequently reminded this was still Indian territory. Young Native Americans in old, run-down cars reminded me of the discussion in my Historical Geography class the previous school year. Indians, more than any other ethnic group in America, struggled to become assimilated into American society. For two centuries, they struggled to figure out if assimilation was what they really wanted. Many preferred the old ways, but it became more and more difficult to sustain themselves as they were pushed into more undesirable and less productive places. A century after Crazy Horse's passing, it seemed like only one notable change had taken place: they were driving old run-down Chevys instead of riding horses.

It was a bit early for lunch when we got to the town of Chadron, but the Pizza Hut was too tempting to pass up. After the feast, we enjoyed our first respite from the easterly wind in many days. However, an afternoon of threatening clouds and thunderstorms again impeded our progress, and we ended up completing less than 80 miles.

As we went further east, the landscape turned boring again. We would remain in the Sand Hills over the next several days and, especially along the Niobrara River plain, it became less scenic and more monotonous. Unbeknownst to us at the time, the much more scenic Pine Ridge ran nearly parallel to US 20 a few miles south of Crawford and Chadron. Named for the fact that it was covered with Ponderosa

Pines, it was home to Chadron State Park and the Nebraska National Forest. It was one of only three small tracts of National Forest in the entire state, primarily because there were only a small handful of notable contiguous woodlands in all of Nebraska.

Missing the National Forest, we continued east toward the Niobrara. When we arrived in the town of Gordon, we were shocked to see an entire city block on US 20 had been flattened by a tornado just a week before. Confirming that tornadoes can be small and their energy incredibly concentrated, the opposite side of the street appeared untouched by the violent storm. I had never witnessed a recent tornado's aftermath and was overcome by the destruction.

I went to Saturday evening mass at Saint Leo's Church, the namesake of my church of 20 years back in Altoona, Pennsylvania. It was always funny to go to church and see the reaction when, often in full cycling regalia, you pulled your bike into the vestibule to assure it wouldn't disappear during mass. I particularly recall the pastor chuckling at both my attire and the coincidence of our churches' names. With no campground in town, we spent the night in Hill's Motel, hoping the thunderstorms would not bring another tornado. Though we were a bit disappointed the weather had decreased our mileage, the less strenuous day, tasty meal, and relaxing evening were welcome diversions.

We started the next day with yet another gusting easterly wind, which seemed at times to bring us to a near standstill. With the exception of a few hours on a single morning, we had been struggling against the wind since we left the snowy Yellowstone National Park a full week before. Everyone we talked with voiced their surprise of these unusual winds continuing for so long. That never happened, they contended, until this summer. No matter our resolve, we simply could not cover the miles we had intended.

Particularly as we progressed through Western Nebraska, we came to notice a repeated pattern. Soon after we would leave one town, we would notice the next town's water tower on the eastern horizon. Seldom was there a single man-made feature between the towns. Whether we said it out loud or not, we inevitably would make an estimate of how far away it was and how long it would take us to get there. But the wind, coupled with our horrid flatland perception, would make our estimates dreadfully inaccurate. It made us seem to go even slower than what was already a crawl. My mental and physical fatigue was tempered only by the fact that John's was an order of magnitude greater. In retrospect, psychiatric counseling could have probably been justified by this, as my frustration would cause me to actually yell at the wind as we struggled down the road.

Yet it got worse. The surface of this lightly traveled part of US 20 was dreadful, and I was beginning to suffer from both saddle sores and cyclist palsy of the hands. The sun was hot and unrelenting until late afternoon, when our daily thunderstorm threat knocked on the door. We came to learn there was a KOA Campground in the town of Valentine, and we were looking forward to the amenities that usu-ally accompanied what had become known as the Holiday Inn of campgrounds.

The Niobrara River's headwaters were just west of the now infamous town of Van Tassell, Wyoming and roughly paralleled US 20 from the Wyoming border to Crookston. It angled toward the town of Valentine and crossed under US 20 just south of town. A direct tributary of the Missouri, it is the only notable river in the northern third of Nebraska. When we crossed it just a few hundred yards from the campground, we were struck that it was one of the few significant chunks of woodland we had seen since the Wind River in Central Wyoming. When we arrived at the campground, we decided we should camp as close to the river as we could so as to enjoy the most scenic feature we had seen in days.

The dinner hour and early evening were thoroughly enjoyable as we ate and relaxed near the shores of the river. Despite a cool shower, it was a shower just the same, and we felt refreshed that we had been able to scrape the road dirt and sweat off our exhausted bodies. We spread out our sleeping bags in anticipation of a peaceful night next to the babbling Niobrara. Niobrara was the Sioux word for "water spread out over the horizon," an indication that even two centuries before, it was recognized the river wandered slowly across the broad floodplain in a braided pattern. This particular rainy summer of 1978, it had more water than usual and brought with it an unwelcome bonus.

As the sun sank into the western sky, we heard the first buzzes. Not long afterward, the swarms of mosquitos were descending upon us. *What were we thinking*, we asked each other. We were two young geographers that should have known better. The Niobrara moved slowly on a good day and even slower under normal circumstances. There were many ideal places for mosquitoes to call home. So close to the river especially, the likelihood of them was even greater. We tried to weather the storm of flying blood suckers only to see the deluge grow more overwhelming as night fell. I had never seen so many mosquitoes and they found every unclothed bit of skin (and much that was covered) on our bodies. We found a campsite a hundred or so feet up the hill and were relieved when the pesky insects were unable to find us. The move simply delayed the inevitable, however, and in few minutes, they found us again.

Like all KOA campgrounds, this one had a recreation room with pinballs and a ping pong table. Now desperate, we decided the rec room was the only way we could get a decent night's sleep. We carted all our stuff to the door of the building but feared it might be locked up. We were delighted to find it was opened, and we found a spot to throw our sleeping bags. Inexplicably, we were overcome with the mosquitoes here as well. We discovered someone had kicked out the bottom of the screen door, allowing the bug's free passage into the space. Now at our wits' end and exhausted beyond words, we decided to try the bathroom. While more bug-free than anywhere else on the property, the smell and inextinguishable lights were nearly as bad as the insects. Now well after midnight, we decided we would try moving toward the highway, as far away from the water as we could get. It might have been the best we could do, but it was still buggy enough to frequently interrupt our sleep. When dawn came, we brushed our teeth and headed down the road. I might have gotten two hours of sleep.

I could not remember being more tired in my entire life. I feared that I might fall asleep while riding the bike. We decided we had to get some sleep and looked for a suitable spot. It was a dozen miles to the next town, Arabia, but we were so tired we wondered if we could make it. When an inviting patch of prairie grass presented itself, John and I threw out our sleeping bags and laid down 30 or 40 feet from

US 20. The grass was high enough that we would have been hard to see from the viewpoint of a passing motorist. Despite the bright sunshine and rapidly increasing temperatures, we fell asleep. The heat, though, became too much a few hours after sunrise, and we dragged ourselves and our gear back to the highway to continue our journey through Futility.

We crawled down the road, wondering just what we should do considering our debilitated state. As the morning progressed, the wind grew even stronger. Coupled with our overwhelming fatigue, the strong wind seemed worse than it had so far. We got to the tiny town of Wood Lake, just 24 miles from where we began our day's ride, and decided we couldn't go another mile. Wood Lake was three by six blocks and had a combination bar/store/gas station just off US Route 20. Down Main Street a short piece was a fire house that protected the town's two dozen homes.

The town park was at the end of one of the streets. Many towns in Nebraska, Iowa, and Indiana had such a park. Most had a picnic pavilion and many had running water. The one in Wood Lake had no pavilion but sat underneath a stand of trees. As we lay on the picnic tables, the leaves rustled in the brisk easterly wind. It was hot but the incessant wind took the edge off the heat. Despite our frustration, the afternoon of relaxation and occasional sleep was a pleasant and peaceful diversion.

Word evidently got around town that a couple young men were camping at the park and we had two rather odd visits from the townies. In midafternoon, two attractive young ladies walked over to our table. John whispered something about jail bait before they were in earshot.

"So where are you guys headed?" one inquired.

"We're riding across the country," John answered.

"Wow, that's quite a trip. Aren't you guys tired?"

Then, in as abrupt a change in conservation as I had ever experienced, one asked, "Will you buy us beer?"

John and I said almost in unison, "No, we can't," further explaining this would not be a good idea for us or them. We both laughed later that we had visions of the newspaper back home: "Local Men Convicted on Corruption of Minor Charges." Their similarly abrupt exit made it clear they were more interested in our capacity to legally purchase alcoholic beverages than they were in any other distractions. The upside to their beer preoccupation, we laughed, was that at least we weren't going to be brought up on sex-related charges.

In the early evening, a middle-aged man wandered toward us.

Without any introduction, he asked us, "What kind of boys are you?"

I wondered if he was inquiring as to our sexual orientation. Had he heard of our encounter with the two teenagers that afternoon? Did he think we were gay because we didn't take advantage of the two girls?

"What do you mean?" we wondered aloud.

"I mean, could we trust you?" he asked.

"Well, sure you could," we responded, as if we would have admitted to being child molesters or horse thieves.

"I own the store and I'm the fire chief. It's supposed to storm tonight and we thought that we'd let you sleep in the firehouse. They're talkin' about the possibility of tornadoes."

We thanked him several times for the offer. On top of the rain, it had been so buggy we were delighted to have the chance to get a good night's sleep indoors.

"I'm taking the family down the road for the fireworks." It was July 3rd and his kids were eager to celebrate the holiday. "I'm not sure how late we'll get back, so let's go up now and I'll show you around."

We pulled our stuff together and went up the street with the chief. The firehouse was immaculate. I was sorry that we had already eaten supper because it was the first time I had been in a full-fledged kitchen since I had left home nearly four weeks before.

"You can throw your sleeping bags anywhere you'd like," the chief told us. "If there is a tornado, the best place to be is under the fire truck," he said as he pointed to the floor underneath the 20-year-old truck. "It will sound like a train coming down Main Street. But the train doesn't go through Wood Lake anymore, so if you hear it, you're in trouble." I imagined John and I huddled under the fire truck as pieces of roof flew through air and rafters fell on the truck.

I lay awake for a little while, fearing the firehouse would be flattened like the supermarket we saw in Gordon two days before. But even the anxiety of a tornado could not keep me awake in my exhausted state. With no fires or tornadoes, we enjoyed an uncharacteristically quiet, bugless night in the Wood Lake Firehouse and decided to take advantage of the situation and sleep in as late as we could. It was only the second truly good night's sleep I had had in nearly two weeks.

I awoke to a flat tire and even the good night's sleep could not alter my foul mood. I had spent part of the afternoon at the Wood Lake Park computing how much I would spend if I continued the trip and how much it would cost to get the bus home. I figured that I'd save at least $25, maybe as much as $50, if I just gave up and went home. My journal entry noted I'd also save myself considerable aggravation and be home living a simpler life much sooner. We judged we were about a two-day ride from Sioux City, Iowa where we could catch a bus east. At that moment, I had a hard time thinking of a good reason to continue.

High Plains Drifter

"I'd love to oblige you. But a man's got to get his rest sometime."

—Clint Eastwood, The Stranger to Sarah Belding
High Plains Drifter
Universal Pictures (1973)

MY FLAT TIRE AND LATE RISING GOT US ON THE ROAD MUCH later than we would have preferred. Once on the road, the easterly wind continued, albeit ever so slightly less rigorously than the previous few days. The sky grew darker as the afternoon wore on, and we decided to grab some food and wait out the storm in the town of Bassett.

Just as in Wood Lake, the Bassett fire chief found us and struck up a conversation. It was about this time I fully realized the importance of small town fire chiefs. It seemed they wielded more power than the mayor, their influence being magnified in unincorporated towns where there was no mayor. The chief was a pleasant and talkative soul. Inevitably our conversation turned toward the weather.

"Hasn't this weather made you a bit crazy?" I inquired.

"You learn to live with it," the chief responded matter-of-factly.

"Hasn't it been a rainy year?" I continued.

"Soggy by Nebraska standards," he quipped.

"This east wind has been discouraging," I mentioned in what could have been the biggest understatement of the summer.

"Yea, that's been a bit strange. Can't recall such a peculiar summer in that regard."

"Lucky us," I sarcastically mumbled to myself.

Though the continental climate that comes to Montana and North

Dakota can bring wild temperature extremes, the winter precipitation can vary wildly. Even a few modest snows can stick around a long time in the northern plains if the cold hangs on. But I wasn't sure how that changed as you moved this far south. Curious about the severity of their winters, I asked the chief, "So do you get much snow in these parts?"

"Depends," he said. "Some winters we don't get too much, other years it can get ass-high to a tall Indian." The way the chief said it, it didn't strike us as a disparaging remark. But we were glad that no Native Americans appeared to be within earshot just the same.

On the advice of the chief, we sat in Bassett for a long time. He had helped us pass the time and had entertained us besides. Yet the day was fading into late afternoon and we knew we couldn't afford to have back to back days under 40 miles. So we finally decided to chance the weather and head off down US 20 again. We couldn't have gotten more than a few miles from Bassett when the threatening western sky became ominously black. We were between a rock and a hard place. Like so many other stretches of roads in this part of the country, there was next to nothing between the last town and the next one, Bassett and Newport on this stretch. As the storm spread eastward, the patch of clear skies ahead got smaller and smaller. It was clear the rain was now imminent, and I rode as hard as I could to stay ahead of the storm. John was soon far behind, and with nowhere to hide I decided to ride on, knowing John would catch up after the storm passed. The hole of sunlight kept shrinking and soon looked like the tiny light at the end of a long tunnel. Unlike a real tunnel, the light got smaller and finally disappeared altogether. With its disappearance came the final realization we were in real trouble and our scary experience in Meteetsee, Wyoming, was to be repeated.

The thunderstorm finally caught me a few miles outside Newport and, like Meteetsee, I found myself in a no-man's land of thunder and lightning. I was relieved this storm did not have the hail of the Meteetsee storm, but I feared I was about to be killed by lightning. Not long after the worst of the storm hit me, I rode up to Spring Valley Park. The historic marker said it was the first roadside rest in Nebraska, built by Vic and Maude Thompson in 1938. A privately run facility, the corrugated steel pavilion looked like it could have been the original structure built 40 years before. But archaic or not, it was a roof in the midst of a wild storm, and I was happy to be there rather than out in the open somewhere. Never mind that the building would become a series of flying shards of metal if the tornado hit.

Again, I was worried about John and hoped he had found safe haven. His slightly slower pace may have been a blessing. Even though he became stranded in a ditch yet again, he ultimately headed back to Bassett and weathered the storm in a more substantial park shelter. Meanwhile, despite being out of the rain, I found myself in a tiny and not particularly substantial picnic pavilion in the most violent storm I had ever experienced. The worst night of the entire trip to be split up, I resigned myself to spending the night alone.

The two previous days had turned very hot and humid, and it was still uncomfortably sticky well after sundown. The thunderstorm did nothing to cool the evening air. I laid out my sleeping bag on the picnic table and tried to go to sleep. After a short reprieve, the howling wind and rain resumed sometime after 10:00 p.m. I was so scared, I pulled the sleeping bag up to my chin, as if it would somehow protect me from flying debris or a lightning strike. I was still wide awake, sweating profusely in my bag an hour later. I feared I was in a storm capable of producing a tornado, and I had no fire truck to crawl under on this night.

As the wind picked up, I contemplated what I should do. Tornadoes can be relatively small and I had this silly idea that I could maximize my chances if I spotted it in time and ran the opposite direction. Certainly, the flimsy picnic shelter would offer me little protection and would likely be blown apart if the winds even approached tornado force. I had everything in easy grasp and looked intently toward the north, ready to run for it if I heard the train-like sound the Wood Lake fire chief had told us about. I was among a group of trees and they were waving wildly. Beyond the fear of being impaled or carried somewhere over the rainbow, I feared one of the trees could fall in the high winds, even if we didn't get a full-fledged tornado.

Then it happened; I heard the sound of a train, the tell-tale tornado sound. It seemed to be coming from the northeast, so I grabbed what I could and prepared to make a run for it. As the sound grew louder, I prayed that it was something else or would move away from where I was. But it kept coming. When I finally saw it, I was overcome with confusion.

Coming toward me I saw the silhouette. It was the silhouette of a train. The train didn't go through Wood Lake anymore but it did sometimes go through Newport. I was never so relieved to see a locomotive in my life. On this July 4th, the fireworks, Mother Nature's in this case, lasted until 2:00 a.m. and the sleep deprived cyclists got yet another abbreviated night's sleep.

Interestingly, the rail line that caused me such anxiety in 1978 was completely abandoned by the early nineties. It eventually became a rail trail, the Cowboy Trail, following the Chicago and North Western Railroad corridor. It carried both freight and passengers from the 1870s to the 1920s and became the driving force behind the settlement that took place near the Niobrara. Among other things, the line carried livestock from the ranches in the Sand Hills through the thirties. But the Great Depression and new highway construction conspired to undermine the demand for the rail transportation. World War II gave the line a shot in the arm, moving Wyoming oil east as well as carrying passengers that, ironically, had limited gasoline for their private automobiles. By 1958, however, demand for service faded and the last passenger train ran that July.[26]

The nightmarish night was transformed into a blissful morning. It was especially appreciated given that we had spent so much of the previous week on the threshold of hell. I waited as close to the road as I could so John would not miss me. He eventually came along and I conveyed the details of my Independence Day fireworks experience.

It is in this part of Nebraska that one can notice the results of higher rainfall and come to better understand the significance of the 100th meridian. Just west of Bassett, we had crossed the most famous of longitude lines in North America. This line has traditionally separated the wetter, more arable Central Lowland Plains from the High Plains. Clint Eastwood's old movie *High Plains Drifter* may capture the essence of the High Plains as well as any movie has ever portrayed a unique geographic place. Even Eastwood's character takes on the ambience of the dusty, windblown landscape west of the 100th meridian. The change can be sensed as one cycles through the region. Hay and marginal pasture land are more common west of the line; a smattering of trees, greener grass, and cropland become more common to the east. As I thought about the subtle changes we were experiencing, I was again reminded it would be more difficult to sense that change had we been buzzing along at 60 miles per hour in an automobile.

Hoping to get halfway to Sioux City on Tuesday, the threatening sky and subsequent storm caused us to fall 50 miles short of our 100-mile goal. Our two-day trip turned into three. During our lunch stop, someone told us there was some construction ahead, but we were reassured we should be able to make it through without too much difficulty. US 20 was being rebuilt around O'Neill, and we stumbled right into the mess. It had been graded but little more had been done. We came to appreciate with a new degree of understanding why they called them the Sand Hills. We plodded through the sand like we were in slush. It may have only been a few miles, but it seemed like a dozen before we finally hit the pavement again. Despite the slow going, the frustration of the sandy interlude, and a thunderstorm in Plainview, it was our best ride in quite a few days. Plainview was a beautiful town appropriately named for its view of the plains, and its town park was especially nice for a dry night's sleep. We appreciated the opportunity to eat and relax under roof after a wild night, the long day, and its annoying detour.

One of the best preserved volcanic fossil deposits in the United States was just a short ride down the road from Plainview, in what would become Ashfall Park. Fossils in sedimentary rocks are most often casts of small shells found in marine environments, but a relatively rapid volcanic ash deposit can freeze whole animals in three dimensions. The ash was laid down ten million years before and preserved rhinos, camels, horses, and other animals where they stood. Stomach contents and unborn animals were even found by the paleontologists that excavated the area.[27]

Though we did not have to worry about any rhino or camel stampedes when we awoke the next morning, we were confronted by threatening skies. The rain began before we got a dozen miles down the road, and we were stuck in the town of Osmond for two hours. As we approached the Nebraska/Iowa line, this delay seemed sadly appropriate. Before I began the trip, I would have expected this 450-mile stretch across Nebraska to have been full of wind-assisted hundred-mile days. With the rain, headwind, unexpected hills, and nightly battle with the mosquitoes, we couldn't do even one day beyond the century mark. What we hoped would take four days took almost a week.

Scenes of Visionary Enchantment

"This immense river waters one of the fairest portions of the globe. Nor do I believe that there is in the universe a similar extent of country. As we passed on, it seemed as if those scenes of visionary enchantment would never have an end."

—Meriwether Lewis
Referring to the Missouri River
Voyage of Discovery Journal (May 31, 1805)

A SMALL TRIBUTARY OF THE MISSOURI RIVER CUT A NOTCH in the bluff of the river near Willis, Nebraska. This made our drop onto the broad floodplain of the Missouri a fairly gentle descent. Even this far north, the floodplain is very broad in places, and Sioux City and its suburbs on both sides of the river sit on very flat land. South Sioux City on the Nebraska side of the border and much of Sioux City on the Iowa side are pancake flat. The Sand Hills fade to loess hills and plains by the time we get to this region of Nebraska and Iowa. The finer wind-blown loess is carried further east, being more easily transported by the wind across the High Plains than the sand. Loess is exceptional agricultural soil and is among the reasons this region is one of the most productive on the entire planet.

We didn't make it to the Missouri River until almost 5:00 p.m. The only way across the river was the US 77 bridge, a narrow two-lane, metal grated structure. Between the rough surface and the impatient drivers, it was as scary a stretch of road as we had experienced. I put my head down and time-trialed across the span as quickly as my legs would power me, cringing every time a car or truck buzzed by. About halfway across, yet another newspaper headline popped into my head: "Pennsylvania Cyclist Plunges to Death in Missouri River."

It was a shame the crossing was so precarious, because the view from the bridge was incredible and deserved more contemplation than I could afford to give it in the horrifying traffic. Lewis and Clark were hundreds of miles from here on the White Cliffs of the Missouri when Lewis wrote of the "scenes of visionary enchantment," but even this part of the river was still spectacular. Just the same, ours was not quite the same experience they had written about on the final day of May 1805.

Frustrated and physically drained, we decided we deserved a good night's sleep and splurged for a room at the Imperial 400 Motel in Sioux City. Though the motel had the same bland architectural style of thousands of other motels built across America, it was clean and met our needs. We particularly welcomed the swimming pool and air conditioning in the still oppressive afternoon heat. We stopped at a market and stocked up on some real food, including a box of macaroni and cheese. I was longing for something besides a cheese or peanut butter sandwich.

Given its weight and bulkiness, neither of us had a cook stove, so when we prepared a meal, it was almost always a cold one. I ate so many sandwiches, I saw them in my sleep. Not eating meat, the sandwiches could become even more monotonous. Changing from Swiss to Provolone became a momentous event. This made the macaroni sound like a gourmet delight. But I failed to consider I really did not have any way to cook it. Like the campfire potato experiment in Oregon, my attempt at a hot meal again was foiled.

Though our mileage had been disappointing the previous week, we had still ridden enough miles to be suffering the plagues of long-distance cycling. While my hands were numb, it was my backside that really bothered me. After a pleasant swim in the still hot early evening, I took a soak in our tub, hoping to relieve the discomfort only a cyclist can truly understand. Taking advantage of real beds and pillows, we slept in as late as we had the entire trip. We were in bad need of a laundromat but it ended up being two miles out of our way. Some mechanical things needed to be addressed, too. Over 2,000 miles into the trip, my back tire was worn to the threads, and I decided it should be replaced in a town that actually had a bike shop. We stopped at a gas station to do the work, but an unusual nozzle on the pump resulted in me pulling the valve off the inner tube. In my continuing string of incomprehensibly rotten luck, my replacement tube had a hole in it. After all this, we wandered around town for another half hour looking for the post office to mail some things back home. We didn't get out of Sioux City until 12:50 p.m.

The Glory of Suicide Machines

"In the day we sweat it out
in the streets of a runaway American dream.
At night we ride through mansions of glory in suicide machines.
Sprung from cages out on highway 9,
Chrome wheeled, fuel injected and steppin' out over the line."

—Bruce Springsteen
"Born to Run"
From the album *Born to Run*
Columbia Records (1975)

THE CHALLENGING MORNING GAVE WAY TO ONE OF OUR best afternoons in many, many days. The wind was actually out of the northwest and we enjoyed our first notable tailwind since Oregon. The thought of abandoning the trip faded in the temporary ecstasy of favorable weather, wind, and the beautiful landscape of western Iowa. The trip once again seemed like an adventure instead of a chore. Despite the very late start, we managed to get in 75 miles, ending up in Early, Iowa. John and I laughed that our ending point was ironically the opposite of our departure time. Early was a beautiful town and their park had a covered pavilion and bathroom, albeit without hot water. John and I stocked up on some provisions, enjoyed some sandwiches, and I filled in my journal before settling down for the night.

We had noticed but not paid particularly close attention to the young, recently-licensed teenagers drifting about town in the early evening. As night fell, the real fireworks began. The town's teenagers, either bored with the monotony of life in rural Iowa or perversely aroused by the sounds of roaring automobile engines (or perhaps both), set off on the cruise through Early. In a ritual I had never understood, they screeched their tires at every intersection and sped down the street until they skidded to stop to begin the process anew. Had the tire screeching become less frequent as the early evening faded toward midnight, it might have been dismissed as adolescent frivolity. When it persisted past midnight, we plotted how we might get away with murdering the perpetrators. Perhaps some judges would have declared the crime justifiable homicide, but we were certain the local counterpart would have thrown us in the clink for a long time.

It was after 1:00 a.m. when the crazed cam heads finally tired of their idiotic exercise and we got to sleep. Despite the good night's sleep we had experienced the night before at the motel in Sioux City, I was still whipped. Once I fell asleep, I drifted into an uncharacteristically deep slumber. Sunrise came early, not much more than four hours after the nonsense of the previous night ended. When I first awoke in the stupor that frequently accompanies sleep deprivation and picnic table sleeping arrangements, I thought I was in my bedroom back in Altoona, Pennsylvania. As I opened my eyes, I expected to see the stereo next to my bed. Alas, it was the cement block wall of the park bathroom instead.

Beyond the disappointment of being on a picnic table a thousand miles from home, I also felt the void of not being able to plug into my stereo. In its absence (coupled with the monotony of the Great Plains), I had taken to singing to myself on the road. The bike was pretty crowded some afternoons, as I was frequently joined by Greg and Duane Allman; Lowell George from Little Feat; David Crosby, Stephen Stills, Graham Nash and Neil Young; the Beatles' Paul McCartney and John Lennon; John Denver; and Mick Jagger and the rest of the Rolling Stones. Many of their songs matched up with the challenges of the road trip. "Born to Run" and its line "glory of suicide machines" came to mind the previous night. The Stones "You Can't Always Get What You Want" had also popped into my mind with considerable frequency during this particularly trying part of the trip.

Though it was hard to sleep in the brilliant sunshine of the nearly cloudless morning, we tried to make up for the late night. Rather than an early Early departure, we had a very late one for the second day in a row. Easterly winds cursed us yet again as the winds whipped clockwise around a high-pressure system (which also brought the sunny morning) parked over central Iowa. Despite the bright morning sunshine, a few isolated thunderheads popped up again in the afternoon. The heavy traffic on the four-lane US 20 prompted us to turn onto Route D25 near Webster City, Iowa. Surrounded by otherwise nearly cloudless skies on the quiet rural road, yet another shower fell upon us from the only notable cloud in the sunny sky. We looked and felt like a couple of cartoon characters. We were the poor souls that were followed by every imaginable stroke of bad luck, standing alone and downtrodden under a rain cloud on a day everyone else was showered in sunshine. The previous day had stopped a streak of ten straight days of rain. We joked that we needed to start another streak.

The wildlife in this part of the trip had not been particularly noteworthy, especially compared to the proliferate antelopes we saw our first week or the incredible variety of big game we witnessed in Yellowstone. The one animal that was conspicuous in Iowa, however, was much smaller in stature than the animals we noticed in the west — the red-winged blackbird. When we first started to see them in big numbers in Nebraska, we found them to be a novel, colorful relative to the all-black blackbird in Pennsylvania. The birds loved the environment common in the roadside ditches, where food, water, and overall friendly habitat were easy to find. Very territorial, they became perturbed when anything got too near their nesting area. They would not hesitate to come after passing cyclists. As we progressed further east, they became more numerous and ornery. It seemed as if we were constantly swatting at them as they swooped unnervingly close to our heads. We felt as if we were in a sequel to Alfred Hitchcock's classic horror film, *The Birds*. It got to the point that we didn't even have to see the bird coming at us. The tell-tale "Damn it!" or "Son of a Bitch!" was a sure sign one was attacking us. After many close calls, John was actually pecked on the back of the head as we approached Fort Dodge.

Despite the bird attack and our late start, we still managed to do

113 miles and cruised into Iowa Falls late in the day. We decided to look for the community park in Iowa Falls but, being a bigger town, it was not so easy to find. We climbed two ungodly hills (proving again that the Plains are not always plains). We made the descent into, and the climb out of, the Iowa River floodplain several times looking for the park. Being a typical man, I wouldn't stop to ask directions. John, working hard to keep up, became furious with me.

"Do you think maybe you could have stopped and asked directions?" he gasped. Particularly after 110 miles into a headwind, tempers could be short.

I had no good answer to his question. "I thought it would be easier to find," I finally explained, having no other excuse.

"Ah, no kidding? Well it wasn't, was it?" he responded in his most sarcastic tone. John and I had come to know each through our academic endeavors in the Department of Geography at Penn State and he, too, was fascinated by the prospect of a cross-country adventure. While we might not have been close friends when we started, the physical demands and psychological strain of the trip would force us to share many ecstatic and traumatic moments. The annoyance he expressed that evening was one of a very few times either of us got really upset with the other. We might have realized it to some degree at that moment, but years later, I came to fully appreciate how important our mutual support was to one another. One or both of us might have persevered by ourselves, but the odds would have been poorer and our sanity stretched further. Though it would greatly understate the difficulty of war to say we forged a relationship like soldiers in combat, there's little question there were some common threads. Like soldiers, when the ordeal is over, you realize that you are stronger and better able to handle the curve balls that life so often throws you.

Like the small handful of times we did get upset, it passed and we moved on. It took us awhile, including those climbs out of the Iowa River floodplain, but we finally found the park. Though it didn't seem worth the trouble at the time, we were happy to find that it was a beautiful park with a band shell at the end of a grassy field. It seemed that the trying day would have a pleasant end.

Central Iowa is one of the flattest places in the Plains, the product of the southern portion of the glacial ice sheets of the last Ice Age. The only notable changes in topography are the floodplains of the Des Moines, Iowa and Cedar rivers. We crossed those rivers at Fort Dodge, Iowa Falls, and Waterloo. Our futile search for the park that day meant that we crossed it several times in Iowa Falls. This glacial plain, sometimes called the Des Moines Lobe, mirrors the shape and size of the southern portion of Lake Michigan 400 miles due east. The last of the glacial intrusions that made the lobe, the Wisconsinan, happened only 10,000 years ago, a mere blink in geologic time.

The glacial till, or sediments, characteristic of the region is underlain by an impressive deposit of gypsum in the Fort Dodge area. The gypsum mining had been going on for more than a century as we passed through in 1978, making Iowa one of the country's most productive gypsum producers.[28] We weren't thinking of glaciers or gypsum as night fell in Iowa Falls; we were just hoping we might get a good night's sleep. Iowa Falls was just big enough, evidently, to have some big city problems. In one of our scariest nighttime incidents since being confronted by the leader of the pack near Portland, Oregon, a drunken man stumbled (quite literally) upon us as we tried to sleep. A rain shower caused John and me to scramble for drier ground and we ended up in the shelter of the band shell, where the homeless drunk managed to find us again. The blowing rain also meant we got wet, even though we were under the shell. Despite all our good intentions, sleep was again elusive.

The rain came with the passage of a cold front and July 9th was marked by cooler temperatures. The wind had correspondingly turned out of the north, not perfect but a far sight better than we had been putting up with. Coupled with the straight, flat road, it would power us to our biggest mileage day, 125 miles, since our marathon into Thermopolis, Wyoming, two weeks before.

Iowa, like most other Midwestern states, is laid out in rectangular townships that are in turn divided into square mile sections. Each township is typically six by six sections, or 36 square miles. For obvious reasons, it is often referred to as the rectangular survey system, but its official name is the Public Land Survey System (PLSS). It was created by the Land Ordinance of 1785. It is a profound contrast to the old

English metes and bounds system that was used in Pennsylvania and eastward. Metes and bounds use local reference points and lines often based on topography or water features. Though metes and bounds may seem less scientific and more random when compared to the rigid straight lines of the rectangular system, it makes more sense in a place like Pennsylvania, where the topography and rivers make natural boundaries that are uncommon in the Midwest. In a place like Iowa, though, the rectangular system is more practical, given the landscape does not often vary much topographically.

US 20 is an interesting study in how the survey system and landscape conspire to make a mostly straight, nearly flat roadway. Like the overwhelming majority of roadways in the central Plains, it is a straight line over a large portion of its path and almost all of the intersecting roads run perpendicular. Especially in the central third of the state, topography alters the straight as-an-arrow highway patterns only when a notable meandering river gets in the way. Though often peaceful and frequently beautiful, the long stretches of straight roads and endless farmland could give the word monotonous a new meaning.

Light at the End of the Tunnel

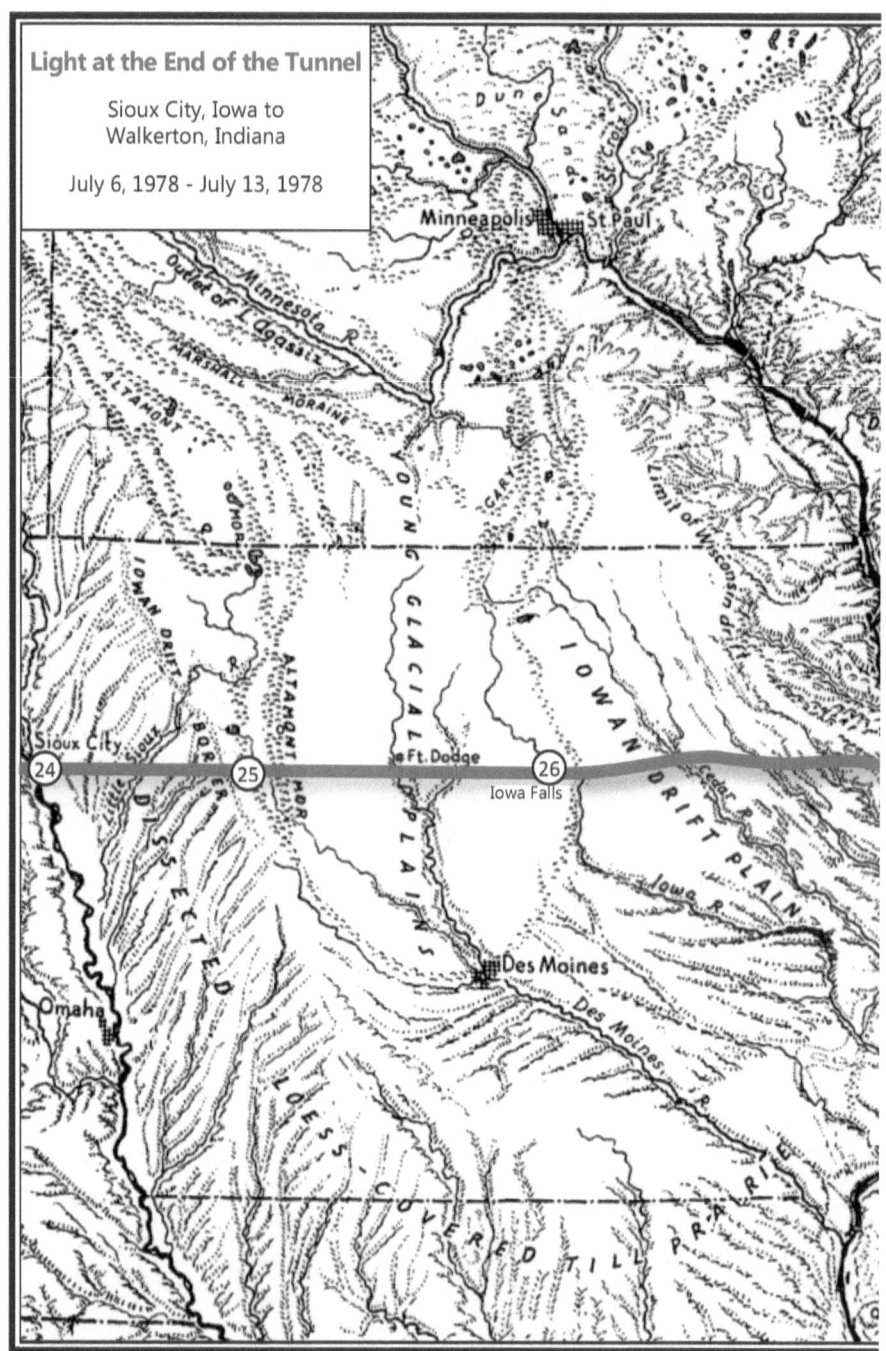

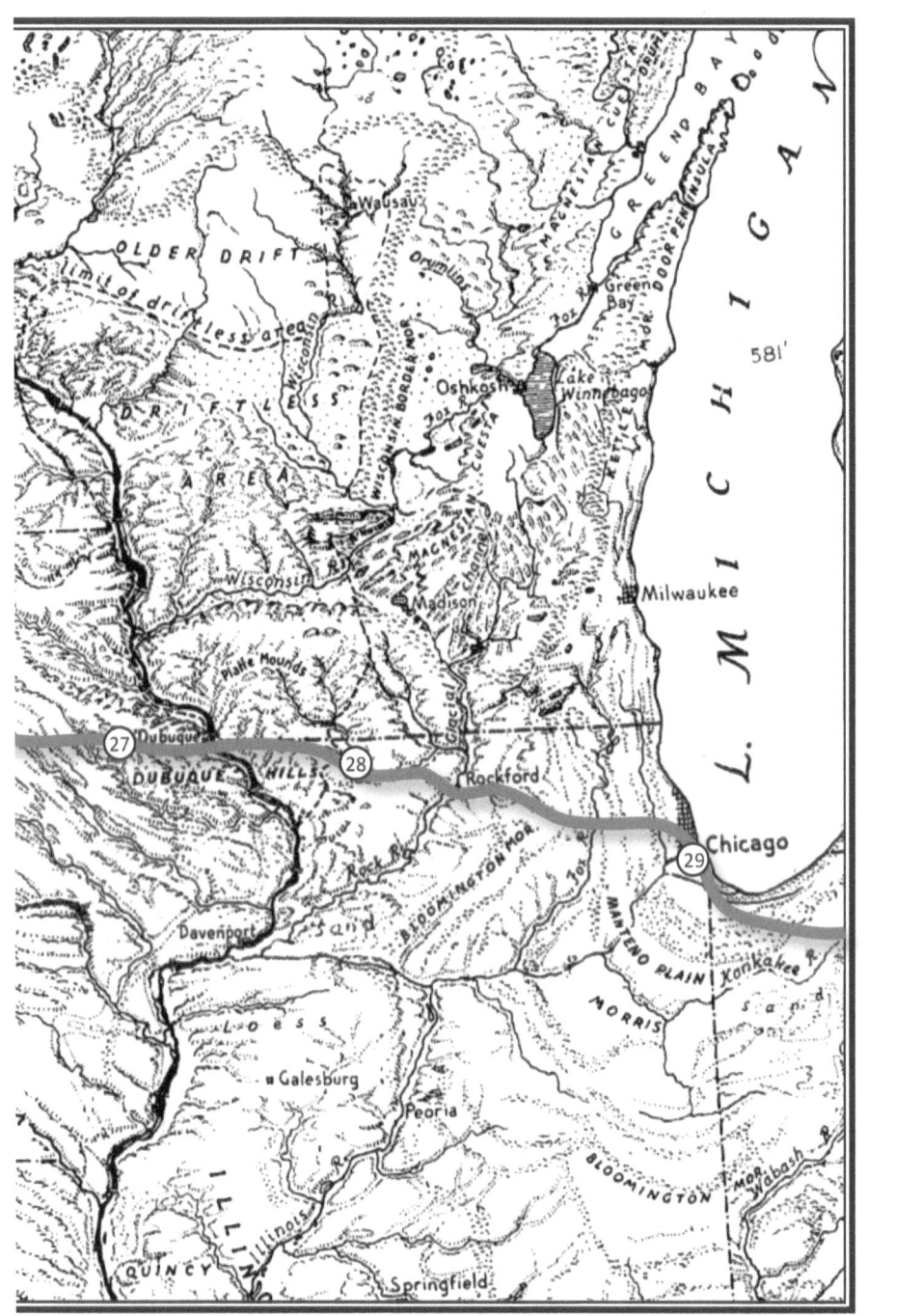

A Field of Dreams

"Ray, people will come Ray. They'll come to Iowa for reasons they can't even fathom. They'll turn up your driveway not knowing for sure why they're doing it... And they'll walk out to the bleachers; sit in shirtsleeves on a perfect afternoon. And they'll watch the game and it'll be as if they dipped themselves in magic waters. The memories will be so thick they'll have to brush them away from their faces. People will come, Ray."

—Terence Mann, played by James Earl Jones
Field of Dreams
Universal Pictures (1989)

SUNDAY MORNING WAS OVERCAST, THE WIND AT OUR BACK and it looked as if all was right with the world again. But as we moved into eastern Iowa, the flat landscape and lightly traveled roads faded, and the traffic became overwhelming. The afternoon portion of the ride became the polar opposite of the flat, pleasantly cool ride of the morning. Despite the afternoon headaches, we were able to pedal 125 miles, our second straight 100-plus mile day after six consecutive rain shortened days the week before.

We pulled into Dyersville, Iowa, in the early evening and found the town park just as a large family get-together was breaking up. We looked for the folks in charge to ask if we could stay in the picnic pavilion and ended up talking with several of the party-goers. Curious to hear about our adventure, the friendly revelers talked with us and wished us the best on the remainder of our trip. Not only did they welcome us to stay the night in the shelter, they told us to help ourselves to whatever leftovers were still around. While most of the substantive food was long gone, there were lots of pretzels, chips, baked beans, and a few desserts scattered about the picnic tables. With no utensils handy, I dipped the barbeque potato chips in the baked beans and discovered a unique flavor and texture that struck my fancy. Since there were plenty around and I was starving, the bean and chip concoction became the main entree of my evening meal. Much to the amusement of family and friends, I would continue that unique picnic practice later in life. Any time beans and chips were on a picnic menu, I would harken back to that summer evening and the nice people in Dyersville, Iowa.

A decade later, Dyersville would become the answer to a cinematic trivia question, having played host to the Kevin Costner and James Earl Jones movie *Field of Dreams*. Particularly in contrast to the much drier climate just a few day's ride west of here, the greener landscape did indeed make this part of Iowa beautiful and fitting for a movie that tried to capture the ambience and character of rural America. Built on the Lansing Family Farm, just outside the town of Dyersville, the field and farmhouse remains a shrine to the movie, much as James Earl Jones' character suggested it would near the end of the film.

It is no coincidence that Kevin Costner's character, Ray Kinsella, grows corn, for Iowa is the nation's biggest corn growing state. It also grows a great many other foodstuffs, producing seven percent of the nation's agricultural goods. And while the fertile soil, higher rainfall, and productive agricultural economy make for a much greener landscape than central and western Nebraska, it can still be a monotonous landscape at fifteen miles per hour.

Though the wide stretches of monoculture fields could give the impression the entire state was one big, flat cornfield, we would find that the region east of Dyersville was a different landscape all together. Commonly called the Dubuque Hills, they were a striking contrast to the flatland over which we had just passed. We were surprised by the topography and the difficulty of negotiating it. The hilly, tree-covered terrain was somewhat similar to our own Appalachian Plateau of Western Pennsylvania, and it reminded us how we had come to treasure our tree-covered mountainsides back home. Just north of us was what had become known as the Driftless Area, a pocket of highlands missed by the most recent continental glaciation. Absent of glacial till or the flat landscape of the Des Moines Lobe, it was a stark contrast to the central part of the state.

Eastern Iowa was beautiful but our enjoyment had been offset by the demands of the hilly terrain. The most demanding and surprising of those stretches would come at the crossing of the Mississippi River. Rivers like the Mississippi carved impressive floodplains that could be very broad. Being so wide, I had always thought a river in the plains could not make a particularly deep floodplain. Nothing could have been further from the truth. We should have figured this out as we came off the bluff on the Iowa side of the river, but in the ecstasy of descending a big hill, a cyclist will often forget an important principle. In the world of long distance cycling, what goes down must come up. The climb out of the Mississippi floodplain surpassed many mountain ascents in the Appalachians for a short but difficult spell. We were initially lulled into a false sense of security as the highway coasted along the river, climbing only slightly at first. Then, with the subtlety of a sledge hammer, the road pitched skyward, climbing back into the Dubuque Hills. Both here and in Sioux City, when we crossed the Missouri, the elevation change was only a few hundred feet. Yet it seemed like much more because they were the only two significant relief changes in a thousand miles.

We were also in the middle of our first three day stretch of rain-free riding since eastern Oregon. I had hoped to do another hundred-mile day, but the hilly riding had taken its toll on John especially. When we found a KOA campground outside Lena, Illinois, along Route 20, it wasn't hard for John to talk me into stopping at mile 82. Its swimming pool sealed the deal. We had finished the day of riding relatively early and the KOA was the nicest commercial campground we had visited the entire trip.

We ate well and enjoyed a relaxing swim while discussing how we would negotiate metropolitan Chicago. Most folks we talked to told us the best strategy was to avoid Chicago all together. John thought there were advantages of going right through the city, primarily because it would be the shortest route. I had ridden in enough cities to know there was no way we could get through Chicago without considerable difficulty. We set off the next morning still not quite sure where we were going in particular. We needed a few things from a bike shop and found one in Freeport. The shop's racing posters and track bikes made it clear we were in one of America's cycling hotbeds. The Kenosha Velodrome, just across the border in Wisconsin, is the nation's oldest cycling track, built in 1927, so the tradition runs deep in the region. I could have talked bike racing to the shop staff all day.

The more urgent conversation, however, was how we would get through Chicago. The boys at the bike shop told us Illinois Route 72 (which paralleled US 20) would be a much more sensible alternative to get us into the western suburbs. We set off on the connecting road, Route 26, a "hardtop road" in the local colloquialism. Hardtop meant it was a narrow tar and chip surface and was rougher than some corrugated metal roofs. Route 72 was almost as bad. I wrote in my journal that it was the roughest stretch of the whole trip. On a journey of more rough roads than we could keep track of, that was saying a great deal. It was of some consolation that most of Route 72 passed through beautiful farmland and was very lightly traveled. We should have savored that more than we did, for it would be the last such riding we would enjoy for two days.

Somewhere around Elgin, as the suburban sprawl really started to sprawl, our route made a left turn at a busy intersection. I was a bit ahead of John, so I stopped at the corner so he wouldn't miss the turn. However, the stop would not go as smoothly as anticipated. Though I traveled as lightly as I could, my bike was still loaded down. The two panniers were full of clothes, tools, the typical toiletries, and whatever food I hadn't eaten at the last meal. I had my sleeping bag on top of the rear rack and had a pair of sneakers secured to the handlebars with a bungee cord. Needless to say, bikes are usually not ridden with such loads and this profoundly affected how mine handled. It also meant that it could fall over much more easily and be harder to stop once it started to waiver. Simply dismounting could be a complicated procedure.

As I slowed to a stop after my left turn, I pulled my left foot out of the toe clip and leaned the bike the same direction, just as I had done a hundred times over the previous three weeks. Only this time, the bike, seemingly with a mind of its own, started to fall to the right, the side that was still firmly secured to the pedal and toe clip. The fall happened quickly, so much so that I was unable to even get my hand out to break the fall. I fell squarely on my right elbow. More concerned about how stupid I looked than any injury I had sustained, I tried to gather myself with some degree of dignity. Sure that my fall looked like the Artie Johnson skit on the old *Laugh In* television show from the sixties, I was certain any witnesses were laughing hysterically. I wiped the blood from my arm and was standing as if nothing had happened by the time John arrived at the corner. We finished the day's ride without further incident and got a motel room in West Dundee, Illinois. Little did I know, the embarrassing tumble would pale in comparison to the struggles that would confound us the next two days.

Some Way Out of Here

"How did I escape? With difficulty. How did I plan this moment? With pleasure."

—Alexandre Dumas
The Count of Monte Cristo
(1844)

WITH TRAFFIC STRUGGLES THROUGH THE WESTERN SUB-urbs and grossly underestimating the mileage, we found ourselves still far from where we hoped to be by lunch the next day. The Lakeshore Trail bikeway and the prospect of riding through the city on a dedicated bike trail gave us renewed hope. The trail was, at first glance, everything we could have hoped for. Running along the shore of Lake Michigan, it was all paved and had no street crossings to speak of. But after the first few miles, the bike traffic became as crazy as the automobile traffic on nearby Lakeshore Drive. We saw two bike collisions, one with fairly serious injuries. We proceeded carefully, so as to avoid a wreck of our own.

The most shocking sight, though, was the number of people openly smoking marijuana on the beach and at the benches along the trail. I suppose John and I were pretty straight-laced guys, but we also knew folks that smoked. In our part of the world, it was a very clandestine activity, and it seemed really odd to see it done so openly, even if it was Chicago. Despite all the shortcomings of the trail ride, we were grateful overall that we were riding on a bikeway instead of a busy highway or a congested street.

But all good things come to an end (especially on this trip) and quite abruptly, the trail ended on one of those congested Chicago streets. We tried to orient ourselves in the sea of humanity and tall buildings and searched for someone that might be able to help. We were relieved to stumble upon a police station. Not daring to let the bikes out of our sight for even a minute, I told John I'd stay with them and he could go in and ask for directions. As John recounted the conversation, it went something like this.

"I was wondering if someone could help a couple of lost bikers find their way out of the city."

"Sure," the desk cop answered. "Which way ya headed?"

"East," John replied. "Gary, Indiana, I suppose."

"Oh, that's an easy one," the cop responded. "Just look for the 90/94 signs a few blocks down the street. You can take the Chicago Skyway right into Gary. If you want to avoid the toll, take 94 down to Lansing. It's a little longer but the traffic is less of a hassle, too."

"The toll road?" John queried. "We can't ride on a toll road. We're on bikes."

"Oh, hell," the policeman moaned. "I thought you were on motorcycles. This is going to be a bit more difficult," he said as he glanced down at the map on the desk.

After clarifying our circumstances, the cop explained to John how to navigate his way through the city streets. John came out and told me the amusing anecdote and then explained how we might start the adventure. I was a bit annoyed with John for dragging us through this Chicago ordeal, but I knew this was no time to say so.

It had been clouding up as the afternoon wore on, and not too many miles from the police station, the skies opened up. It was as hard a rain as we had experienced in a while, one of those typical summer downpours on a hot, oppressive day that left us soaked to the bone in less than fifteen seconds. Being in the heart of the city, we didn't see many affordable lodging options. We asked some locals where we could go in this neighborhood and they pointed us toward Midway Airport. They weren't the nicest places, they warned, but it was the best we could do under the circumstances. We paddled down the street a modest distance and found the Airliner Hotel. Having ridden the last three miles in the downpour, we must have looked like a pair of drowned rats when we entered the lobby.

Whether it was circumstances, bad luck, or bad judgment, many times I found myself in some unpleasant lodging situations during my bicycling career. But this was among the worst. It was directly across the street from the southeastern-most runway of the Midway Airport. Its grimy double-paned windows were supposed to assure that the rooms were "soundproof." As I researched for the book many years after our visit, I came upon a matchbook image of the hotel, circa 1955. It had the same "soundproof" and "air conditioned" notation as the hotel had on its sign 25 years later. Little had changed in the quarter century since the original matchbook had been printed. I'm certain it was the same carpet. I couldn't be sure, but there was strong evidence to support the possibility that the blanket on the bed had not been changed in the ensuing years either.

Considering the proximity to the runway, the room was as quiet as a room could be just a few hundred feet under departing planes. We slept moderately well, for it was, after all, under roof in the midst of a series of nasty thunderstorms. Despite the sleep, we were anxious to vacate the room the next morning, but the persistent showers would keep us there until nearly ten. When it finally stopped, we went to the White Castle restaurant around the corner for breakfast. The stainless steel interiors of White Castles were a trademark of the establishment in the seventies. The motif permeated every nook and cranny of the eatery, even the bathrooms. I inhaled three of their delicious cheese danishes, unconcerned that I had likely consumed a week's worth of saturated fat in one sitting.

We heard a report that this part of Illinois had received four times the normal amount of rainfall since the first of June. It had been the same scenario through the entire western plains. That this weather pattern had become commonplace across most of the Central United States did little to ease our frustration. When we finally got on the road, the traffic added insult to injury. Even as we moved toward Hammond, Indiana, the traffic persisted. We hoped things would ease as we got further from center city Chicago, but our problems were simply transformed. The traffic was ever so slightly lighter, but the stop lights became the real challenge as we approached and traveled through the not-so-fair city of Gary.

The string of signal lights would have been bad enough by themselves, but their timing became the greater source of frustration. Synchronized more to facilitate the smooth flow of motor vehicles, the lights changed too quickly for our two-wheeled self-propelled vehicles. Of the many lights (seeming to number more than a hundred), we could count the number of times we got two straight green lights on one hand. Just as we got up to speed, we would get to the next light as it was flipping to red.

Such a stop and go ordeal might have been somewhat tolerable had we been riding along the beach or through a charming downtown. But this section of Gary, Indiana, was quite the opposite. Though I had been through slums and low-income housing projects during my life, this was the first time I had peddled through an expansive area of such blight and poverty. The fact that such poverty existed in a place that had been one of the hotbeds of the steel industry seemed to be a paradox. Even though we were in the midst of a decline, my bus trip through the region a month before testified there were still many jobs to be had in the steel industry. At one time, the Gary Works was the biggest steel-making facility in the world, and the view from the bus in 1978 still showed a skyline of manufacturers and refineries. Yet the poverty in this part of Gary was overwhelming and the resulting ghettos were the manifestation.

Gary was founded in 1906 by the US Steel Corporation. The location was attractive to the industry because of its convenient rail access and the possibility of building its own docks on the shores of Lake Michigan. Not surprisingly, the city grew and flourished with the steel industry. But when the industry's fortunes faded, so did Gary's. The city lost 30,000 people in the seventies and crime rates rose as the economy turned sour. Gary's mayor at the time, Richard Hatcher, perhaps put it best when he noted, "This has never been a rose garden," in a 1979 newspaper interview.

Two nasty gangs, the "Black P Stone Nation" and "The Family" were terrorizing Gary in those days, and their crime rate was the highest in the country among mid-sized cities. Mayor Hatcher was encouraged the year after we rode through when Gary finally lost their grip on the infamous top spot.[29] John and I did not need to read the statistics at the time; it was clear to us this was not a safe place to ride, and we only paused when the endless red lights forced us to.

The geology and landscape of northwest Indiana and the Lake Michigan shore was a sharp contrast to the urban decay of Gary. The shore was incredibly beautiful and was home to Indiana Dunes National Lakeshore and a nearby state park by the same name. The region was occupied by a Native American society that was part of the Hopewell tradition from 200 BC to 400 AD. Unfortunately, the mounds built during the era in this area have disappeared for the most part, the victim of cultivation and looting. I came to realize that the region had gone backward in some ways, both socially and environmentally, in the two millennia that had passed since the Native Americans built the mounds.

Even after getting through Gary, the traffic remained heavy and many of the miles were riddled with potholes and washboard pavement. We came upon a long underpass east of Gary in the midst of the heavy traffic, and it seemed like a good idea to get through it as quickly as we could. John entered the dark roadway first, and I passed him about halfway through. The traffic was so heavy that he thought I was a car about to run him over. He was badly startled and let me know in no uncertain terms. It had not been a good day of riding and my act of thoughtlessness had been the final straw for John.

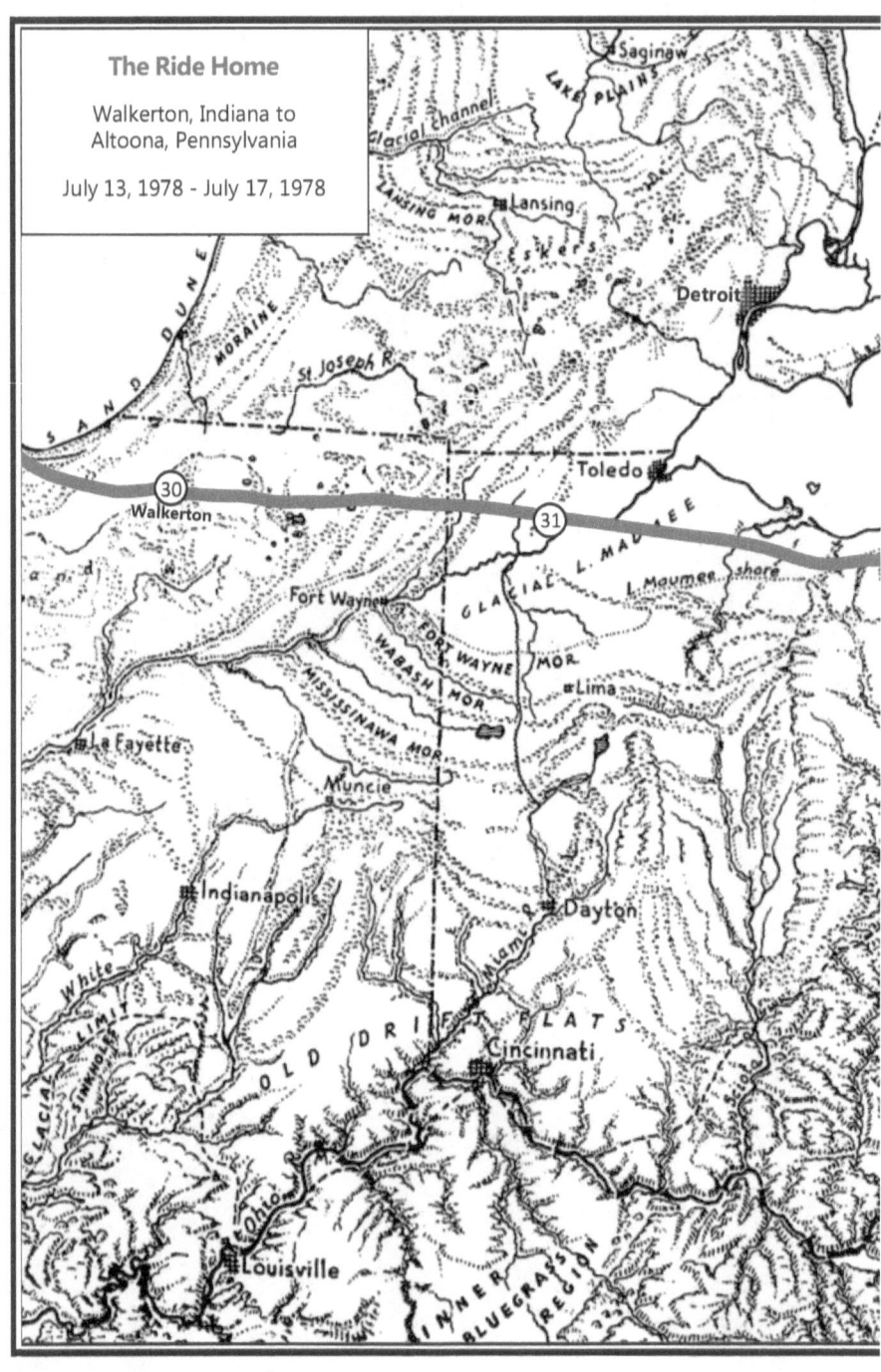

The Ride Home

Walkerton, Indiana to Altoona, Pennsylvania

July 13, 1978 - July 17, 1978

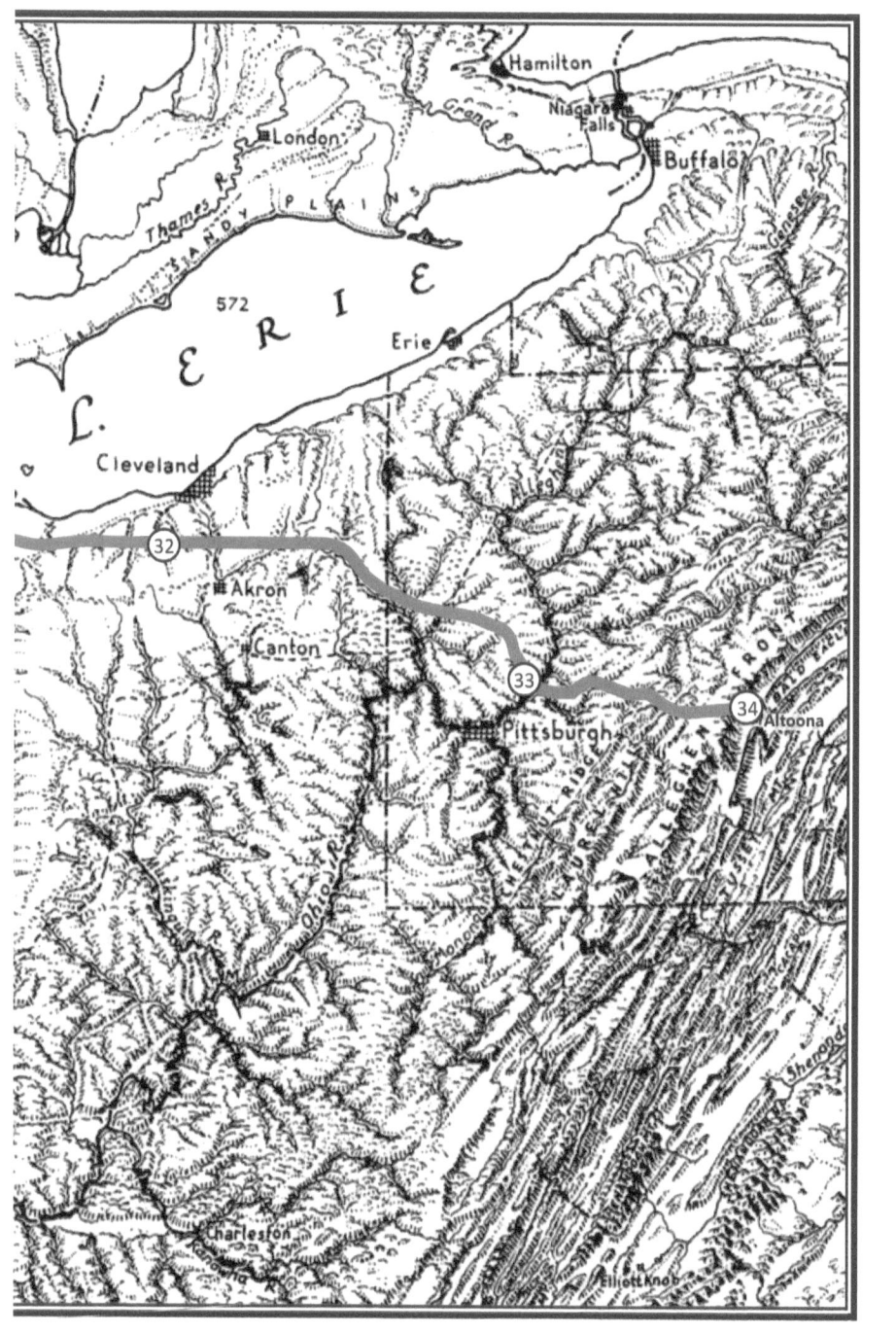

The Good Samaritan

"But a certain Samaritan, as he traveled, came where he was. When he saw him, he was moved with compassion, came to him, and bound up his wounds, pouring on oil and wine. He set him on his own animal, and brought him to an inn, and took care of him."

—Saint Luke
Chapter 10
The Holy Bible

AFTER MANY FRUSTRATING AND SCARY MILES, THE SLUMS of Gary and other eastern suburbs finally faded into the flat farmland of central Indiana. As early evening approached, we came upon a peaceful roadside rest area a few miles west of Walkerton, Indiana, on US Route 6 and decided it looked like a great place to camp for the night. It was nestled back in a patch of trees and bushes and had a pair of picnic tables for us to sleep on. We enjoyed a hearty supper (at least by our lax standards) and cleaned up. Unfortunately, the scourge that had followed us since western Nebraska came down upon us yet again just as the sun faded in the western sky. We were soon enveloped in the buzzing biting fog of mosquitoes. Just beyond the line of bushes, it turned out, was a drainage ditch filled with water, which made an ideal breeding ground for the dirty little bloodsuckers.

We tried to weather the storm for a short while but finally succumbed and decided we had to look for other sleeping provisions. Blessed by a bit of moonlight, we set off down the road sometime well after ten. We did not have any lights so, hoping not to be run over, we would pull off the road whenever a car passed. Fortunately, traffic was very light and it was a pleasant evening for such a moonlight ride.

As we rode down Route 6, we passed a large sign but were unable to read it in the darkness. It turned out to be the sign stating we had passed into Eastern Time. We entered the town of Walkerton under the cloak of darkness and found the Dairy Queen to be one of the few places still open. In conversations with the locals, we came to understand the town was big enough to have a DQ in 1978, but there was no lodging of any kind. The next town was La Paz, but it was smaller than Walkerton. Bremen was the next place that might have lodging, but it was eighteen miles away. For a couple of bicyclists wandering around in the dark, it might as well have been in Georgia.

So we sat at the Dairy Queen, milking our milkshakes as long as we could. As midnight approached (or 11:00 p.m. in Central Daylight Time a few miles away), we were politely reminded the establishment would be closing shortly. As the desperation crept into our situation, I prayed for divine intervention. It appeared in the person of Carl Nixon. As we sat on the bench at the side of the DQ, Carl struck up a conversation with us and we explained our plight.

"Where you guys headed on bikes this late at night?" Carl inquired.

"We're in a bit of a bind. We tried to camp out at a roadside rest a few miles outside of town but the mosquitos overwhelmed us," John explained. "We hoped there would be someplace to stay here in town, but we can't find a thing."

Spooning a bite of his banana split into his mouth, Carl peered at us. "I got a rec room off the house. What would you think about stayin' there? You'd be out of the bugs."

We could hardly contain ourselves. Certain that we would be sleeping in some mosquito-infested town park, the prospect of sleeping indoors was beyond our wildest expectations just a few minutes before we met Carl Nixon. His pickup truck made it possible for us to get there without riding through the dark July night.

A few miles north of town, we came to Carl's place. He had fashioned a rec room out of a small block building next to the house. A pool table sat in the middle surrounded by some modest furniture. A small bathroom provided us with all the comforts of home. Carl bid us a good night and we thanked our lucky stars for his kindness. The Good Samaritan lived on and the two Johns enjoyed a good night's sleep.

We didn't get to bed until after midnight, so we slept in and left Walkerton much later than we would have liked. We awoke to a perfect day for riding, something we had come to appreciate because it had been so uncommon during our four weeks on the road. As I had come to learn during my first trip through Indiana with my aunt five years before, this part of Indiana is one of the flattest places in America. Despite the flatness, the underlying geology is more complex than what it might appear from the surface. Many terminal moraines, the piles of glacial junk that accumulated at the end of continental ice sheets, can be found across Illinois, Indiana, Michigan, and Ohio. As we moved across Indiana into western Ohio, we crossed two of those terminal moraines. Even moving along at the speed of a bicycle on the back roads, we rode through them without realizing they were there.

As boring a landscape as this could be, the mostly smooth and flat roads of Indiana were a welcome relief after the many trials and tribulations we experienced. A rare favorable wind blew us along and the morning sun beat down upon our faces. As we passed into Ohio, the landscape didn't change at all. The sign that welcomed us to Ohio was the only indication of change. We pulled into Napoleon, Ohio, in early evening, having ridden 125 miles despite the late departure from Carl Nixon's place. We decided to stay at the Napoleon Inn since the bugs had become bad even during the daylight hours.

Napoleon sat on the Maumee River, and we crossed the Lake Erie tributary the next morning and continued east. The Maumee has the largest watershed of any Great Lake tributary, stretching from Fort Wayne, Indiana, to Toledo, Ohio, and north into Michigan. Though not a deep floodplain by any stretch of the imagination, waterways were the only place we usually saw any noticeable change in topography in this very flat landscape. Beyond the flatness, US Route 6 was as straight as a road could be, only wavering from a due east direction to go around the city of Bowling Green and toward the town of Bradner.

We crossed the Sandusky River in the town of Fremont in mid-afternoon. John had decided his trip would be coast to coast and he would go through Northern Pennsylvania and into New York to reach the Atlantic, where he had some family. Since I had ridden to the Jersey coast with my cousin Brian in 1975, I did not feel the urgency of riding the whole way to the Atlantic after a trying month in the saddle. I just wanted to sleep in my own bed.

Fremont was the place he decided to part company with me. We had spent nearly five weeks with each other morning, noon, and night and shared one of the toughest things we had done to that point in our young lives. Really not commemorating the moment with the fanfare it deserved, we shook hands and bid each other farewell and safe travels. Perhaps it occurred to one or both of us, but we did not mention that we might not ever see each other again.

John's route initially would take him along the shore of Lake Erie and the continuingly pancake-flat landscape we had been enjoying since Central Illinois. His march across Pennsylvania would not be nearly as pleasant, as US Route 6 through the Northern Tier was one dreadful hill after another through the northern portion of the badly eroded Appalachian Plateau. The traffic was similarly terrifying, especially the seemingly unending parade of coal trucks. While I would have to deal with coal trucks on my route, I found out afterward that my more southerly track would spare me from the many close calls John endured.

All Alone on the Road

"When the traveler goes alone he gets acquainted with himself."

—Liberty Hyde Bailey
Cofounder of the American Society for Horticultural Science
(1858-1954)

THOUGH HAVING A TRAVELING PARTNER MADE THE cross-country ordeal much more pleasant, I was determined to pile up the miles more quickly when I was by myself. Especially since I was so close to home, I was additionally motivated to make some hay as I went through Eastern Ohio and on into Western Pennsylvania. After parting company with John in mid-afternoon that day, I did 80 more miles by the day's end.

Though I was not at all concerned about riding by myself, I began to worry I was going to run out of money. In addition to my bus ticket to the West Coast, Mom and Dad gave me $300 in traveler's checks for my trip as a college graduation gift. I had a little bit of cash in addition to the traveler's checks but no credit card and no plan if I ran out of money. I'm not quite sure why $300 was the magic figure, but it turned out to be incredibly close to what I would need. Had the weather been more cooperative and the mosquitoes less prolific, I might have had some to spare. We camped much less (and spent more on lodging) after we crossed the Missouri River in order to stay out of the weather and away from the bugs. We did enjoy a few rain-free days in Indiana and Ohio, but there had been so much rain that summer the mosquitoes were awful even on days it didn't rain. The drier weather allowed us to get in a few big mileage days, as we enjoyed a flat and fast 125-mile day in the glacial plains before hitting the rolling hills of central Ohio.

It was Saturday afternoon, so I looked for a church when I rolled into Brunswick, Ohio. I got to Saint Ambrose Church just as the evening mass was ending. I told the pastor I had ridden across the country, slipped in mention of my dire financial situation, and asked if I could stay in the church hall overnight. He couldn't let me in the hall, but he knew the manager at the Willow Haven Motel and called ahead to make arrangements. I'm not sure if the priest paid the bill or the owner treated me, but there was no charge for the room. While it was not a five-star establishment in anyone's lodging guide, it seemed like a luxury hotel when compared to the flea bag we suffered through in Chicago a few days before. I was happy to be out of the mosquitoes and able to sleep in a bed after nearly 130 miles in the saddle.

The pastor greeted me the next morning at early mass, happy to see I really was a faithful, practicing Catholic after all. I would have never entertained the thought of skipping mass, though. Despite trekking through some incredibly isolated places, I realized that morning I had managed to find a church every weekend I was gone. Mom and Dad, evidently, had raised a fine Catholic boy after all.

While formal nourishment of the soul was addressed each weekend, the body's fuel tank needed more frequent refilling, particularly on these incredibly high mileage days. All-you-can-eat deals are especially lucrative to long-distance athletes and salad bars had become the rage in the mid-seventies. When I found one at a fast food place in Canton, Ohio for lunch the next day, I jumped at the opportunity. I went back to the buffet at least ten times. I suspect the workers talked about the famished cyclist for days afterward.

Given the unpredictable nature of such a bike trip, there were few days when we planned our endpoint and stuck to an itinerary. This penultimate day of the trip would be an exception. Come hell or high water (both of which we had experienced on the trip), I was determined to get to my great aunt and uncle's house in Freeport, Pennsylvania by the end of the day. Aunt Perta and Uncle Lee's modest home sat upon the shore of the Allegheny River, the northern tributary that joins the Monongahela to form the Ohio (making Pittsburgh's "Three

Rivers"). Their house was separated from the river by railroad tracks across the street, and the house shook when a train passed. We had visited them once or twice a year when I was little, and we always had a good time. Uncle Lee would take us to their town park, and Aunt Perta would always cook a great meal with a tasty dessert. One year, Uncle Lee took me fishing in the Allegheny, the only time I ever held a fishing rod.

It was more than 140 miles from Brunswick, Ohio to their home in Freeport, and I suspected the topography would make for tough riding as well. It would turn out to be even hillier than I feared. The drastic change from the pancake-flat glacial plains of Indiana and Ohio made it seem even worse. Eastern Ohio marked the western edge of the Appalachian Plateau and my house sat at the base of the eastern edge of the highlands. That meant that nearly 200 miles of up and down purgatory lay before me as I rode through the badly eroded plateaus.

Beyond the hills, the road surfaces were equally abysmal. The white line marking the edge of the running lane of traffic was often painted on the gravel, as the macadam had crumbled from neglect and heavy coal truck traffic. The coal of the Appalachian Plateau, then, could be blamed at least in part for the deplorable condition of the roads. Coal trucks are among the heaviest things ever found on secondary roads in this part of the country, and their toll on the roads can be staggering. Even when roads are bonded and coal companies must pay for the damage they inflict, it's difficult for the state to keep up with the necessary repairs.

Two things took the edge off the rough ride: the natural beauty of Western Pennsylvania and the fact that I was so close to home. Just how close I was became clear when I arrived at Lee and Perta's house. When I hugged Aunt Perta and shook Uncle Lee's hand, it was the first pair of non-cycling familiar faces I had seen in five weeks. Like my visits as a youngster, the incredible food was one of the things that made the visit even more special. It had been that same five-week span since I had enjoyed a real home-cooked meal. The taste of the hot apple pie she served for dessert is still well entrenched in my memory.

Though I had religiously kept a journal of the trip and called home every few days, this was the first opportunity I'd had to talk to someone I knew face-to-face about my month long adventure. I can't help but think, in retrospect, they might have been tempted to stuff a sock in my mouth after the long spell of storytelling. Having enjoyed their company more than I could express, I was not in an overwhelming rush to set off the next morning. Besides, I knew Aunt Perta would insist upon cooking a hot breakfast. Clearly, it would have been impolite to refuse her offer. After inhaling a slew of homemade pancakes, I finally set off for the final leg of a most extraordinary journey.

Much of the ride proved to be even worse than the previous day, the broken-up roads and nasty climbs made even worse by more coal truck traffic. Just west of Indiana, Pennsylvania, about 70 miles from home, a loaded coal truck ran me off the road and would have clipped me had I not bailed out onto the gravel berm. A few hours later, just six miles from home, a car decided to pass another car on two-lane Sugar Run Road, despite my clear presence in the oncoming lane. It occurred to me that the two closest calls I had experienced since the mobile home ran me into the guardrail in Oregon were within three hours of home. I had traveled nearly 3,000 miles without incident only to be treated poorly in my own backyard. To many Pennsylvania drivers in those days, a bicyclist was a road hazard and nuisance that deserved to be treated with blatant disregard. Whether they heard me or cared, both drivers on this day got a shower of curse words befitting their boorish road manners.

I pulled into a small country store in Homer City just before lunch. I opened my wallet and pulled out my last traveler's check. I snickered to myself again that I had uncannily estimated my expenses so precisely. I placed the change in my bag, figuring that I'd still have a few bucks left when I landed in Altoona four or so hours later. Beyond the relief of having the financial resources to make it home, I was further consoled by the prospect of seeing a familiar landscape on a road I had ridden before. It happened just west of Indiana, where we had begun our cross-state ride two summers before. Though I was tired, my backside sore and my hands numb, the anticipation of seeing my family and jumping in our swimming pool was enough to push me home in good time.

Living on a hill on the edge of Altoona, even my last mile was uphill. Though still carrying a substantial load of gear, I made the final ascent without much pain or strain. It made me realize how the anticipation of a long-awaited destination can level out the steepest of climbs. How appropriate that my final miles were yet another metaphor for life.

Epilogue: Another Story

"But that's another story."

—Rudyard Kipling
Private Mulvany from *Soldiers Three* (1888)

THE NEXT FEW YEARS WOULD BRING THEIR OWN SET OF fascinating cycling adventures, with just enough misadventure to make the tales interesting enough for yet another book. It would be racing that would be at the center of my life for the next half decade and though the experiences would be of a different sort, the stories are every bit as compelling.

I hung onto many of the same cycling mates that got me excited about the sport, but also met some new ones, too. As I share in this book, some were not on the same page I was philosophically, but that's another one of the things that makes the story interesting. After all, it would be a boring place if we all saw the world through the same lens.

I traveled far and wide to races with my family and a handful of friends. In the process, they all became enthusiastic and knowledgeable fans of the sport, and a few become impassioned bike racers in their own right. I had the chance to meet and compete against the best cyclists in North America. I had an opportunity to experience even more of America in the process.

Toward the end of my racing days, I set off on a geology field study that was intended to begin my post-graduate studies. This five-week-long trip (that included, of course, many miles on the bike) to the Rocky Mountains and the Western canyon lands in 1983 could itself fill its own volume.

Though life went on, just like the previous five years, the bike seemed to have a connection to nearly every day. When I wasn't riding, I was doing something else to make me a better rider. Many things took a back seat to the bike and my pursuit of being the best cyclist I could be.

Sometimes we become so focused on our destination, we don't enjoy the journey. Bike racers, in their preoccupation with being the fastest rider possible, sometimes lose track of the adventure that cycling should be. I would like to think that I never lost track of my roots—roots that remained firmly imbedded on the roads and mountains of south central Pennsylvania. These dual pursuits—striving to become faster while enjoying the rides—were not mutually exclusive. Together they made for an even more unusual and surprising journey.

But that's another story…

Endnotes

1. Lehigh Earth Observatory, "Walking Purchase", www.leo.lehigh.edu/envirosci/watershed/pjournal/section3/18/index.html
2. "On the Pioneer Trail in Rural Cambria County" October 2002, www.cambriacountyhistorical.com/.../PioneerTrail/pioneer-trail-pg2.doc
3. East Broad Top Railroad & Coal Company, "History of EBT", 2003, www.ebtrr.com/history.html
4. Kris Jenkins, "Gregory Links CIA to Kennedy Murders." *Altoona Mirror*, February 5, 1975: 1, 3.
5. Perdue and Martin-Perdue, "Appalachian Fables and Facts," 91; Perdue and Martin-Perdue, "To Build a Wall Around These Mountains," 53; Lambert, *The Undying Past of the Shenandoah National Park*, 231, 254-255.
6. NOAA Central Library, U.S. Daily Weather Maps Project http://docs.lib.noaa.gov/rescue/dwm/data_rescue_daily_weather_maps.html
7. www.centrecountyhistory.org/history/ABCsP.html
8. Glenn Trewartha. *The Earth's Problem Climates*. 1961, University of Wisconsin Press, p. 259
9. Friends of Old Fort Stevens, "History of Fort Stevens (1863-1947)," http://www.visitftstevens.com/history.htm, Hammond, Oregon, Referenced 1/1/09
10. Elizabeth Orr, William Orr and Ewart Baldwin. *Geology of Oregon*. Kendall/Hunt Publishing, 1992, 4th edition.
11. Oregon State University: *Northern Coast Range Adaptive Management Area*; Chapter 2: Physical and Biological Environment
12. Wood and Kienle, *Volcanoes of North America: United States and Canada*: Cambridge University Press, 1990, pages 170-172

13. Stephen L. Harris, *Fire Mountains of the West: The Cascade and Mono Lake Volcanoes*; Mountain Press Publishing, Missoula MT, 1988, 1st edition, page 209
14. Steve Brantley and Bobbie Myers, "Mount St. Helens — From the 1980 Eruption to 2000", 2000, U.S. Geologic Survey, http://pubs.usgs.gov/fs/2000/fs036-00/
15. University of Oregon. "Mineral Ages Show Blue Mountain Rocks Related To Klamath, Sierra Nevadas." Science Daily. 31 October 2007. www.sciencedaily.com/releases/2007/10/071029092031.htm
16. Oregon Genealogy, "Durkee Valley, Baker County, Oregon", 2005, http://www.oregongenealogy.com/baker/durkee/durkee_valley.htm
17. http://en.wikipedia.org/wiki/Brownlee_Dam
18. Mark Masarik, "Triumph Mine Tailings Piles", February 2007, United States Environmental Protection Agency, Referenced 6/25/09 http://yosemite.epa.gov/r10/nplpad.nsf/8f2c285be1a7a1fa882568d-b00688860/18bead6a3f7e283485256595005342b1?OpenDocument
19. Idaho National Laboratory, "Experimental Breeder Reactor-I," http://www.inl.gov/factsheets/ebr-1.pdf, U.S. Department of Energy, Idaho Falls, ID,
20. Eugene P. Kiver, David V. Harris; *Geology of U.S. Parklands:* Fifth Edition, (New York; John Wiley & Sons; 1999; pages 592-596) ISBN 0-471-33218-6
21. United States Geologic Survey, "Geological Survey Bulletin 1347 The Geologic Story of Yellowstone National Park", http://www.nps.gov/history/history/online_books/geology/publications/bul/1347/sec3.htm
22. Gregg F. Gunnell, William S. Bartels, Philip D. Gingerich, and Victor Torres, "Wapiti Valley Faunas: Early and Middle Eocene Fossil Vertebrates from the North Fork of the Shoshone River", Contributions from the Museum of Paleontology; Ann Arbor, Michigan; The University of Michigan; December 15, 1992), pages 250-260
23. Wyoming Geologic Survey, "Owl Creek and Bridger Mountains", www.wsgs.uwyo.edu/StratWeb/OwlCreekMts

24. *The Adventures of Captain Bonneville*, Digested From His Journal, Author: Washington Irving 1837
25. Stennett, William H. A history of the origin of the place names connected with the Chicago & Northwestern and Chicago, St. Paul, Minneapolis & Omaha Railways. Chicago: 1908.
26. *Ghost Towns*. http://www.ghosttowns.com/states/wy/vantassell.html.
27. Mike Voorhies, "Ashfall: Life and Death at a Nebraska Waterhole Ten Million Years Ago", University of Nebraska State Museum, *Museum Notes No. 81*, Feb 1992 http://www.unl.edu/museum/research/vertpaleo/ashfall.html
28. Iowa Geologic Survey, *Geologic Points of Interest in the Fort Dodge Area*, Geologic Society of Iowa, September 11, 1976
29. David Smothers,"'Bitter' Too Mild to Describe Gary's Mayor's Race", *Sarasota Herald-Tribune*, May 5, 1979

About the Author

JOHN FREDERICK IS AN HONORS GRADUATE OF PENN STATE University's Geography program, where he also began his cycling career on the university's championship road race team. Following a cross-country trek after college graduation, he embarked on a racing career which produced an additional set of adventurous stories. He discovered that he could use his bicycle to challenge himself while experiencing the natural environment at the same time. His interest in physical geography would initially take him into the classroom as a high school Earth and Environmental Science teacher. Ultimately, he had the opportunity to return to one of his other passions, writing, when he began working with environmental professionals and organizations. In addition to that writing and editing, he authors a popular newspaper column on science and environmental topics, entitled Earth Matters. The father of two sons, he lives with his wife, Kathy, near Altoona, Pennsylvania.

www.ingramcontent.com/pod-product-compliance
Lightning Source LLC
Chambersburg PA
CBHW030106100526
44591CB00009B/294